Triadic Exchanges
Studies in Dialogue Interpreting

Edited by
Ian Mason
Heriot-Watt University, Edinburgh
Centre for Translation and Interpreting Studies in Scotland

St. Jerome Publishing
Manchester, UK & Northampton MA

Published by
St. Jerome Publishing
2 Maple Road West, Brooklands
Manchester, M23 9HH, United Kingdom
Tel +44 161 973 9856
Fax +44 161 905 3498
stjerome@compuserve.com
http://www.stjerome.co.uk

ISBN 1-900650-36-3 (pbk)

© Ian Mason and Contributors 2001

All rights reserved, including those of translation into foreign languages. No part of this publication may be reproduced, stored in a retrieval system or transmitted in any form or by any means, electronic, mechanical, photocopying, recording or otherwise without either the prior written permission of the Publisher or a licence permitting restricted copying issued by the Copyright Licensing Agency (CLA), 90 Tottenham Court Road, London, W1P 9HE. In North America, registered users may contact the Copyright Clearance Center (CCC): 222 Rosewood Drive, Danvers MA 01923, USA.

Printed and bound in Great Britain by
T. J. International Ltd., Cornwall, UK

Cover design by
Steve Fieldhouse, Oldham, UK (+44 161 620 2263)

Typeset by
Delta Typesetters, Cairo, Egypt
Email: delttyp@starnet.com.eg

British Library Cataloguing in Publication Data
A catalogue record of this book is available from the British Library

Library of Congress Catalging-in-Publication Data
Triadic exchanges : studies in dialogue interpreting / edited by Ian Mason.
     p. cm.
Includes bibliographical references and index.
  ISBN 1-900650-36-3 (pbk.)
  1. Simultaneous interpreting--Congresses. I. Mason, I. (Ian), 1944-
II. Title.
  P306.95 .T75 2001
  418'.02--dc21

00-013223

Contents

Introduction Ian Mason	*i*
Transcription Conventions	*vii*
Part I – *Research Directions*	1
Interpreting Expert Witness Testimony Challenges and Strategies Cynthia Miguélez	3
How are Courtroom Questions Interpreted? An Analysis of Spanish Interpreters' Practices Sandra Hale	21
Interactional Pragmatics, Face and the Dialogue Interpreter Ian Mason and Miranda Stewart	51
Interpreting in Crisis The Interpreter's Position in Therapeutic Encounters Cecilia Wadensjö	71
How Untrained Interpreters Handle Medical Terms Bernd Meyer	87
Part II – *Traditions*	107
The Rebirth of the King's Linguist Pierre Kouraogo	109
***Oranda Tsûji* and the Sidotti Incident** An Interview with an Italian Missionary by a Confucian Scholar in Eighteenth-century Japan Yukino Semizu	131
Part III – *Issues in Training*	147
First Steps on Firmer Ground A Project for the Further Training of Sign Language Interpreters in Austria Nadja Grbic	149

Teaching Liaison Interpreting 173
Combining Tradition and Innovation
Annalisa Sandrelli

Notes on Contributors 197

Index 201

Introduction

IAN MASON

In June 1995, a conference was held in Geneva Park, Canada, entitled *The Critical Link – Interpreters in the Community*. It brought together practitioners, trainers and researchers of various modes of interpreting, all united by the common thread of serving the community and by seeing themselves as fundamentally different from those active in the field of conference interpreting. The latter had become a recognized profession and academic discipline in its own right at a much earlier stage, with specialist training in prestigious interpreter schools, a strong professional association, the AIIC (*Association Internationale des Interprètes de Conférence*), and an emerging research discipline based on rigorous methodological principles. In comparison to all this, community interpreting, as it has come to be known, had for too long been the poor relation. There was relatively little professional organisation, training in some countries and for some professional tasks was virtually non-existent, and, as a field of study, this mode of interpreting had suffered from neglect. By the mid-1990s, all this was beginning to change. Whether cause or effect, the Geneva Park conference marked a turning point. Such was its success that *Critical Link II* was held three years later in Vancouver. Practising interpreters from fields as diverse as medical interpreting, war crimes tribunals, immigration hearings and sign-language interpreting in a whole range of contexts were exploring an array of common interests and shared experiences. At the same time, a number of key publications were beginning to appear: Gentile *et al.* (1996); Carr *et al.* (1997); Wadensjö (1998); Mason (ed. 1999); and Roy (2000) have been among those endeavouring to stake out the discipline and determine appropriate methods for its systematic study.

The picture that emerges, not just from the studies mentioned above but also from the experiences related by practitioners at conferences such as *Critical Link*, is an extraordinarily complex one. To the multi-tasking processes involved in all interpreting (simultaneous listening/watching, discourse processing, speaking, self-monitoring) is added constant (re-)negotiation of role, turn management and general monitoring of the unfolding of the talk exchange, in which at least three parties are involved. Moreover, the interpreters are subject to conflicting pressures – from employers, clients and other participants, in the face of which it becomes very difficult to maintain impartiality and professional detachment. That major problems are encountered even by the most seasoned interpreters should hardly be surprising. Rather, we should marvel that the whole process is even possible and that it is carried out successfully, to the satisfaction of users of the service, on a daily basis wordwide.

Enough is now known about the processes involved for us to be able to posit some basic principles. Firstly, the activity we are talking about involves a three-way exchange, in which each party, including the interpreter, is a full participant. It has been well enough established – by Berk-Seligson (e.g. 1990) and Hale (e.g. 1997) among others – that, even in courtroom situations in which interpreters are expected to act as verbatim relayers of others' talk, the interpreter cannot avoid becoming involved as a participant, whether through their own translational filter (e.g. subtle modifications to the register or pragmatics of source speech) or through the need to comment on their own or others' linguistic behaviour. Such comments may arise either on the initiative of the interpreter (see, e.g., Berk-Seligson 1990:65-74) or at the behest of a judge (see, e.g., Pym 1999:277). The invisibility of the courtroom interpreter is, quite simply, a myth.

Secondly, within the three-way exchange between the interpreter and those for whom she or he is interpreting, there are shifts of 'footing' (Wadensjö 1998). For example, one participant may address the interpreter directly, referring to the other participant in the third person ('Tell him that ...') or address the other participant directly and expect the interpreter to reflect this direct address. The interpreter will often shift footing within an exchange. Sometimes, sub-dialogues are initiated within the overall exchange between the interpreter and one of the other parties. Clients will sometimes make observations which they do not expect the interpreter to relay to the other party. In all such cases, clues to the footing being adopted may be signalled by subtle changes in gaze, posture or tone of voice. Consequently, this form of interpreting cannot be studied just as a series of oral texts, in complete isolation from paralinguistic and other contextual features. The title chosen for this volume – **Triadic Exchanges** – reflects the importance of viewing interpreted events as three-way interactions.

Thirdly, the distribution of power within the exchange exerts a determining influence on who says what, when and how. The interpreter's ability to manage the exchange is affected by this. Some interlocutors may interrupt or be interrupted, others may not. The dynamics of the exchange in terms of power and distance – and also in terms of who, within the exchange, is truly monolingual and who, in addition to the interpreter, is actually bilingual (cf. Pym 1999:271-2) – are of primordial importance in seeking to understand what is going on linguistically. For that reason, such issues cannot be set aside in any analysis of interpreter performance.

Lastly, these triadic exchanges take place at the intersection of competing discourses, ways of saying and expressing that typify social groups and institutions. The discourse of the prosecuting attorney will not, in general, be that of the witness. The medical practitioner's discourse will be at variance, on the same topic, with that of the patient. The competing discourses of immigration officer and asylum-seeker are a constant source of problem-solving activity on the part of the interpreter. The negotiation of these "socio-textual practices" (Hatim and Mason 1997:18) is always prominent in interpreted events of these and many other kinds.

These then are some of the characteristics shared by the various fields of community interpreting. But they are not limited to what is normally viewed as community interpreting – i.e. legal, medical and social services settings. They are also prominent in business negotiations, for example, in the field of diplomatic interpreting or interpreting in broadcast interviews (cf. Baker 1997). To cater for the whole range of fields in which these issues, among others, deserve investigation, we are using the term **dialogue interpreting**. In advancing this term, we hope to focus attention on precisely those features – of dialogic interaction – which are shared by all the seemingly disparate event-types mentioned above.

The studies brought together in this volume reflect a variety of different aspects of and approaches to dialogue interpreting. In Part One, we present some **Research Directions**. Each of these is a small-scale study which points up the need for further large-scale investigation of the phenomena observed. **Cynthia Miguélez** re-examines the notion that the main difficulty involved in interpreting the expert witness in the courtroom is access to the specialised terminology which they are bound to use. Working on a 75,000-word corpus of attorney/expert witness exchanges in United States courtrooms, she finds very little in the way of specialised jargon or technical terminology. Conversely, there are many problems of textual coherence, involving incomplete or inconsistent syntax, embedded phrases, false starts and so on. The main challenge to the interpreter is thus one of re-establishing coherence (for the benefit of a defendant with no knowledge of English) rather than access to specialised lexis.

Sandra Hale conducts a fine-grained analysis of courtroom questions in English and Spanish. In particular, she details the pragmatic effects of each question type, providing insights which are not readily available in standard linguistic descriptions such as those contained in grammars. Naturally, there is no one-to-one equivalence between question forms in the two languages. She shows the ways in which question form is closely bound up with an attorney's whole strategy in cross-examination and the interpreters' difficulties in establishing pragmatic equivalence. Yet close equivalence of pragmatic effect is achievable, provided that due attention is paid to it, and the findings of Hale's study, like those of Miguélez in a different way, have something of consequence to offer to those designing interpreter training programmes.

Courtroom interaction also features in **Ian Mason**'s and **Miranda Stewart**'s examination of the pragmatics of interpreting from the perspective of politeness and the negotiation of face. By comparing two very different events – cross-examination of a Spanish-speaking witness at the O.J.Simpson trial in the United States and interviews by immigration officials of illegal Polish immigrants – they are able to show that the inherently face-threatening nature of the events themselves (the witness whose credibility is being undermined, the immigrant who is about to be deported) leads to a great deal of face-work in the speech of questioner and interviewee alike. Relaying this attention to face appears to be problematic, regardless of which of two very different interpreter styles is adopted.

The participation framework and footing within the triad are alluded to in both Hale's and Mason and Stewart's contributions. **Cecilia Wadensjö** then takes up a particular issue regarding the triadic relationship, namely proxemics, the spatial positioning of the interpreter with respect to the other two parties. She examines this within the framework of psychotherapy sessions, in which patients, prompted by therapists, recount traumatic events from their recent past. In this highly sensitive environment, the interpreter him/herself is subject to a great deal of stress and may suffer 'burnout'. But Wadensjö presents evidence which suggests that something as apparently simple as seating arrangements may have considerable impact both on the experience of the participants and on the outcome of the exchange. Specifically, the inclusion of the interpreter within a shared 'communicative radius' (opportunities for eye-contact, shared sight-lines) with the other participants appears to have a positive effect on the quality of the experience for all concerned. The paper opens up a rich seam for further research.

Bernd Meyer pursues another of the themes mentioned earlier, that of the competing discourses at work in many dialogue interpreting settings. Working with untrained interpreters in medical encounters – a not uncommon situation even now in many countries – he observes tendencies which, although they are no doubt also present in the behaviour of professional dialogue interpreters, are perhaps more prevalent or more readily observable in the spontaneous behaviour of non-professionals. Like Miguélez, he finds that the problem is not just that of knowing correct terminology. Rather, particular solutions adopted for rendering particular terms (when is a bruise a 'bruise' and when is it a 'haematoma'?) have more to do with the participation framework, power, (lack of) distance between participants and the professional stance adopted by the interpreter than with any notion of technical equivalence. The implications of Meyer's work relate closely to those of the other papers mentioned above.

To counter-balance these prospective research directions, we have included a section consisting of two papers which relate to **Traditions**. Relatively little is known about the details of the ways in which dialogue interpreting encounters were conducted in the distant past. Researchers have however been able to piece together enough evidence from historical records to provide ethnographic (rather than linguistic) accounts of key cross-cultural encounters such as the interpreting services provided by La Malinche for Hernán Cortés during the conquest of Mexico or Etienne Brûlé's role among the Algonquins during the colonisation of French Canada (see Delisle and Woodsworth 1995; Karttunen 1994). In this volume, **Yukino Semizu** presents evidence of the work of interpreters in an entirely different historical setting, the isolationist period in Japan (1641-1867). When an Italian missionary was captured after landing on the Japanese coast in 1708, the government enlisted the services of its sole authorised interpreters, the *Oranda tsûji*, or Dutch language officers, to assist in the interrogation of the captive. The event turned out to be a highly significant one in terms of the subsequent intellectual history of the country. Despite the lack of a genuine common language, comunication took place and Semizu shows that some of the problems involved, such as role conflict or the lay person's beliefs about what interpreting involves, are those familiar to the modern dialogue interpreter.

Pierre Kouraogo explores traditional approaches to interpreting from another angle. In the practice of untrained interpreters currently working in Burkina Faso, he finds a reflection of the skills and strategies deployed by what were known in pre-colonial times as the king's linguists, a kind of public interpreter responsible for relaying the speech of a chief to assembled audiences. Kouraogo finds that, far from resembling the performance of the conference interpreter, these untrained interpreters display many of the performance characteristics of the dialogue interpreter, responding as participants in face-to-face interaction. Moreover, their work fills an absolute need, that of interpreting using indigenous languages, not otherwise catered for in the country. He concludes that observation of their performance can be an important input into the design of appropriate training programmes.

All of these papers, then, have something to say to the interpreter trainer. In Part Three, **training issues** are addressed in two papers which, from entirely different points of departure, explore the design of training programmes for particular purposes. Whereas in some countries (Australia, for example), the process of defining standards and accreditation of training is well advanced, there are others where much work remains to be done. **Nadja Grbic** describes the huge effort of consciousness-raising needed to ensure the proper professional recognition of sign-language interpreting. She describes a course of further training for sign-language interpreters offered at the University of Graz, Austria. By monitoring participants' reactions to and evaluation of the course, she gains insights into changing perceptions of the activity and the need to involve the Deaf themselves as training providers.

Annalisa Sandrelli starts from the perspective of the skills needed by graduate linguists in a European context. The training course which she describes does not purport to train professional dialogue interpreters but rather to offer liaison interpreting skills to language learners, thereby offering them an insight into the professional world and a range of transferable skills. An important part of this article is its investigation of the tools needed for autonomous learning and preparation for interpreting performance. She describes an innovative use of computer-based learning to enhance learners' awareness of what interpreting involves and to provide practice in a number of the required skills. There can be no doubt that some of the principles involved in this computer-based programme are transferable to the professional trainee and to the design of trainee support systems.

This collection of articles on dialogue interpreting offers a wide variety of perspectives on what is a very diverse field of activity. There have, hitherto, been far too many artificial divisions between various fields and modes of interpreting, with much emphasis on what is distinctive (and therefore separate) in each professional context and not enough exploration of areas of common concern and interest. It is hoped that this volume can make a modest contribution towards reinforcing the identity of the fast-developing field of dialogue interpreting.

References

Baker, Mona (1997) 'Non-Cognitive Constraints and Interpreter Strategies in Political Interviews', in Karl Sims (ed) *Translating Sensitive Text*, Amsterdam: Rodopi, 113-131.

Berk-Seligson, Susan (1990) *The Bilingual Courtroom: Court Interpreters in the Judicial Process*, Chicago & London: The University of Chicago Press.

Carr, Sylvana, Roda Roberts, Aideen Dufour and Dini Steyn (eds) (1997) *The Critical Link: Interpreters in the Community*, Amsterdam & Philadelphia: John Benjamins.

Delisle, Jean and Judith Woodsworth (eds) (1995) *Translators through History*, Amsterdam: John Benjamins.

Gentile, Adolfo, Uldis Ozolins and Mary Vasilakakos (with Leong Ko and Ton-That Quynh-Du) (1996) *Liaison Interpreting: A Handbook*, Melbourne: Melbourne University Press.

Hale, Sandra (1997) 'The Treatment of Register Variation in Court Interpreting', *The Translator* 3(1): 39-54.

Hatim, Basil and Ian Mason (1997) *The Translator as Communicator*, London: Routledge.

Karttunen, Frances (1994) *Between Worlds: Interpreters, Guides, and Survivors*, New Brunswick: Rutgers University Press.

Mason, Ian (ed) (1999) *Dialogue Interpreting*, special issue of *The Translator*, 5(2).

Pym, Anthony (1999) '"Nicole Slapped Michelle": Interpreters and Theories of Interpreting at the O.J. Simpson Trial', in Ian Mason (ed), 265-284.

Roy, Cynthia (2000) *Interpreting as a Discourse Process,* Oxford: Oxford University Press.

Wadensjö, Cecilia (1998) *Interpreting as Interaction,* London & New York: Longman.

Transcription Conventions

[ ] [ ]	Simultaneous or overlapping talk
,	Continuing intonation (rising or level tone)
.	Terminating intonation
?	Questioning intonation
⌈	Rising tone
⌉	Falling tone
…	Open-ended intonation (fading or ambiguous tone)
e: or e:::	Long or lengthened vowel sound
(.) or (…)	Short pause
(2)	Two-second pause
+++	Omission
/	Abandoned utterance or repair
(looks up)	Non-verbal feature
CAPS	Emphasis, stressed syllable or loudness
º º	Uttered quietly or as an aside
(xxx)	Inaudible
→	Line in transcript referred to in discussion
italics	English back-translation of talk in other languages

NB – Contributors make use of few, many or all of these conventions, depending on the relative delicacy of transcription needed for the analysis.

Part I

Research Directions

Interpreting Expert Witness Testimony
Challenges and Strategies

CYNTHIA MIGUÉLEZ

> *One of the most challenging assignments a court interpreter faces is interpreting for expert witnesses. Advances in science and technology over the last few decades and the 'beyond a reasonable doubt' standard have made the use of expert witnesses from a wide variety of fields a common practice in American courtrooms. It has generally been assumed that the testimony of an expert witness is challenging substantively but not formally. Preparation has focused on specialized vocabulary and phraseology. However, after reading several hundred pages of transcribed courtroom testimony we saw that expert witness testimony from a number of different fields was not as lexically specialized as one would believe, but that it did contain many more grammatical, structural and syntactic errors than would be expected. In this study we have classified the most frequently occurring errors found in this transcribed testimony, and have noted the strategies used by both novice and experienced interpreters to deal with these challenges.*

1. Introduction

The aim of this article is to identify the characteristics of expert witness testimony in order to establish strategies and techniques that will enhance the interpreter's ability to successfully manage this type of interpreting assignment. The use of expert witnesses is becoming more and more common in court proceedings in the United States. The demands of the 'beyond a reasonable doubt' standard are leading both defense attorneys and prosecutors to offer 'scientific' evidence as proof in a growing number of cases. Crimes and crime scenes are becoming more complicated, and this, coupled with the era of specialization in which we live and the availability of increasingly sophisticated technology for the analysis of virtually everything from gunshot residue to document age and authenticity, has made the expert witness a key player in many legal cases.

A quick search on the internet or a look at a legal resources publication[1] produces a mind-boggling array of experts and fields of expertise available to litigators. In addition to the forensic scientists, crime scene specialists and ballistics experts that are among those most commonly called upon to give testimony

---

[1] Several directories and on-line listings exist including Expert Pages, ExpertLaws.com, *and* Trial Experts. The National Directory of Expert Witnesses *is available in both book form and on-line and boasts 1500 experts in over 400 categories.*

in U.S. courts, these listings show that experts on topics such as doll collectibles, golf course design and even sports figures have testified. The range of possible expert testimony is understandably intimidating to court interpreters, who must consistently meet the same high performance standards regardless of the type of testimony being given. When faced with a challenging interpreting assignment that includes expert testimony – and assuming that notice is given prior to the proceeding regarding the nature of the testimony – an interpreter usually attempts to become familiar with the terminology related to the specific field in question. Specialized dictionaries and glossaries are sought out and studied, equivalent texts are culled for words and phrases, consultations with fellow interpreters are made. The interpreter then enters the courtroom with enhanced confidence and some sense of preparedness. However, a study of the testimony given by experts from a number of fields shows that the language used by expert witnesses and by attorneys when addressing them, is often grammatically faulty, convoluted, imprecise, repetitive and lacking in coherence. Therefore, preparing vocabulary, while useful, will not guarantee success, given that the challenges in comprehending and interpreting expert testimony are not always strictly – or even principally – lexical in nature.

2. Legal language

In the 1970s and 80s, several studies were published that attempted to define the specific characteristics of legal language. A number of scholars[2] did seminal work on American legal language in its written form. Crystal and Davy (1969) had done similar work on British legal language and had come up with several of the same conclusions. Legal language was found to be replete with passives, nominalizations, multiple negatives, misplaced or intrusive phrases, unusual and complex embeddings and unusual prepositional phrases and clauses. Other characteristics included lengthy sentences, limited verbal groups, and frequent post-modification in nominal groups. On the discourse level, legal language was found to be lacking in cohesion due to unusual use of anaphora, confusing repetition, and a mix of extreme precision and intentional ambiguity.

At approximately the same time these studies were being done, similar studies were being done on spoken legal language. O´Barr and his colleagues Conley and Lind[3] developed schemata for the registers of spoken language in legal settings based on their field work in North Carolina courtrooms, and González (1976 and 1977) undertook a study in Arizona to determine the complexity of the speech of judges, attorneys, experts and witnesses in order to devise indices

---

[2] See Charrow, V. (1982); Charrow, V., J. Crandal and R. Charrow (1982); Danet, B. (1980); and Danet et al. *(1976).*
[3] See O'Barr (1981 and 1982); O'Barr and Conley (1976) and O'Barr and Lind (1981).

that could be used as a set of constructs for a test of functional English proficiency. A decade later, Berk-Seligson (1987, 1988, 1990) studied speech styles and how they affect the outcome of legal proceedings. These studies show that testimony given in courtrooms and the language used in other legal settings (police stations, detention centers, county jails, attorneys' offices) for other legal purposes (arrest, booking, initial attorney-client interview, depositions) spans the range of registers from the highly frozen and formulaic language often used by judges and attorneys to the highly colloquial language used by defendants and witnesses to describe individuals and recount events. Slang, regionalisms, jargon, dialectal variations and even idiolectal idiosyncracies appear frequently in spoken legal language. Moreover, participants in court proceedings or legal interactions often make use of and mix several registers or speech styles in their discourse. Other paralinguistic elements of speech such as hedges, hesitations, false starts, self-corrections, inconsistencies and misspeaks are all common in the spoken language used in court.

3. Expert witnesses

In the United States, expert witnesses can be called either by the prosecution or by the defence to clarify a controversial point in a criminal or civil case. Their credentials must be established at the outset of their testimony, and the Court must formally recognize them as professionally qualified to give the specialized information that is being sought. The general perception of expert witnesses is that they are well-educated, well-versed in their fields and well-spoken. They are presumed to be experienced at and comfortable with discussing their area of specialization with other professionals as well as with the uninitiated. As they are not directly affected by the outcome of a trial, their anxiety level as regards testifying in a court of law is thought to be lower than that of defendants or other participants such as eyewitnesses or third parties. As a result, it is widely assumed that expert witnesses will produce coherent, understandable speech that may be substantively, but certainly not formally, challenging. However, an analysis of several examples of expert testimony shows that this assumption is false and that the speech produced by expert witnesses is often as challenging in form as it is in substance. Additionally, the range of registers, speech styles and paralinguistic elements that were found to exist in general courtroom language are also typical of expert witness testimony. All of these elements contribute to the general difficulty that interpreting for expert witnesses entails.

4. The study

During my time as a visiting research scholar at the National Center for Interpretation Testing, Research and Policy (University of Arizona, USA), I was involved in a project to prepare training materials for aspiring court interpreters. Several thousand pages of authentic transcribed courtroom testimony were combed for materials for this project[4]. Early on in that process, the following text was encountered:

> Q: Now referring to the other areas that you mentioned, density, what is density?
> A: This is the weight of the mass of an object, the weight in air as against water. It was the old Greek principle when Archimedes got into the bathtub and there was so much water came out that was specific gravity so much water displaced. The density of an object is measured in this relation between the relation of its weight and mass in air as against its weight and mass in liquid. In the laboratory the way we run density we actually take a glass particle and we bounce it in a liquid mixture and in this case the mixture is 'Bromifoam alcohol'. Bromifoam being a heavy liquid on which you can float the rocks and alcohol being very light and you put in a glass particle and it neither rises nor falls in that liquid. You can either do that by two ways, by heating the liquid and making it lighter and the object will fall. If you cool it and make the liquid denser the particle will rise. Here is a point where we actually balance it in liquid, neither rises nor falls, a little particle so small you have to use a magnifying glass. At that time when we finally let it down, the equilibrium, we have a definite balance and we take the count of liquid which gives us our density reading. So, we read the density of the liquid, which is very sensitive, much more sensitive method, much more sensitive than the old method they have of giving the specific gravity.

Upon reading this fragment, we were above all struck by the fact that there was virtually no specialized jargon here and yet the answer was quite incomprehensible. This response to a seemingly straightforward and simple question posed to a recognized expert was so convoluted that it led us to question whether this type of language use by experts was a fluke or a regular occurrence. We therefore decided to pull out all of the examples of expert testimony we came across as we read through the court transcripts. The result was some 300 pages of text, which produced a corpus for study of approximately 75,000 words. This number is based on the entire attorney-witness exchange, in other words, attorneys' questions and experts' responses, as limiting the corpus to true expert testi-

---

[4] The transcripts used are all in the public domain. Although a few were obtained from on-line sources, the great majority were in the possession of the National Center for Interpretation Testing, Research, and Policy of the University of Arizona. Peter Lindquist of the NCITRP did the original read-through of the transcripts available and was instrumental in the selection of excerpts to be studied. He also assisted in identifying and classifying language samples for the study. All names, dates and other identifying information have been changed or deleted.

mony would decontextualize those responses. Excerpts were taken from both federal and state court cases and fields of expert testimony included accounting, fingerprinting, serology and blood typing, hair and fibre analysis, pathology, biological sciences, geology, botany, minerology, chemical sciences, mechanical engineering, firearms and ballistics, crime scene management including collection of evidence, chain of custody and crime scene illustration, and social work, substance abuse and family therapy.[5]

An initial reading of the transcripts produced a preliminary categorization of items of linguistic interest, ranging from simple grammatical errors to complex stylistic problems. Subsequent readings were carried out to cull the texts for examples that would correspond to the categories that had been established and to allow for modification of the original schemata. While the exact number of occurrences was not tabulated, categories were only created when several examples could be found in the testimony of different experts so that a category did not reflect any one individual's idiolect. Given that the study was carried out on written transcripts of oral testimony, special efforts were made to exclude items which might be attributable to court reporter transcription error. The idiosyncratic use of punctuation and the general absence of marks such as ellipses or dashes that would reflect pauses, hesitations and other extra-linguistic elements of spoken language also had to be addressed. Excerpts were read aloud and/or taped to see if a spoken version produced a different effect from the one produced by the written text. Sometimes it seemed quite clear that a visual cue or gesture of some sort must have accompanied an utterance, adding the missing link for complete comprehension. This type of gesture was sometimes annotated in parenthesis in the written transcript but this was the exception, not the rule. The categories of items considered to be of 'linguistic interest' for this study included obvious grammatical errors, structural or syntactic irregularities and the misuse, unusual use, or repeated use of a linguistic or para-linguistic device which somehow affected the coherence of an utterance, thereby adding to the interpreter's decoding and encoding tasks and further complicating the extremely complex cognitive processes that take place during interpretation.[6]

Most expert testimony in U.S. courtrooms is given by individuals who share

---

[5] Approximate word counts for the different areas of expert testimony are serology and blood typing 6,000; hair and fibre analysis 6,500; crime scene management including collection of evidence, chain of custody and crime scene illustration 16,500; pathology 3,600; firearms and ballistics 3,600; biological sciences including geology, botany, and minerology 4,500; chemical sciences 2,000; mechanical engineering 7,500; social work in the areas of substance abuse and family therapy 15,600; accounting 3,800; and fingerprinting 4,650.

[6] For a discussion of the complexities involved in simultaneous courtroom interpreting see the theoretical models presented in González et al., *1991, especially the explanation of the Simultaneous Human Information Processing (SHIP) model.*

the language of the court, so the mode of interpretation used is simultaneous.[7] Therefore, selected texts were recorded, and interpreted renditions (into Spanish) were obtained from a small group of both experienced and aspiring interpreters[8] in order to analyze the strategies they used when confronted with the irregularities encountered in this type of testimony.

5. Results

5.1. Lexicon

Surprisingly, very little specialized jargon or technical terminology was found in any of the transcripts studied. Only a handful of terms could be identified including *rifling, lands and grooves, hammer* and *barrel* (ballistics and weapons), *Section Eight housing* (social work), *glutination, serum* and *blood typing* (serology), and the chemical substance *diphenylamine*. However, some lexically-based examples of interpreter challenges are worthy of mention. One example is when common terms take on uncommon meanings in a specialized context. Consider the following examples, in which bold print is used to highlight the term glossed between parentheses.

1. What is the **proximation**? (*distance*)
2. Was she **consistent** in coming to see you? (*Did she come regularly?*)
3. The officer then **ran the plates**. (*checked on the vehicle´s registration and ownership*)
4. The date of **intake** was last year. (*admission*)
5. We were able to **lift latent prints** from several surfaces ... (*get a copy of fingerprints*)
6. In the laboratory the way we **run** density ... (*measure, determine*)

In these cases, the interpreter must be aware of the meaning of these words or

---

[7] There are cases, although not many in comparison, in which a non-English speaking expert witness is called; the mode of interpretation used is then consecutive. Whether consecutively or simultaneously interpreted, these interactions remain instances of dialogue interpreting in that the witness gives evidence in response to attorneys' questions and the interpreted evidence may then lead to further questions. They are not monologic in the same way as are conference speeches, interpreted simultaneously by interpreters in soundproof booths.

[8] Renditions were obtained from certified and practising court interpreters in the United States, experienced conference interpreters in Spain and students in their final year of an undergraduate degree programme in Translating and Interpreting at the University of Alicante (Spain). The target language was Spanish.

phrases as used in the specific context and take special care not to render a literal translation if the same effect would not be produced in the target language. Often structural accommodations or functional equivalents are required, so immediate comprehension is needed. For example, the phrase '*Was she consistent in coming to see you?*' would have to be structurally modified in some languages to what might be equivalent to '*Did she come to see you regularly?*', as an appropriate adjective that would correspond to the original word '*consistent*' might not be available. Likewise, a literal translation of '*ran the plates*' or '*run density*' would be incomprehensible in most languages, and the interpreter would have to make use of a descriptive or functional equivalent such as the ones given in parentheses above. In the simulation, the experienced interpreters were able adequately to render these utterances in the target language; however, the interpreters-in-training tended to use a more literal approach or lost the concept altogether. The cognate '*consistente*' was used for '*consistent*' even though the result is not correct Spanish usage, and '*hacer*' (the verb '*to do*') was the closest the trainees came to a valid rendition of '*run*' density.

The use of analogies, comparisons and metaphors was also a common strategy used by experts to explain a concept or the appearance or functioning of a piece of equipment or device when they thought that a more technical explanation might be beyond the grasp of the lay person. For example:

7. I could best describe a hair, the scales from a cuticle on the hair and a hair could be compared to **a wooden lead pencil that is painted yellow** and the scales surrounding the outside of the hair shaft have an overlapping, **much like the scales of a fish**.
8. Well, I sequentially looked at the entire item back and forth**, as if you were mowing grass**, you would go sequentially back and forth.

Generally, these comparisons and metaphors enhance comprehension and would not in and of themselves tax an experienced interpreter. The difficulty often lies not in the images themselves but rather in the way they are structured in the sentence. For instance, in 7 above we find a syntactically convoluted sentence in which the two relatively easy comparisons are embedded, while in the second we find a shift in perspective from first person to second person universal. The second example was included in the simulation and the most frequent strategy for rendering this utterance was to maintain the shift, but instead of it being from first to second person, it was from first person to a commonly used passive reflexive construction (roughly equivalent to '*as if grass were being mowed*') which maintained the impersonal and universal intent of the use of the second person form in English.

Along the same lines as the use of analogies or metaphors is the use of complicated definitions for simple terms:

9. ... a reddish fluid substance in a plastic container, snap-on top, with black writing on a white band tape with information written on it. (*Labelled vial of blood*)
10. The crystalline form of recrystallized ammonium nitrate is in a different **visual form**. *(shape)*

Sometimes a definition such as 9 is requested by an attorney if it has not yet been established that the *reddish fluid substance* is blood (although a simple *red fluid* or red *liquid* would probably suffice). At other times, however, such as in 10 above, the word choice is more likely the expert's. Interpreters usually render these descriptions or usages as given.

Finally, polysemy and words used for two different grammatical functions in the same utterance also occur occasionally. For example:

11. Firearms identification is the ability to identify a particular bullet or cartridge **case** or whatever the **case** might be, as having been fired in, or in the **case** of a projectile, fired from a particular weapon.
12. So far as the double **action** of the **function** of State's Exhibit 1. ... I found this did not **function** properly in the double **action** of the State's Exhibit 1. After a cartridge was fired, it was necessary to slightly pull the hammer back to a first position causing a small click as it makes contact with the mechanism before the **action** of the **function** of the weapon would be free enough to **function** as double **action** where you actually depress the trigger...

5.2. *Grammar and syntax*

While there was less lexical specialization than expected, exactly the opposite was true of basic grammatical errors and structural or syntactic irregularities. While some of these could be considered simple mis-speaks or confusions, other more complex examples could not be so easily explained.

As regards basic grammatical errors, those most frequently found include lack of subject/verb agreement, misused anaphora, and faulty use of prepositions, as exemplified in the following extracts.

13. **This is** some of the **characteristics** we look for in hair.
14. The Smith and Wesson **weapon**, State's exhibit 1, **are** rifled with five lands and grooves twisting to the right.
15. Q: Do they have your writing on the outside of **them**?
    A: That is Sergeant Brown's writing on **it**.
16. There was still **some** that you can see **in** the dress and I picked off **a quantity** of this **vegetation** (...) and packaged **them** separately.
17. Q: Doctor, may I interrupt you here again and ask you if you will describe the best you can recall, the depth of the **lacerations** and their length

if you can?
A: The **two lacerations** which were over the left eye were about a half to one inch in length. The edges were ragged and **this** also almost penetrated to the bone.
18. I found particles of broken glass which I did compare **against** the glass with a broken lens.
19. This is a photograph of exhibit 654 (...) again while it [the bullet] was embedded **into** the doorframe.
20. ... and I'm referring **in** a matter of days ...
21. ... she died **between** this period of time ...

Simulated interpretations of texts including these kinds of errors showed which of them presented the most significant challenge to interpreters. For example, none of the interpreters reproduced the subject/verb agreement errors (examples 13-15 above). However, misuses of anaphora were sometimes more challenging as a lack of agreement between pronouns and their antecedents can cause confusion. In the simulation, some errors in anaphora provoked only a slight hesitation at the initial decoding stage but there were other cases in which the interpreter had to use a noun rather than a pronoun in the target language to maintain accuracy, completeness and clarity. When pronoun-antecedent agreement was not consistent in the source language (15 and 16 above), the interpreter had to add that monitoring function to the myriad of decoding and encoding processes already underway. As regards prepositions, since none of the errors included in the simulations were so ambiguous as to preclude comprehension, interpreters were able in all cases to select the appropriate preposition in the target language.

Several examples of sequence of tense and tense agreement irregularities were also encountered in the texts studied.

22. Q: Showing you State's exhibit No. 40, when **did you first see** this exhibit 40?
A: **I have seen** this on the morning of 9-27-69.
23. Q: In regards to the child issues, what type of issues **did you deal with** in that area?
A: **We deal** with issues about, I think, four of the kids that were with the grandmother.
24. And she was the one who **came in** and basically mentioned the fact that **they have broken up** and other – and M. **had left** the relationship, so she **deals** with some of the anger about the relationship.
25. Q: Before we get to that, **there are** other systems as well for analyzing a person's semen, more esoteric systems, **aren't there**?
A: Yes, **there would be**. (...)

These irregularities were not reproduced in the simulations. However, the following example did produce a variety of strategies in the interpreted renditions.

26. Q: Now, before you began the search, did you brief your team members on what you wanted them to do?
A: Yes, I briefed them on the process of how to collect the evidence, record it, package it. If we were going to photograph it, I assigned a photographer to do that. If we were going to do a sketch of the area that we were searching, I assigned a sketch artist to sketch that area and to locate items that we recovered on that sketch.

In this case, a question is posed in the simple past tense and refers to a specific situation. The first sentence of the response appropriately reflects that tense and the specificity involved. However, the speaker then shifts from the simple past to a compound progressive past tense in an if-clause construction. This shift takes the listener from a concrete situation to a hypothetical one and creates confusion. In the interpreted versions, some interpreters gave a literal rendition, maintaining the use of *if* and the past continuous. Another approach was to use a restatement with a slight semantic shift whereby '*If we were going to photograph it ...*' became something like '*If I wanted [someone] to photograph it ...*' or '*If I wanted it to be photographed*'. Two of the experienced interpreters omitted the if-clause, simply stating '*I assigned a photographer and a sketch artist to sketch that area ...*'.

Other irregularities in sentence structure affect coherence and comprehensibility. Especially challenging are those cases in which a thought is not completed or an element essential to comprehension is omitted. As with all speech, the receiver needs and expects some type of closure and completion, and when the speaker stops mid-phrase, embarks on a different syntactic structure or inadvertently omits an essential element of a sequence, the receiver is perplexed. When an intepreter is faced with rendering an incomplete sequence or an essentially flawed utterance, she or he has the additional concern of knowing that the target language receiver may think that the incoherence is due to her/him rather than the witness.

In example 27 below, not only is there an inconsistency in anaphora which creates confusion – the lack of agreement between the possessive adjective used in the question (**her** *attendance record*) and the object pronoun in the response (*from* **him**) – but the final sentence of the response lacks coherence.

27. Q: ... how would you describe her attendance record?
A: Very good, very good. It wasn't until March 17th I haven't heard from him.

In order to remedy the problem and achieve comprehension, syntactic restructuring and a modification of terms (*until* → *since*) are needed, such as '*I haven't heard from her since March 17th*'. Another possible solution would also entail a modification in word choice (*I haven't heard* → *that I stopped hearing*). A review of the simulated renditions shows that in general, the more inexperienced interpreters gave a literal translation and reproduced the problem, while the more experienced interpreters were able to capture the intended meaning and render it in appropriate target language expression.

In examples 28 and 29, an essential element is missing, thus greatly affecting the coherence of the utterance. The problem could be solved by simply inserting a verb into each of the utterances, such as the one I have included in brackets:

28. Q: In regards to employment, what areas did you deal with?
    A: Employment issue, one of the things [was] that he used to do a lot of odd jobs in a sense.
29. State's Exhibit 59 I determined to be some microscopic marks of possible value and I would have to determine whether [there was] a sufficient amount at a later time under a higher powered microscope.

These examples were not included in the simulation.

The final example in this category – an incomplete sentence made up of an introductory clause and two relative clauses – is more difficult for an interpreter working in the simultaneous mode to render. Either an entire final clause is missing, or the conjunction '*and*' should be omitted, thereby converting the question into one related to the blood type of a specific sample. Given the question as stated, it is difficult to understand how the expert could answer at all.

30. Q: Was the sample you received and had the name of Mrs. Stevens on it, which you received on the 30th and which you examined and was typed 'O'?
    A: That's right, sir.

Less experienced interpreters tend to reproduce this type of utterance as given, while more experienced interpreters can monitor and/or correct their renditions upon hearing the witness' response, often restating the final portion of the question without the conjunction.

5.3. *Style and diction*

Many elements related to style and diction were found to complicate the comprehensibility of expert witness testimony. Simple redundancies, embedded phrases, hedges, false starts and repetitions often made the language produced by these witnesses appear convoluted. Some of these elements seemed to occur most often when a witness was offering a correction or clarification, most likely in an attempt to aid comprehension but often with just the opposite effect. Some of the categories proved to be relatively minor obstacles to interpreter performance (redundancies, some repetitions, some self-corrections and hedges), while others (false starts and embeddings) often proved to be more difficult to process. Consider the following examples:

Simple redundancies
31. **Continue on**, doctor.
32. **Approximately about** six o´clock this morning ...
33. Would you be able to **recall from recollection** ...

None of these presents any significant difficulty to interpreters. The utterances are easily understood and the redundancies are not reproduced in the target language.

Repetition
34. As police illustrator I generally go to the **scene of an occurrence** or the **scene of a crime** and **measure** the pertinent area to **measure** and transfer these **measurements** to a large chart for court illustration.
35. I, prior to examining and **comparing** the test bullets that I **obtained from State's Exhibit 1** or that I **observed from State's, Exhibit 1**, I made a side by side **comparison,** using the **comparison** microscope (...). The **field of view is divided by a hairline, divided by a hairline** which is the prism which **divides** the **field of view**.
36. The vehicle was in the Sheriff's compound. It is just a **wire enclosed Anchor wire enclosed** in the rear of the Sheriff´s office.

Less experienced interpreters tended to render the repetitions as they heard them, reproducing some of the stylistic awkwardness found in the original. More experienced interpreters were able to omit some of the repetition, such as '*divided by a hairline*' in example 35. Example 36 proved most confusing to the interpreters as a group, seemingly due more to the lack of a noun to complete the descriptive nominal phrase '*wire enclosed Anchor wire enclosed* [area, lot]' and to the use of the brand name *Anchor* than to the mere fact that part of the phrase was repeated.

Embeddings
Embedded phrases are quite a common occurrence in expert witness testimony and in speech in general. They usually reflect the spontaneity of spoken language and the thought processes that underlie speech as the speaker attempts to remember and relate details and order them in a comprehensible way. Consider examples 37 – 40.

37. Q: What about the barrel characteristics?
    A: The Smith and Wesson weapons are normally – **and the same in this case, Exhibit I** – rifled, and when I refer to rifled, I refer to the number of lands and grooves.

38. Basically there was some – an anger issue related to that because they didn't feel – **I'm talking about M... and his wife at the time** – that they, the children, should have been taken away from them ...
39. One time they were working together in a – **how would I put it?** – I believe it was in the hotel ...
40. The first night of the, the bombing on the 19th, we had people from the different law enforcement agencies there, and someone – **and I don't know who** – or a group of people, painted pink circles around items of – such as this tyre rim that they felt could be significant pieces of evidence.

When the embedding comes at a logical juncture in the utterance, comprehension is still achievable as meaning is partly conveyed through pause and intonation (examples 39 and 40 above). However, when the embedding comes at an unnatural juncture in the utterance, such as between an adverb and the verb it modifies (example 37) or at the end of a clause as opposed to next to the noun being modified (example 38), processing by the interpreter becomes more complicated.

Clarification and self-correction
Speakers unconsciously monitor their own speech, and when a mis-speak occurs or when an expert witness realizes that perhaps further clarification is needed, an attempt is often made to provide the additional information or make the correction. Examples 41 and 42 below show the repair process at work.

41. Q: Now I will show you State's Exhibit 78 and ask you if this is a true Xerox copy of the **original page** of State's Exhibit No. 77, **the first page** of that tablet?
    A: Without going into all the other material on the page, the **label is**, the **Xerox is** a copy of the label which is on the sheet.
42. State's Exhibit 47 contained full length pubic red hair, **of pubic, of Caucasian** origin.

In the simulation, interpreters incorporated the corrections into the target language. In the first example, the mis-speak and correction were both reproduced. However, since the word '*Xerox*' has not been universalized in Spanish to represent copying as it has been in English, the interpreted version was generally '*the label is, the photocopy is of the label which is on the sheet*'. In the second example, the fact that in Spanish adjectives follow nouns made it quite easy for interpreters to omit the misuse of '*pubic*'.

Another type of self-correction is the false start. This occurs when the speaker changes direction mid-utterance and instead of completing his original thought, embarks on a totally new one. Sometimes false starts consist of only a word or two and are easily negotiated by an interpreter (example 43 below), but as we can see in 44-46, comprehension can be greatly affected.

43. What ... were you able to reach any conclusions with respect to possible comparisons?
44. Q: Can you say that this photograph fairly and accurately depicts the parking lot as you saw it?
    A: In general, from a general ... just passing by, but not in particular.
45. Q: Doctor, could it be probably that either State's Exhibit No. 3 or State's Exhibit No. 1 could have inflicted the lacerations or some of the lacerations?
    A: Well I don't think I can say anything about probability as to its – all I can say is it is possible, if we are trying to determine what could have inflicted these lacerations.
46. Q: And are you aware of whether or not she was with – approximately within legal limits with the Section Eight housing?
    A: That – when we are talking about Section Eight housing, it's a cloudy issue. And she – and it's usually – they are more the middle people that set it up between landlord and tenant.

In these cases, interpreters use many strategies including ignoring a clear and easy-to-omit false start (example 43), reproducing the phrase that comprises the false start using prosodics to help convey meaning and ensure comprehension (examples 44 and 45), or waiting to grasp the meaning of the utterance and eliminate the false start (example 46). As a simultaneous rendition of expert testimony provided to the defendant in order to protect his/her due process rights does not become part of the record or contribute to a judge's or jury's perception of credibility or trustworthiness, the primary goal becomes achieving communication. Hence, the high degree of equivalence required for interpreted testimony that does go on the record is not required in these instances.

As regards hedges, those produced by the speaker were sometimes reproduced and sometimes omitted, often depending upon placement in the utterance. Examples of speaker-produced hedges include the repeated use of 'okay', 'all right', 'well' and so on at the outset of a question or response. Consider the following attorney-expert exchange.

47. Q: **Okay**. Explain briefly what the enzyme typing method is.
    A: **Well**, in as I said in semen where there´s possiblity of having A, B, O substance present, there is also possible to have the enzymes, **okay**, present in semen as the enzymes are present and found in blood and it is a tool to again further individualize a person's seminal fluid particularly in semen. This is one enzyme which is used quite exclusively, that is what is known as PGM and this is an enzyme which has a various break down among the population and is used to further individualize a person's semen.
    Q: **All right**. Under the PGM enzyme system there is three categories,

PGM I, PGM II, PGM I and II.
A: Yes.
Q: **Okay**. Is there any correlation between PGM enzyme break down and the ABO blood typing?
A: No.
Q: **That is to say**, a person just because a person is a type O or A or B he could be any one of the three enzyme system?
A: That's correct.

Initial hedges were reproduced as uttered in the interpreted versions. However, a hedge found in the middle of an utterance, such as the use of 'okay' in the second line of the first response was omitted by both more and less experienced interpreters. Further examples of this phenomenon are found in exchange 48.

48. Q: How did it improve?
A: **Well**, she was doing her hair and she was wearing, **I guess**, nicer clothes. She was even putting **just** light makeup on. (...)

In this case, the hedge '*well*' at the beginning of the outset was maintained, while the other two found within the utterance were omitted.

Equally as interesting were those hedges that were introduced by the interpreter, often to mitigate the effects of a mis-speak or false start. In the renditions of examples 49 – 51 given by the more experienced interpreters, we find the insertion of hedging devices to signal a correction or redirection of the utterance in order to aid comprehension. The hedges inserted by the interpreters are shown in Spanish where they occur in the rendition, with an English gloss provided in italics.

49. Thank you. When you first/ have you seen any improvement ...?
    bueno (*well*)
50. I would say that she/ we had to postpone not more than two meetings.
    bueno (*well*)
51. Dr. V. testified that she would use/ that she would fall back to using
    digamos (*let's say*)
    drugs if/ when depressed.
    o sea (*that is*)

A final category includes what I shall call 'semantic ambiguities' or total loss of coherence. This category contains examples of what are almost nonsense utterances, given that the misuse of language affects comprehension so completely that communication is not achieved. These often appear comical but in reality are an interpreter's nightmare.

52. Why it is important here is if Mrs. X, no matter what you say, you can argue that it couldn't happen here.
53. I checked the speedometer reading from the general reading to the decimal indicator at the end of the reading from one point to the next and then in sequence and then got at the mileage by subtraction.
54. At this time I obtained test bullets using 38 S&W calibre ammunition of Winchester Western manufacture or loaded with bullets which were copper-coated lead and recovered test bullets from State's Exhibit I.
55. Q: What determines the barrel's general condition?
    A: Primarily due to wear, corrosion and misuse of the weapon allowing it to have condensation build up in the barrel and not cleaning it properly gives it a very definite pattern through the particular weapon and the care of the weapon during the years.

In these cases, the interpreter has no choice but to render an ongoing interpretation of what she/he hears as it is virtually impossible spontaneously to correct or improve the quality of spoken language when cohesion and coherence are so totally lacking. On some occasions, the context and previous testimony aid comprehension by both the interpreter and the target language receiver and, of course, their willingness and desire to achieve communication also plays a significant role.

6. Conclusions

Interpreting expert testimony is an intimidating assignment for even experienced interpreters. How best to prepare for this type of testimony should be based on an understanding of its characteristics. Of course, it is impossible to guarantee that there will not be a significant amount of specialized terminology in a given expert's testimony. The findings of this study are not intended to suggest that adequate lexical preparation is not wise, especially considering the fact that searching for equivalent terms or concepts results in an enhanced knowledge of the topic, which in turn contributes to successful interpreting. However, the findings do suggest that much of the difficulty that comes with expert testimony has more to do with how language is used by these experts than with the specialized words they employ. By understanding that the speech of experts is fraught with the same types of inconsistencies as any other spontaneous speech and has many of the characteristics found in spoken legal language in general, the misconception that expert witness testimony is lexically but not formally challenging can be overcome. In this way, interpreters will realize that honing their discriminatory listening and comprehension skills and improving their overall interpreting skills will also contribute greatly to the success they will achieve when interpreting for specialists from even the most esoteric of fields.

References

Berk-Seligson, Susan (1987) 'The Intersection of Testimony Styles in Interpreted Judicial Proceedings: Pragmatic Alterations in Spanish Testimony', *Linguistics* 25: 1087-1125.

------ (1988) 'The Impact of Politeness in Witness Testimony: The Influence of the Court Interpreter', *Multilingua* 7(4): 431-449.

------ (1990) *The Bilingual Courtroom: Court Interpreters in the Judicial Process*, Chicago: University of Chicago Press.

Charrow, Veda (1982) 'Linguistic Theory and the Study of Legal and Bureaucratic Language', in Obler and Menn (eds) *Exceptional Language and Linguistics*, New York: Academic Press, 88-101.

------ J. Crandal and R. Charrow (1982) 'Characteristics and Functions of Legal Language', in Kittredge R. and J. Lehrberger (eds) *Sublanguage Studies of Language in Restricted Semantic Domains*, New York: Gruyter, 175-190.

Crystal, David and Derek Davy (1969) *Investigating English Style*, Bloomington & London: Indiana University Press.

Danet, Brenda (1980) 'Language in the Legal Process', *Law and Society Review* 14(3): 445-564.

------ K. Hoffman, N. Kermish, H. Rafn and D. Stayman (1976) 'An Ethnography of Questioning in the Courtroom', in R. Shuy and A. Shnukal (eds) *Language Use and the Uses of Language*, Washington, D.C.: Georgetown University Press, 222-233.

González, Roseann Dueñas (1976) *English Language Handicap Diagnostic Instrument no. 1*, Tucson: Pima Superior Court, Justice Interpreters Model Development.

------ (1977) *The Design and Validation of an Evaluative Procedure to Diagnose the English Aural-Oral Competency of a Spanish-speaking Person in the Justice System*, unpublished doctoral dissertation, University of Arizona.

------, Victoria Vásquez & Holly Mikkelson (1991) *Fundamentals of Court Interpretation. Theory, Policy and Practice*, Durham, N.C.: Carolina Academic Press.

Mellinkoff, D. (1963) *The Language of the Law*, Boston: Little, Brown.

O'Barr, W. M. (1981) 'The Language of the Law', in C.A. Ferguson and S.B. Heath (eds), *Language in the U.S.A.*, New York: Cambridge University Press, 386-406.

------ (1982) *Linguistic Evidence: Language, Power and Strategy in the Courtroom*, New York: Academic Press.

------ and J.M. Conley (1976) 'When a Juror Watches a Lawyer', *Barrister* 3: 8-11.

------ and E.A. Lind (1981) 'Ethnography and Experimentation – Partners in Legal Research', in B.D. Sales (ed) *Perspectives in Law and Psychology: The Trial Process*, New York: Plenum Press, 181-208.

Solan, Lawrence (1993) *The Language of Judges*, Chicago: University of Chicago Press.

How are Courtroom Questions Interpreted?
An Analysis of Spanish Interpreters' Practices

SANDRA HALE

> Questions in the adversarial courtroom are used strategically by counsel to guide, control and constrain the information presented in evidence. This is achieved partly by the content of the question, but also by the form of the question. Different types of questions predominate in either examination-in-chief or cross-examination to suit the purpose of each. Whereas the questions used in examination-in-chief tend to be more open and less constraining (e.g. Wh- questions), those used in cross-examination tend to be more coercive and aggressive (e.g. declaratives, tag questions). When cases involve speakers of different languages, interpreters are required. It is essential that interpreters understand the purpose of questions in the courtroom and the pragmatic effect of each type in order to render accurate interpretations. This paper will report on the results of empirical research into the way Spanish interpreters interpret English questions into Spanish in thirteen Local Court cases in Australia. The main aim of the study was to ascertain whether interpreters maintain the form as well as the content of the question in their interpretation, and if they do not, the possible reasons why and the implications of their choices.

1. Introduction

The adversarial courtroom constitutes a very ritualized speech event, where participants have inflexible roles to play and where the rules of evidence dictate certain behaviours and constrain others. Cases are based primarily on oral evidence which must be presented in the form of 'questions and answers'. However, only the powerful participants in the courtroom, the lawyers and the Bench, are permitted to ask the questions. The role of the witness/defendant/accused, whatever the case may be, is to provide a relevant answer to the questions put to them. The lay person is barred from asking questions, making comments or refusing to answer questions. This unequal relationship between questioner and respondent, gives counsel the power to control the exchange and to construct a 'story' (Bennett and Feldman 1981) that suits his/her case, in a way that is relevant to the court. As Walker (1987:57) states "attorneys are aware of the essential imbalance of power that operates in any... adversary legal interview, and ... they employ this power in conscious ways in an effort to influence the outcome of their cases by controlling a witness's line of testimony". Such control is exerted through the strategic use of questions.

Questions in this speech event are generally not asked in order to elicit information unknown to the questioner, but to elicit information or responses that would either favour or discredit a particular case. The pragmatic function of lawyers' interrogations varies according to the intention behind them, regardless of their grammatical form. As Dunstan (1980: 64) points out:

> ...such turns are only 'minimally describable' as questions for they are also variously produced and treated primarily as accusations, counter-denials, displays of disbelief, repair initiations, pre-sequencers, and so on. Furthermore, in only a small fraction of instances are the questions asked in cross-examination genuine requests for information. It is, as consultation of trial manuals will reveal, a primary 'rule' for cross-examination, that one should never ask a question to which one does not know the answer.

Schegloff (1973) compares a question in everyday conversation with a summons. In the courtroom this metaphor becomes reality, since a refusal to answer a question can be regarded as contempt of court. Harris (1984: 6) argues that "...questions are the accepted means of determining what is talked about in particular cases, the form the discourse takes, and ultimately the structure of the information transfer in a court situation". The pragmatic function of the majority of lawyers' courtroom questions is in essence that of ordering a response rather than seeking new information. As aptly put by Walker (1987:59-60) "in a legal adversary interview a question becomes more than that: it becomes an order that the respondent's knowledge be displayed in an appropriate form".

The purpose of examination-in-chief and cross-examination determines the discourse practices used in the presentation of evidence. Each lawyer presents his/her version of the facts through the use of questions in examination-in-chief in a manner that is convincing and favorable to their case. The evidence presented in examination-in-chief is then challenged in cross-examination by the opposing lawyer, to try to discredit the version presented by the other party. It is to be expected then, that the questions in cross-examination will be more accusatory, more aggressive and more coercive, constraining the witness's answers to a limited choice. In examination-in-chief, leading questions, which tell more than they ask, are permitted only to elicit non-controversial, initial information, such as personal details. In all other instances they are disallowed by the rules of evidence. The reason for this is that the evidence must come from the witness's mouth, unprompted by the lawyer. However, in cross-examination, leading questions are encouraged, as counsel's objective is to coerce the witness into giving a damaging answer.

2. Question type

Among other approaches to studying courtroom questioning is the analysis of question type. This entails the classification of every question or lawyer's turn into a characteristic type. The main reason behind analysing the types of questions used in the courtroom has been to ascertain whether the type of question makes a contribution to the overall presentation of evidence, and if it does, the way in which it constrains the answers. According to Loftus (1979: 90-91), "the form in which a question is put to a witness exerts a strong influence on the quality of the answer". A number of different studies have been presented. The table below shows the different classifications of questions according to four different studies. Loftus (1979) and Maley and Fahey (1991) speak of two broad categories of questions, whereas Danet and Bogoch (1980) and Woodbury (1984) categorize them into smaller, more specific groups, although Woodbury initially speaks of two broad groups, Wh- versus yes/no questions. The table clearly shows both match and overlap across the authors.

Loftus (1979)	Danet and Bogoch (1980)	Woodbury (1984)	Maley and Fahey (1991)
1. Free Report / narrative form question	1. Declaratives – with or without tags	1. Tags a. Copy tags (+dec./+tag) b. Confirmatory tags (is that/isn't that correct) c. Checking tags (+dec./-tag & -dec./+tag)	1. Confirmation Seeking questions a. Declaratives – with or without tags: -probing tags (+dec./+tag) -assumption tags (+dec./-tag & -dec./+tag) -ratification tags (is that/isn't that correct)
ø		2. Prosodic questions (in the form of declaratives)	
ø	2. a. Interrogatives Yes/No questions	3. Grammatical yes/no qns a. Negative yes/no questions b. Positive yes/no questions	b. Polar interrogatives
2. Controlled Narrative questions	b. Choice questions	4. Alternative questions	ø
	3. Interrogative Wh- questions	5. Wh-questions a. Narrow Wh- questions b. Broad Wh- questions c. Reduced Wh- questions	2. Information Seeking questions Wh- questions
ø	4. Requestions	ø	ø

ø = no equivalent

Table 1: Question type taxonomies

3. Courtroom questioning through the use of an interpreter

Although there is a considerable volume of work on courtroom questions, it is mostly based on English discourse alone. There has been some limited work on the impact of interpreters in courtroom questioning. Berk-Seligson (1990:25) states that "the court interpreter affects the verbal outcome of attorney's and judges' questions" and that interpreters "interfere with the attempts of examiners to get out their questions in the way they want to". Rigney (1997, 1999), using examples from a Spanish speaking witness' testimony in the O.J. Simpson trial, presents some interesting results of the interpreter's effect on question type. She found that the interpreter tended to alter "the pragmatics of certain types of English questions when translating them into Spanish" (1997:14). Her studies demonstrated that English tag and declarative questions were particularly challenging for Spanish interpreters as they would need to resort to "additional linguistic resources" in order to convey the same pragmatic meaning in Spanish (1999:104). Berk-Seligson (1999:50) also found, in a recent study of Spanish court interpreters in the United States, that although equivalence of propositional content is generally maintained, they "inadvertently *alter* the pragmatic force of attorney's questions", systematically weakening the coerciveness of leading questions.

3.1. The data

Thirteen English-Spanish interpreted Local Court hearings held in New South Wales, Australia, during the years 1993 to 1996, form the data for this study. Local Court hearings in NSW are routinely audio tape-recorded by the court monitor, hence there was no researcher intrusion in the data collection process. Each case was transcribed including as much detail as was audibly possible. All questions were numbered, amounting to a total of 1957 questions asked by counsel, 1028 in English and 929 in Spanish. As the numbers show, some of the English questions were not translated into Spanish because some of the Spanish-speaking witnesses understood some of the questions and answered them directly before the interpreter had time to interpret. The questions were then divided for analysis into cross-examination and examination-in-chief, with an end result of 631 English and 550 Spanish interpreted cross-examination questions; and 397 English and 379 Spanish interpreted examination-in-chief questions. The term 'question' is used loosely to refer to any turn taken by the lawyer in addressing the witness. A number of these turns are not grammatical questions but require a response from the witness nonetheless.

All questions were coded for syntactic type, after which all types were quantified in each language and percentages calculated. The questions fell into one of three broad grammatical categories: interrogatives, declaratives and imperatives, under which there are a number of subtypes.

In this study I aimed to discover the following: 1. whether the pattern of courtroom questions found in studies conducted in other Common Law countries is also found in Australia; 2. whether the interpreted questions kept the same form as the original English questions; 3. if there were differences between the English and the Spanish questions, what were the differences and possible reasons for it; 4. what effect may such changes have on the answers.

3.2. Question type in cross-examination and examination-in-chief

As in previous studies, it was found that the type of question used relates to the type of examination. Table 2 below outlines the distribution of question type in cross-examination and examination-in-chief with frequencies and percentages, in order of occurrence.

Cross Ex. questions	Ex. in chief questions
1.+ Polar Interrogative = 164 (25.99%)	1.+Polar Interrogative= 151 (38%)
2.+/- Declarative= 159 (25.19%)	2.Wh Interrogative = 70 (17.63%)
3.Wh Interrogative = 64 (10.14%)	3.+/- Declarative= 59 (14.86%)
4.+ Dec. with +tag= 51(8%)	4.Modal Interrogative = 59 (14.86%)
5."I put it to you" Dec.= 47 (7.45%)	5.+ Dec. w/ rising intonation = 29(7.3%)
6.+ Dec. w/ rising intonation = 45(7.13%)	6.+ Dec. with +tag= 12 (3%)
7.+ Dec. with –tag= 39 (6.18%)	7.Forced choice Interrogative= 6 (1.5%)
8.- Dec. with +tag= 24 (3.8%)	8.Imperatives = 6 (1.32%)
9.Modal Interrogative = 12 (1.9%)	9.+ Dec. with -tag= 3 (1.5%)
10.Rep. Speech Dec.= 8 (1.27%)	10.- Dec. with +tag= 2 (0.50%)
11.Forced choice Interrogative= 7 (1.10%)	- Dec. w/ rising intonation = 0
12.- Dec. w/ rising intonation = 6 (0.95%)	- Polar Interrogative = 0
13.+ Polar Interrogative = 3 (0.47%)	- Dec. with –tag= 0
14.- Dec. with -tag= 1 = 0.16%	'I put it to you' Dec.= 0
15.Imperatives = 1 (0.16%)	Rep. Speech Dec.= 0
Total = 631	Total = 397

Table 2 : Cross-examination and examination-in-chief question types
(in order of occurrence)

3.2.1 Quantitative results

The quantitative results of this study corroborate those of previous studies on question type. Firstly, the most commonly used type of question in both examination-in-chief and cross-examination was the positive polar interrogative, since it allows the lawyer to maintain full control of the evidence presented. This corroborates Rigney's (1997) results. Secondly, question type differs according to the type of examination. We can clearly see in Table 2 that there is not a one-to-one correspondence of question type in cross-examination and examination-in-chief. A wider range of question types is used in cross-examination. Some of the more aggressive and coercive types of questions either do not appear at all in examination-in-chief or are insignificant. 'I put it to you' declaratives, reported speech declaratives, negative declaratives with rising intonation, negative polar interrogatives and negative declaratives with negative tags are not used in examination-in-chief at all. Declaratives with tags in general comprise a very small percentage (5%) of the questions in examination-in-chief. On the other hand, some of the types that yield high percentages in examination-in-chief either have lower percentages in cross-examination or hardly feature at all. For example, modal interrogatives form 14.86% of examination-in-chief questions and only 1.9% of cross-examination questions. Wh-interrogatives, as in other studies, also feature more prominently in examination-in-chief, although the difference is not so striking (17.63% vs 10.14%). When the questions are grouped into two broad categories, Information Seeking Questions (ISQ) and Confirmation Seeking Questions (CSQ), the difference between examination-in-chief and cross-examination becomes more obvious. The great majority of questions in cross-examination (87.85%) were CSQ or yes-no questions, providing information rather than seeking it, with only 12.04% being ISQ, comprising Wh- questions and Modal questions. In examination-in-chief, 67.98% were CSQ and 32.49% ISQ. Although CSQ comprise the majority of questions in both examination-in-chief and cross-examination, Information Seeking Questions were 20.45% more popular in examination-in-chief, and Confirmation Seeking Questions, were 19.87% more popular in cross-examination, a finding that corroborates Maley and Fahey's (1991) results. This is consistent with the rules of evidence that prevail in the courtroom that allow a very limited use of leading questions in examination-in-chief, but encourage its use in cross-examiantion.

4. Grammatical differences between the formulation of questions in English and Spanish

The main object of this study was to ascertain whether interpreters maintain the form of the question in their interpretation, and if they do not, the possible reasons why and the implications of their choices. Before comparing the differences found between Source Language (SL) and Target Language (TL) questions, an overview of the grammatical differences found in English and Spanish in the formulation of questions will be provided.

4.1. Formulating questions in English

In English there are three major classes of questions, broadly divided according to the type of reply each can typically expect: those that expect affirmation or negation, as in yes-no questions, those that expect a wide range of replies, as in Information or Wh- questions, and those that present two or more options, as in alternative or forced choice questions. Yes-no questions are usually formed by placing the operator, that is, the first auxiliary verb or form of 'do', in front of the subject, and generally giving the sentence a rising intonation. Wh- questions are formed by fronting the Wh-word, except in very few cases as in the fronting of a preposition 'To what do you attribute that?'. Generally, unlike yes-no questions, Wh- questions have a falling intonation. Alternative questions can resemble either of the two classes already mentioned and are formed in the same way with the addition of options at the end, as in 'Do you want tea or coffee?' or 'What did you say, this or that?' Into the class of yes-no questions fall two subclasses, that of tag questions and declarative questions. Tag questions are formed by combining a statement with a tag question appended at the end. Declarative questions are simply statements with a rising intonation. Each of these classes will be discussed in more detail as they arise later in the text. There are two minor classes of questions in English, exclamatory and rhetorical, which I will not mention as they are not pertinent to this study (Quirk *et al.* 1985: 806-826).

4.2. Formulating questions in Spanish

Spanish questions can also be divided into three major classes: Yes/no questions, Information questions and Alternative questions. However, they differ in form from English, the major difference found in the formulation of yes/no questions. As Spanish is a highly inflected language grammatically, its word order is much freer than that of English. Questions are asked intonationally, hence the position of the clause elements does not make any grammatical difference. In essence all polar questions in Spanish are statements with rising intonation, the equivalent of the English declarative question.

> Any declarative sentence can become a general interrogative without the need to alter its syntactic structure. The assertions *Tu hermano está mejor* ('your brother is better') or *Está mejor tu hermano* ('is better your brother'), adopt the form of questions when saying *¿Tu hermano está mejor?* or *¿Está mejor tu hermano?*. This freedom of construction is due to the particular interrogative melodic curve found in Spanish questions from the beginning

of the utterance, and not only at the end, as is the case in other languages. Spanish orthography reflects well the reality of oral speech by requiring the question marks (¿...?) both at the beginning and at the end of the question. (Real Academia Española 1981: 396 – my translation[1]).

It is also worth noting that Spanish has no equivalent of the English dummy operators (Quirk *et al.* 1985: 133) such as 'do', a fact which causes major difficulties in the translation of tag questions. However, although word order does not affect the grammaticality of the sentence, it affects its illocutionary force. Thematic choice in questions is much wider in Spanish than in English.

The verb can precede or follow the subject and any of the other elements in general interrogatives with the same freedom as in the construction of declaratives, from which they are only different in intonation...The interest of the moment dictates in each case the position of the sentence elements, with a tendency to front what is considered to be most important or expressive. (Real Academia 1981: 359-60 – my translation[2]).

For instance, any of the clause elements, subject, predicator, object, complement or adjunct, can be fronted in a question. Table 3 is an attempt to illustrate this point.

3/1 ¿*Todos vienen a la cena?* 'Is everyone coming to dinner?'	Question – rising intonation – subject fronted
3/2 ¿*Vienen todos a la cena?* '**Everyone's** coming to dinner?'	Question – rising intonation – predicator fronted
3/3 ¿*A la cena vienen todos?* 'Is everyone coming to **dinner**?'	Question – rising intonation – adjunct fronted

Table 3: Word order in questions

---

[1] "Cualquier oración enunciativa puede convertirse en interrogativa general sin necesidad de alterar su estructura sintáctica. La afirmación *Tu hermano está mejor* o *Está mejor tu hermano*, adopta forma de pregunta diciendo ¿*Tu hermano está mejor?* o ¿*Está mejor tu hermano?*. Esta libertad de construcción se debe a que la curva melódica interrogativa adquiere en español su carácter peculiar desde el comienzo de la pregunta, y no solo al final, como ocurre en otras lenguas. La ortografía española traduce bien la realidad del habla oral al exigir los signos de interrogación (¿...?) al principio y al fin de la pregunta."
[2] "El verbo puede anteponerse o posponerse al sujeto y a los demás elementos de las interrogativas generales, con la misma libertad de construcción que en las enunciativas, de las cuales no se diferencian más que en la entonación... El interés del momento regula en cada caso la posición de los elementos oracionales, con tendencia a anteponer el que se siente como más importante o expresivo."

In Table 3 I have tried to provide a pragmatic near equivalent of the different questions in Spanish. As explained before, any of the sentence elements can be fronted without any change in the propositional content. However, the illocutionary force is slightly altered. This is related to the level of markedness of each choice. According to Boretti de Macchia (1996: 100) and Pórtoles (1988: 80), the Subject-Verb order in Spanish is equivalent to the English interrogatives. I therefore propose (based also on my native-speaker competence) that the least marked choice for interrogatives would be question no. 3/1, which fronts the subject; hence I have provided the least marked option in English for its translation, *¿Todos vienen a la cena?* – 'Is everyone coming to dinner?'. Fronting the predicator in Spanish, as in question 3/2, makes the question slightly more marked and gives more prosodic emphasis to the subject. The stress naturally falls on *todos* when asking this version of the question. The stress cannot fall on any other element and sound natural. For this reason, I believe a declarative question in English which fronts the subject and stresses it prosodically, is the closest equivalent. The last version which fronts the adjunct is the most marked and would only be used when emphasising 'the dinner'. This question in Spanish implies that we are specifically talking about the dinner and not about the dance or anything else. Since in English it is grammatically incorrect to front the adjunct of place in an interrogative, the only way of achieving the same effect would be by stressing it intonationally. Note that the adjunct of place can be fronted in a declarative in English, as in 'To the dinner we all come', although this is highly marked. Table 4 shows available options when personal pronouns are involved.

4/1 *¿(Tú)Compraste bananas?* 'Did you buy bananas?'	question – rising intonation – subject fronted (subject conflated)
4/2 *¿Compraste bananas tú?* 'Did **you** buy bananas?'	question – rising intonation – predicator fronted
4/3 *¿Bananas compraste?* 'You bought bananas?'	question – rising intonation – object fronted

Table 4: Word order in questions: subject pronouns and verbs

Since in Spanish the verb marks for person as well as tense, number and aspect, the personal pronoun is not necessary unless an emphasis is required. Therefore, in question 4/1, although the verb is what appears first in the sentence, the subject *tú* is tacit, but it is still in first position, making it an unmarked question. Question 4/2, which no longer conflates the subject with the predicator, becomes more marked and implies an emphasis on the person. In English this is once again achieved prosodically. The third question which fronts the object is the most marked and can best be translated with a declarative question in English.

5/1 ¿*Lleno está?* 'Full, is it?'	question – rising intonation – complement fronted

Table 5: Word order in questions: complement fronting

Finally, fronting the complement as in Table 5 is only common in conversation when the other elements of the sentence are ellipted. Since the pronoun is conflated in the verb *estar* in Spanish, we can say that the English version is structurally equivalent to the original Spanish. The difference lies in the fact that Spanish is ellipting the subject *Lleno está el coche?* and the English question is ellipting both the initial verb and subject 'Is the car full, is it?', making the 'is it' into a constant declarative tag.

To sum up, the pattern that I am suggesting here is that equivalence of the pragmatic function of questions in English and Spanish relates more to levels of markedness than to grammatical form. Since questions in Spanish are formulated intonationally, regardless of the order of the clausal elements, I have proposed that the fronting of specific elements has pragmatic significance. Unlike English, the Spanish unmarked question fronts the subject and not the verb. Therefore, unmarked English polar interrogatives which front the verb or relevant auxiliary or dummy operator, would be equivalent to the Spanish polar interrogative which has the form of a declarative with rising intonation and the subject in front position. I then suggest that since the theme position of the verb in Spanish questions is slightly marked, this would be closer pragmatically to the English declarative question. Some of the other versions of Spanish questions which front elements such as objects, adjuncts or complements can mostly be rendered into English by way of stressing the element that is thematized in Spanish, even if it does not appear in front position in English. Therefore, I suggest that matching the level of markedness is more important than matching the grammatical form in aiming to achieve pragmatic equivalence.

5. English original questions and interpreted Spanish questions

A quick glance at the percentages of the English questions as compared to the percentages of the same types in the interpreted Spanish versions (see Tables 6 and 7) indicates that there is not a one-to-one correspondence. This shows that the interpreter changed the form of some of the questions when interpreting them into Spanish. The tendency is more prevalent in some types of questions than in others. Tables 6 and 7 show that all declarative questions in English have no counterparts in Spanish. For the grammatical reasons already outlined, all Spanish questions are declaratives with rising intonation. Hence they were all classified as polar interrogatives, since they expect either an affirmative or a negative answer. In the original classification, there was no consideration of the order of the sentence elements in the Spanish questions, as outlined in section 4.2 above; hence all Spanish yes/no interrogatives fall into the same category, regardless of their syntactic structure.

Question type	English original questions	Spanish interpreted questions
Wh-Interrogative	64 = 10.14%	58 = 10.54%
Positive Polar Interrogative	164 = 25.99%	199 = 36.18%
Negative Polar Interrogative	3 = 0.47%	19 = 3.45%
Positive Declarative with rising intonation	45 = 7.13%	0 N/A
Negative Declarative with rising intonation	6 = 0.95%	0 N/A
Positive Declarative with neg. tag	39 = 6.18%	9 = 1.63%
Neg. Declarative with pos. tag	24 = 3.8%	6 = 1.09%
Pos. Declarative with pos. tag	51 = 8%	32 = 5.82%
Declarative	159 = 25.19%	170 = 30.90%
Neg. Declarative with neg. tag	1 = 0.16%	1 = 0.18%
Modal Interrogative	12 = 1.9%	5 = 0.90%
Imperatives	1 = 0.16%	5 = 0.90%
'I put it to you' Declaratives	47 = 7.45%	35 = 6.36%
Forced Choice Interrogatives	7 = 1.10%	5 = 0.90%
Rep. Speech Declaratives	8 = 1.27%	6 = 1.09%

(631 English qns. 550 Spanish interpreted qns.)

Table 6: Cross-examination English and interpreted questions

Question type	English original questions	Spanish interpreted questions
Wh-Interrogative	70 = 17.63%	79 = 20.84%
Positive Polar Interrogative	151 = 38%	162 = 42.74%
Negative Polar Interrogative	0	2 = 0.52%
Positive Declarative with rising intonation	29 = 7.3%	0 (N/A)
Negative Declarative with rising intonation	0	0 (N/A)
Positive Declarative with neg. tag	3 = 0.75%	3 = 0.79%
Neg. Declarative with pos. tag	2 = 0.50%	1 = 0.26%
Pos. Declarative with pos. tag	12 = 3%	11 = 2.9%
Declarative	59 = 14.86%	69 = 18.21 %
Neg. Declarative with neg. tag	0	0
Modal Interrogative	59 = 14.86%	36 = 9.50%
Imperatives	6 = 1.5%	9 = 2.37%
'I put it to you' declaratives	0	0
Forced Choice Interrogatives	6 = 1.5%	7 = 1.85%
Rep. Speech Declaratives	0	0
Uncoded questions	4	

(397 English qns, 379 Interpreted qns)

Table 7: Examination-in-chief English and interpreted questions

6. Cross-examination questions and their interpretations

Since the interpreters' alterations of question form differed according to type of courtroom examination, the analysis of the translation of the questions will be covered in two different sections, one on cross-examination and one on examination-in-chief. When types are grouped into broader categories, the differences become more pronounced (see tables 8 and 9). One major difference which is to be expected is found in the translation of prosodic declarative questions. A great number of prosodic declarative English questions were translated as polar interrogatives in Spanish, which explains the higher percentage of this type of question in the interpreted text, 39.64% as opposed to 26.46% in English. The rest were translated as simple declaratives, with no rising intonation. This difference means that overall, the English cross-examination questions have a higher percentage of declaratives than interrogatives (59.11% vs 46.90%).

Since declaratives are said to be more coercive (Danet and Bogoch, 1980) than interrogatives, such a difference seems to suggest that the English interrogation is more coercive than the Spanish interrogation. As can be seen, the trend is reversed in the Spanish questions, with 46.9% declaratives and 53.09% interrogatives. Therefore, the lawyer's level of control over the witness may have been altered in the translation.

English	Spanish
Declaratives with tag = 115 (18.23%)	= 48 (8.73%)
Declarative & Imperatives = 207 (32.8%)	= 210 (38.18%)
Dec. with rising intonation = 51 (8%)	= 0
Total = 373 (59.11%)	Total = 258 (46.9%)

Table 8: Cross-examination declaratives

English	Spanish
Wh- Interrogatives = 64 (10.14%)	= 58 (10.55%)
Polar Interrogatives = 167 (26.46%)	= 218 (39.64%)
Forced Choice Int. = 7 (1.11%)	= 5 (0.9%)
Modal Interrogatives = 12 (1.9%)	= 5 (0.9%)
Rep. Speech Declarative = 8 (1.27%)	= 6 (1.09%)
Total = 258 (46.90%)	292 (53.09%)

Table 9: Cross-examination interrogatives

By looking at the figures we can clearly see that there is a very significant difference between the percentage of declaratives with tags in the original English text (18.23%) and the percentage in the Spanish interpreted text (8.73%). The data show that the interpreters tended simply to omit the tag question and translate such questions as either simple declaratives or as polar interrogatives. This matches Rigney's results on the translation of tag questions (1997:20).

6.1. Tag questions

Tag questions were identified as one of the types that caused interpreters most difficulty. This finding is consistent with Rigney's (1997, 1999). The data show that interpreters omitted the tag 52.12% of the time. There are a number of explanations for this phenomenon. As Hale and Gibbons (1999) suggest, one possible reason why interpreters tend to omit what they consider to be 'irrelevant' is that they are pressured to offer a quick delivery so as to not waste the court's time. Berk-Seligson (1990) also found that interpreters who tried to please the court by making things 'easier' and saving time were appreciated more. Another plausible reason for such omissions may be that interpreters do not realize the importance of question form and concentrate on translating the propositional content alone, in whatever form they randomly choose at the time. However, I will argue that there are both grammatical and pragmatic differences across both languages that impose a difficulty on the translation of tag questions from English into Spanish.

6.2. Tag questions in English

Tag questions in English express maximum conduciveness and they are considered to be a type of yes-no question. They are formed by a statement and a tag question appended to the end, with either a negative or a positive orientation. Quirk *et al.* (1985) mention seven types of tag questions that appear in the English language. I will refer only to the six types that appear in the data. The four main types of tags in English are:

Type 1. Positive statement with falling tone followed by negative tag with rising tone
Type 2. Negative statement with falling tone followed by positive tag with rising tone
Type 3. Positive statement with falling tone followed by negative tag with falling tone
Type 4. Negative statement with falling tone followed by positive tag with falling tone.

The difference between these four types is in the assumption presented by the statement and the expectation indicated in the tag.

1. She likes school\ Doesn't she?/
2. She doesn't like school\ Does she?/
3. She likes school\ Doesn't she?\
4. She doesn't like school\ Does she?\

Both sentences 1 and 2 present a positive and a negative assumption respectively in the statement, and a neutral expectation in the tag. In other words, the tag in rising tone invites verification from the hearer and is a genuine question. Sentences 3 and 4 with tags with the falling tone have either a negative (3) or a positive assumption (4). Such tags, however, expect confirmation of the statement, having the force of an exclamation rather than of a genuine question.

These last two types of tag questions are the type of tag found in cross-examination (Quirk *et al.*, 1985:810-811).

A fifth and less common type of tag is what some researchers have named 'constant polarity tag'. This type of tag question has both a positive statement and a positive question. These are the most pragmatically loaded tags.

Type 5. She likes school\ Does she?/

> The tag typically has a rising tone, and the statement is characteristically preceded by *oh* or *so*, indicating the speaker's arrival at a conclusion by inference, or by recalling what has already been said. The tone may sometimes be one of sarcastic suspicion... Its effect may be scalding *(Oh, you've had another accident, have you?)*, sarcastic *(So that's your game, is it?)*, or sarcastically contradictory *(So your car is outside, is it?)*. (Quirk *et al.* 1985:812).

The sixth type of tag that appears in the data is what other researchers have named 'ratification tag', or what are called 'invariant tag questions' by Quirk *et al.* Unlike the other types of tag, these have the same form regardless of the polarity of the statement. For example, both 'you were there that night' and 'You weren't there that night' can have appended to them a tag like 'Is that correct' or 'Isn't that correct', as in Type 6. below. These generally have a rising tone, but a falling tone is sometimes used to indicate more insistence.

Type 6. They {forgot/didn't forget} to attend the lecture {am I right?/isn't that so?/ don't you think?/ wouldn't you say?/right?/ etc. (Quirk *et al.* 1985:814).

6.3. Tag questions in Spanish

English has a wider range of tags than does Spanish. The only tag questions that have a direct equivalent in Spanish are the ratification or invariant tag questions. Such tag questions do not appear as a separate entry on question types in any Spanish grammar. They are regarded as simple yes/no questions. The possible tags in Spanish include among the most common: *¿no es cierto?* ('Isn't that right?'), *¿cierto?* or *¿es cierto?*, *'¿no es verdad?* ('Isn't that true?'), *¿verdad?* or *¿es verdad?*, *¿No es así?* ('Isn't it so?'), *¿Es así?*, *¿No es correcto?* ('Isn't it correct?'), *¿correcto?* or *¿es correcto?*.

The reason for the lack of equivalence of all other types of English tags is that Spanish grammar does not allow for the use of auxiliary verbs (Have you?), copula verbs (Are you?) or dummy operators (Do you?) in questions. One type of tag that Spanish uses is the ellipted tag *¿no?* and *¿o no?*. There is no account of the pragmatic use of these tags in the Royal Academy's Spanish grammar, except a small mention that "the use of *no* at the beginning or the end of a sentence tends to indicate that an affirmative answer is expected or insinuated" (Real Academia Española 1981:360 – my translation[3]). This means, that interpreters need to make a number of choices when confronted with English tag questions, hence a difficulty in matching not only the form of the question but also the tone of the tag question in English. Table 10 lists all the possible English tag questions and what I consider to be pragmatic Spanish equivalents.

As Table 10 shows, some difficulties arise in trying to translate the illocutionary force of English tag questions when there are no exact equivalents in Spanish. Invariant tag questions can be translated without any problem, since close equivalents do exist. Constant polarity tags, which according to Quirk *et al.*, mostly indicate sarcasm and can be preceded with '*Oh*' or '*So*', do not have a direct equivalent in Spanish. However, the illocutionary force can be rendered by adding the *Así que* ('So') at the beginning of the question and giving it a falling declarative intonation. Checking tags can be translated as invariant tags in Spanish or as declaratives with a *¿no?* or *¿o no?* tag. This type of tag is potentially the most aggressive and coercive in Spanish, since it insinuates agreement with the main statement.

Each type of tag question as it appears in the data will now be discussed in relation to the interpreters' rendition into Spanish.

6.4. Invariant tag questions – Positive declarative with positive ratification tag – 'Is that right?' / 'Is that correct?'

The least aggressive tag questions are the invariant tags, also known as ratification tags, or checking tags. These seek confirmation of the statement and usually do not contain contentious information. This is evident in the context in which they are used. In examination-in-chief, 10 out of the 15 tag questions are ratification tag questions, used to elicit non-controversial information quickly, such as personal details. In cross-examination they are usually used to reiterate information that has already been presented by the witness during evidence-in-chief, although this is not always the case.

As explained before, invariant tags should cause no problems for the interpreter because they are readily translatable into Spanish. Table 11 shows all instances of this type of tag in cross-examination and their translations. As can be seen, this type of question formed 5.86% of all cross-examination questions, which is 34% of all tag questions. The majority of these questions, 70.27%, were translated using the same form and apparently caused no problems to the interpreter. However, 29.73% of them were translated in a different form: 16.12% as simple declaratives, 10.81% as polar questions, and 2.7% as a declarative

---

[3] "El uso del *no* al principio o al fin de la oración suele indicar que se espera o insinúa una respuesta afirmativa."

with a negative tag. In all instances, the translation was less coercive and less aggressive in tone than the original English version.

English	Spanish pragmatic equivalent
1. Invariant tag questions - Positive declarative with positive ratification tag, or tag with copula omitted. – Seeks ratification, expects a positive answer. - These are common in examination-in-chief when asking non contentious information such as personal details. E.g. *You called your sister. (Is that) correct/ right?*	1. *Usted llamó a su hermana. ¿Verdad?/¿Correcto?* ('You called your sister. True?/ Correct?')
2. Invariant tag questions - Positive declarative with negative ratification tag. - Content of declarative is usually not meant to be contentious. The tag seeks confirmation. (Maley and Fahey,1991) - These are common in examination-in-chief when asking non contentious information such as personal details. E.g. *You live in a flat. Isn't that correct/right?*	2. – *Usted vive en un departamento. ¿No es cierto? / ¿No es así?* ('You live in a flat. Isn't that right?/so?')
3. Constant polarity tag - Positive declarative with positive auxiliary tag - Its tone may indicate sarcastic suspicion, with a scalding, sarcastic or contradictory effect. It can be preceded by 'oh' or 'so'(Quirk *et al.* 1985). - It allows questioner to probe (Maley and Fahey 1991). E.g. *You called your sister, did you?*	3.- *Así que usted llamó a su hermana.* ('So you called your sister') - Since there is no equivalent of this type of tag, an initial *Así que* ('So') gives it the closest force.
4. Checking tag (Falling intonation) - Positive declarative with negative auxiliary tag - Expresses a stronger assumption and expects confirmation of statement (Maley and Fahey 1991; Quirk *et al.* 1985). -Typically used in cross-examination to challenge the witness's testimony. E.g. *You wanted to take advantage of that. Didn't you?* *You're lying. Aren't you?*	4. a- *Usted se quería aprovechar de eso. ¿No es cierto?/¿No es así?* (rising intonation) ('You wanted to take advantage of that. Isn't that true?/so?') 4.b- *Usted se quería aprovechar de eso. ¿No?* (rising intonation) 4c-*Usted se quería aprovechar de eso. ¿O no?* (falling intonation – more aggressive tone)
5. Checking Tag (Falling intonation) - Negative declarative with positive auxiliary tag. - Expresses a stronger assumption and expects confirmation of statement (Maley and Fahey 1991; Quirk *et al.* 1985). -Typically used in cross-examination to challenge the witness's testimony. E.g. *You haven't got the money. Do you?*	5.a- *Usted no tiene el dinero. ¿verdad?* (rising intonation) ('You haven't the money. True?') b- *Usted no tiene el dinero. ¿No?* (rising intonation)

Table 10: Tag question taxonomy as used in the courtroom

TOTAL = 37 (5.86% of all Cross qns.)	
1 translated with a negative tag	2.7%
26 translated with positive tag	70.27%
6 translated as a simple declarative	16.12%
4 translated as a yes/no question	10.81%

Table 11: Positive declaratives with positive ratification tag – 'Is that right?' / 'Is that correct?'

The following are two examples of this type of question that were translated as positive polar interrogatives.

Extract 1[4]
QU   Yes you recognize that as a letter you wrote to the defendant regarding the alleged arrears and the rental, is that right?
INT   Y ¿usted conoce que esta es la carta que le escribió a la demandada, eh, relacionada con el dinero que le debía, por renta?
      And, do you recognize that that is a letter that you wrote to the defendant, uh, about the money that she owed, for rent?

Extract 2
QU   That's because you you still wanted to fight with Mr Petro, is that correct?
INT   ¿Usted todavía quería pelear con él?
      Did you still want to fight with him?

Both translated versions are less confrontational than the original in English. In both examples, the information is put to the witness as a fact, as an allegation that is likely to spark contention. The tag question provides the witness with an invitation to respond to the allegation. The Spanish translations change the statements of facts into polar yes or no questions that do not assume or expect either a positive or a negative response. They appear to be 'asking' rather than 'stating', as do the original versions. The translated versions can be said to be less coercive since, as there is no apparent expected answer, the witness is not constrained into giving any one answer and hence has more freedom of choice.

This type of tag question was also translated as declarative statements, which are closer to the original in illocutionary force but still not quite the same. Whereas the original questions contain an explicit invitation to respond, the translated version does not. The following are two examples.

---

[4] In the quoted extracts, QU = question; INT = interpreter; A = answer.

Extract 3

QU And, because you wanted to assault him, is that correct?
INT Porque usted quería agredirlo.
    Because you wanted to assault him

Extract 4

QU Now, in this bag that you uh, only carry books, is that correct?
INT En esa bolsa usted lleva puro libros.
    In that bag you carry just books

6.5. Invariant tag questions – Negative declarative with positive ratification tag – 'Is that right?' / 'Is that correct?'

Extract 5

QU Uh, and when you came back from the city, uhm, you couldn't find your car, is that correct?
INT Y cuando usted regresó de la ciudad no pudo encontrar su coche, es eso correcto?
    And when you returned from the city you could not find your car, is that correct?

There were only 6 instances of this type of question, comprising a mere 0.95% of all examination questions, and 6.9% of all tag questions. There was no problem whatsoever in the translation of these questions. They were all translated in the same way, with the tag *¿es eso correcto?* ('Is that correct'). Although the small percentage of this question type does not allow us to make reliable generalizations, the result may indicate that interpreters do not omit translating the tag when it causes no translation difficulty, but only do so when finding an appropriate pragmatic equivalent becomes more problematic, as is the case with checking tags, which will be discussed next.

6.6. Constant polarity tag – Positive declaratives with positive auxiliary tag – 'You work all night, do you?'

This type of tag, which was very rare in Woodbury's (1984) study, comprised 12.79% of all tag questions used in cross-examination in my study and was not used at all in examination-in-chief. The question type is normally used in the data to express surprise or sarcasm on the part of counsel, which is consistent with Quirk *et al.*'s description of the function of this type of tag question (1985:812). It usually follows an unexpected answer, one that provides new information (extract 6) or an answer that contradicts the question put to the witness before (extract 7).

Extract 6

A	Yo le hablé y le dije 'yo no te dije a vos que no quiero que hablés con personas que no conocés?'
INT	I talked to her and I said 'didn't I tell you not to speak to people you don't know?'
QU	Right. You had previously told her not to speak to people she didn't know, had you?
INT	Así que usted claramente le había dicho que no hablara con gente que no conocía?
So you had clearly told her not to speak to people she didn't know?

Extract 7

QU	And Mr X made these arrangements for you to find your car at Goulburn
INT	Y el Sr X organizó para que usted encuentre su coche en Goulburn
A	Antes no, hasta ese día que llegué él preguntó a los relativos, que fueran a al policía a preguntar
INT	Not before but when I got there then he called his relatives to tell them to go to the police to ask
QU	You met him by accident, did you?
INT	Usted se encontró con él por accidente, verdad?
You met him by accident, true?

This type of tag question can be problematic for the interpreter because a translation of the tag as a positive tag in Spanish, using any of the ratification words such as *verdad* ('true'), *no es así?* ('isn't that so?'), will not maintain an equivalence of pragmatic force. To say 'You saw him by accident, did you?' is not the same as 'You saw him by accident, true?'. The first one is rectifying a false prior belief by stating what the speaker now understands to be the case. The second one is stating what the speaker believes to be the case and asking for ratification of the same. The best way to translate these into Spanish is by prefacing the question with *así que* ('so') or *entonces* ('then'), depending on the propositional content of the question. Returning to the questions quoted above, 'So you met him by accident then' would be a closer approximation to the original intended meaning. When we observe Table 12, it becomes immediately clear that this type of question caused problems for the interpreters.

TOTAL = 11
1 translated as a positive tag *verdad?*   9%

2 as a simple declarative	18.18%
7 as a yes/no question	63.63%
1 as a question prefaced with *así que*	9%

Table 12: SL positive declaratives with positive auxiliary tag

There was only one instance where this type of question was translated with the use of an initial *Así que* ('So'), namely, the question that appears on extract 6. Over half of these questions (63.63%) were translated as polar interrogatives (see extract 8). This change is significant. Polar interrogatives do not state a newly acquired piece of information, like the tag question does; they ask for new information. The illocutionary force of these two types is very different. In the rest of the instances, these questions were translated as a declarative (see extract 9), which once again does not reflect the original intention of the question.

Extract 8
QU   You'd seen it before, had you?
INT   ¿Usted la había visto antes?
      Had you seen it before?

Extract 9
QU   It was just a screen door, was it?
INT   Era como una mampara.
      It was like a screen

6.7. Checking tags

Checking tags include positive declaratives with negative auxiliary tags and negative declaratives with positive auxiliary tags, with rising or falling intonation. All of the instances of this type of tag found in my data had a falling intonation. Other researchers have not mentioned the intonation of the tag in their discussions and have grouped all checking tags together, claiming that they are the most aggressive, coercive and controlling type of question. "Checking tags are used during cross-examination in order to make innuendos, to accuse, and to cast doubt upon previous testimony... The form and content of these questions suggest that the expected answer will incriminate the witness. Lawyers choose checking tags when they wish to pounce on a witness" (Woodbury 1984:223). Woodbury's statement is consistent with the purpose behind cross-examination, to challenge and discredit the witness's evidence-in-chief, and agrees also with the function of checking tags with falling intonation as explained by Quirk *et al.* (1985). These tags, when uttered with a falling intonation, present a strong assumption and expect an answer that agrees with that assumption. They are not genuine questions. The cross examiner will put to the witness contentious propositions as fact, with checking tags expecting an answer that agrees with the assumption of the statement. Since the witness will mostly disagree with such assumptions, such contradiction will constitute a battle of wills between counsel and the witness, with the witness often being forced to half-heartedly agree with counsel. This is frequently achieved through the use of modality and repetition as shown in the following example, drawn not from the corpus but from a monolingual case:

Counsel You remember what you said on the day of the interview, don't you?
Witness No, not exactly.
Counsel Do you agree that you could have said 'I wanted to call him'
Witness Yes, I suppose so.
Counsel Now that's not the same as what you just told us a minute ago, is it?
Witness No.

This type of question is obviously a very important strategic tool in cross-examination. Although Woodbury found a small frequency of this type in her data, they formed 5.22% of all cross-examination questions and 40.74% of all tag questions in my data. This shows that their use is probably more prominent in Australian courts.

SL Positive declaratives with negative auxiliary tag **TOTAL = 20** (3.16% of all cross questions)	
4 maintained a negative tag	20%
5 simple declarative – tag omitted	25%
2 declarative with positive tag	10%
7 declarative with an added initial *pero*	35%
2 yes/no interrogative	10%
Negative declarative with positive auxiliary tag **TOTAL = 13** *(2.06% of all cross questions)*	
2 maintained a positive tag	15.38%
3 translated as simple dec.	23.07%
3 translated as yes/no interrogatives	23.07%
5 translated as dec. with initial *pero*	38.46%

Table 13: Declaratives with auxiliary tag

Table 13 shows the different ways these tag questions were translated by the interpreters. The great variety of versions demonstrates a difficulty in the translation of this type of tag question. As explained earlier, there is no direct equivalent in Spanish for this type of tag, hence the interpreter has to choose between omitting the tag altogether, translating it as an invariant ratification tag such as 'is that correct?', translating it as a Spanish ¿no? or ¿o no? or replacing it with an initial discourse marker. What makes these questions so strong in tone is the expectation implied in the tag, which coerces the witness into answering in a certain way. In an adversarial situation the tag has a falling intonation rather than a rising one, which can be the case in other, non-confrontational situations. Thomson and Martinet agree with Quirk *et al.* in saying that "when question tags are used the speaker doesn't normally need information but merely expects agreement. These tags are therefore normally said with a falling intonation, as in statements" (Thomson and Martinet 1983: 97). Extract 10 from cross-examination illustrates this.

Extract 10
You were yelling and screaming at this stage, WEREN'T (\you?

The tag is stressed, with the verb 'weren't' said in a louder voice and the pronoun 'you' with a falling intonation, indicating a fact rather than a question. The difficulty in Spanish is that the subject of the statement cannot be repeated in the tag. Hence, the emphasis cannot lie in the tag and the accusing tone is lost. The interpreter translated the above example as *Usted estaba gritando y y y y ah hablando en voz alta en ese momento, no es cierto?* ('You were screaming and and and uh talking in a loud voice at that moment, isn't that true?') in a flat tone. A more forceful and aggressive way of asking this question, would be to replace the ratification tag with a *¿o (\NO?*. Such a negative tag can be stressed with a louder voice and can only be said in a falling intonation. These tags are used only in confrontational discourse, whereas all other tags in Spanish are used in friendly conversational contexts. Although this is not a perfectly equivalent option, it is pragmatically closer to the original than any other form. Interestingly enough, none of the interpreters opted for this version at any time, presumably because it is always easier to resort to a more literal translation when placed under pressure.

The tag was omitted more frequently by the interpreters when it was a positive tag than when it was a negative tag. In positive declaratives with negative tag questions, the tag was translated only 20% of the time. The tags used in Spanish were: *¿no es cierto?* ('Isn't it true?'), and *¿no es así?* ('isn't it so?'). In negative declaratives with positive tags, the tag was translated even less, in 15.38% of the cases, making it the least popular option for the interpreters . The tag used for this question type was *¿verdad?* ('True?'). Interestingly, interpreters opted for a different strategy to attempt to maintain the level of aggressiveness of these checking tag questions. The preferred translation for both types of checking tags, 35% of positive declaratives with negative tags, and 38.46% of negative declaratives with positive tags, was a declarative statement with an initial *pero* ('but') as in extract 11.

> **Extract 11**
> QU   He didn't shout anything of the kind, did he?
> INT   Pero no le gritó nada por el estilo.
>   But he didn't shout anything of the kind

The disjunctive conjunction 'but' is used to indicate a contradiction between what the witness had previously said and what the lawyer is putting to him/her. Still, the illocutionary force is not the same as the original. Starting the declarative with a 'but' and ending the question with a negative tag *No es cierto?* would have achieved a closer equivalent.

This question type was also translated as a simple declarative, with the tag omitted 24.42% of the time (see extract 12), as a polar interrogative 15.15% of the time (see extract 13).The polarity of the tag was reversed 6% of the time, with a negative tag being translated as a positive tag (see extract 14).

> **Extract 12**
> QU   You say, you're making this all up, aren't you?
> INT   Usted está inventando todo esto.
>   *You are making all this up*

> **Extract 13**
> QU   Mr Petro, you don't like Mr Carro, do you?
> INT   Señor Petro, a usted no le gusta el señor Carro?
>   *Mr Petro, don't you like Mr Carro?*

> **Extract 14**
> QU   Well, you remember the roundabout, don't you?
> INT   Se acuerda de la rotonda, ¿verdad?
>   *You remember the roundabout, right?*

7. Examination-in-chief questions through the interpreter

English	Spanish
Tag questions = 17 (4.28%)	= 15 (3.95%)
Statements = 65 (16.37%)	= 78 (20.58%)
Prosodic declar. questions = 29 (7.3%)	= 0
Total = 111 (27.96%)	Total = 93 (24.54%)

Table 14: Examination-in-chief declaratives

English	Spanish
Wh- open-ended questions = 70 (17.63%)	= 79 (20.84%)
Yes/No questions = 151 (38%)	= 164 (43.27%)
Closed option questions = 6 (1.5%)	= 7 (1.85%)
Modal questions = 59 (14.86%)	= 36 (9.50%)
Total = 286 (72%)	Total = 286 (75.46%)

Table 15: Examination-in-chief interrogatives

As mentioned earlier, the nature of examination-in-chief is very different from that of cross-examination, and this is reflected in the type of questions used, a finding that corroborates all previous studies on question type. In examination-in-chief, declaratives with tags are not a very popular type of question. Only 4.28% of all questions fall in this category as compared to 18.23% in cross-examination. None of the other types of declaratives is prominent either, amounting to only 16.37% as opposed to 32.8% in cross-examination. Even the instances of these types of questions show that although the form may be coercive, the content tells otherwise. As can be seen, the differences found between the original English questions and their Spanish translation is not great. One significant difference lies in the higher percentage of statements in Spanish, 20.58% as opposed to 16.37% in English. However this increase can be attributed to the fact that the prosodic questions were translated at times as simple statements and at times as polar interrogatives, which explains the slight increase in the percentage of this type of question in Spanish. The most noticeable difference is found in the occurrence of modal interrogatives. Indirect requests formulated in the form of modal interrogatives are common in examination-in-chief. 14.86% of examination-in-chief questions were asked in this form, whereas only 9.50% appear in the Spanish version. Interpreters translated modal interrogatives into one of the following question types: a Wh- question, an imperative, a polar interrogative or a modal interrogative (see Table 16).

Wh- questions	Imperative	Modal interrogative	Polar interrogative
46.2%	34.62%	11.53%	7.7%

Table 16: Examination-in-chief modal interrogatives

Modal interrogatives were translated as Wh- questions 46.2% of the time, being the most popular choice. By doing this, the interpreter omitted a great proportion of the original question, maintaining only the essence of the question. Extracts 15 and 16 below are representative of this type of omission by the interpreter. In this category, not only does the modal verb 'can' go missing, the entire reference to all participants, 'you' and 'the court' or 'us' is also omitted. Two main elements are altered in the interpretation. Firstly, by using the modal interrogative question type, the lawyer is indirectly making a request to the witness. The pragmatic function of such questions is that of a request or a command. Therefore, while maintaining politeness in the use of indirectness, the lawyer establishes his/her control and authority over the witness, by indirectly saying 'tell the court what happened'. By turning an indirect request into a direct question, that level of authority disappears. Secondly, a change in tenor occurs (Halliday and Hasan 1985). Tenor reflects the negotiation of social relationships between participants in the relevant field or context. In this case, the question makes it explicit that there are three participants in the activity type of the hearing: the lawyer who asks the question, the witness who is to answer and the courtroom or 'us', to whom the information is directed. In essence, one participant, the lawyer, elicits the evidence from the witness for the benefit of a silent but most important participant, the courtroom. Hence, the relationship between the witness and the courtroom is a mediated and evidently distant one. This insight into the dynamics of courtroom interaction disappears in the interpretation.

Extract 15
QU   Yes, can you tell the court what happened?
INT   ¿Y luego qué pasó?
       And then what happened?

Extract 16
QU   Not precisely, OK, can you tell us how you remember the screen was when you saw it?
INT   ¿Cómo estaba esa partición cuando usted la vio? ¿En qué posición estaba?
       How was that partition when you saw it? In what position was it?

The next most popular translation choice for this type of question was the use of the imperative, with a 34.62% occurrence. Here the interpreter simply kept the function of the question, by making an indirect command into a direct one, as shown in extracts 17 and 18.

Extract 17
QU   Right, well so could you just tell us what damage was done to your car?
INT   Diga solamente qué daños se le hizo a su auto.
       Just say what damages were done to your car

Extract 18
QU   Ah Mr ah Mr Ramos, could you please give your full name, ad-

	dress and your occupation to the court?
INT	Diga su nombre, ocupación y dirección.
	Say your name, occupation and address

As can be seen in the above two examples, once again both the modal verb and the reference to the court go missing in the interpretation. This time however, the intention of command is maintained with the use of an imperative. Nevertheless, the fact that Spanish tends to use the imperative more frequently than English does not make such translations inappropriate or impolite, but simply more direct (Hale 1997).

Modal interrogatives were translated as the equivalent type in Spanish only on three occasions (11.53%), two of which were uttered by the same interpreter, indicating a lack of preference for the maintenance of this feature in the Spanish translation (see extracts 19 and 20). This can be due to a number of reasons. As mentioned before, the use of the imperative is much more frequent and appropriate in this context in Spanish, hence it may be cognitively quicker to access by the interpreter within the time constraint. Modal interrogatives can lend themselves to confusion by being indirect speech acts. They can be interpreted as indirect requests or as genuine questions on ability or desire. The fact that they are not as common in Spanish as they are in English can add to this possibility. Interpreters, in an attempt to avoid miscommunication, may subconsciously clarify or disambiguate utterances. A third possible reason for any omission of form by retaining substance alone is the misconception that certain discourse features may be irrelevant or superfluous, adding to the memory burden and impinging on the time constraint placed on interpreters. Interpreters will then scan utterances and retain only what they regard as relevant.

Extract 19

QU	Yes, now, can you tell the court what happened?
INT	¿Puede decirle a la corte qué pasó?
	Can you tell the court what happened?

Extract 20

QU	Can you look at that quickly please?
INT	¿Quiere mirarlo rápidamente por favor?
	Do you want to look at it quickly please

The last and possibly most serious alteration to the modal interrogative question type is its conversion to a polar interrogative. Fortunately this change only took place on two occasions (7.7%), uttered by two different interpreters, and cannot be claimed to be a common tendency.

Extract 21

QU	Can you describe it to the court?

INT ¿Tú reconoces este documento?
Do you recognize this document?

Extract 22
QU   Yeah, can you tell the court to the best ... to the best of your recollection, to the best of your memory?
INT ¿Pero algo recuerda usted?
But you remember something?

As extracts 21 and 22 show, both original questions are indirect requests for information. The first requests a description of a document and the second a narration of events. Both questions were translated as polar interrogatives which require a yes or no answer.

8. Conclusion

This paper has dealt with question form and question type in the courtroom. It was highlighted through the existing literature on courtroom questioning that lawyers use questions strategically to control and manipulate the evidence. The term 'question' was assigned to lawyers' turns in the adjacency pair, even though their function is clearly not always a question or their form always interrogative. A number of studies have classified courtroom question types, generally dividing them into two major categories: Information Seeking Questions, comprising Wh- and Modal Interrrogatives, and Confirmation Seeking Questions, comprising declaratives with and without tags and polar interrogatives. The effect of question type on the answers was discussed in terms of levels of coerciveness, control, tone and illocutionary force. It was argued that question type was highly dependent on whether the questioning was part of cross-examination or examination-in-chief, with the most coercive, controlling and aggressive types predominating in cross-examination, and the freer, less constraining and friendlier types, predominating in examination-in-chief.

A quantitative analysis of the question types found in my data, together with their respective interpreter's renditions, were presented. The patterns found on the use of different question types in my data corroborated those of previous studies. In terms of the interpreters' renditions of questions into Spanish, it was found that there was a tendency on the part of the interpreter to omit certain types, with the ones that caused most difficulty being declaratives with tags and modal interrogatives. It was concluded that the main reason for the interpreters' omissions of certain features was a lack of syntactic and semantic equivalence. However, it was proposed that pragmatic equivalence, which maintains the same or similar illocutionary force, can be achieved. If interpreters are to interpret accurately they must maintain equivalence not only of content but of pragmatic meaning and force. This is of particular importance in the adversarial courtroom, where questions are used strategically to manipulate the flow and content of the evidence. If accuracy of pragmatic meaning is not maintained, counsels' strategies will be lost in the interpretation.[5]

References

Bennett, M.S. and W. L. Feldman (1981) *Reconstructing Reality in the Courtroom*, London: Tavistock Publications.
Berk-Seligson, S. (1990) *The Bilingual Courtroom Court Interpreters in the Judicial Process*, Chicago: The University of Chicago Press.
------ (1999) 'The impact of court interpreting on the coerciveness of leading questions', *Forensic Linguistics* 6(1): 30-56.
Boretti de Macchia, S. (1996) *Estructuras interrogativas. Análisis de actos de habla coloquiales,* Buenos Aires: A-Z editora.
Danet, B. and B. Bogoch (1980) 'Fixed fight or free for all? An empirical study of combativeness in the adversary system of justice', *British Journal of Law and Society* 7: 36-60.
Dunstan, R. (1980) 'Context for coercion: Analysing properties of courtroom 'questions'', *British Journal of Law and Society* 7: 61-77.
Hale, S. (1997) 'Interpreting Politeness in Court. A study of Spanish-English interpreted proceedings', in S. Campbell and S. Hale (eds) *Proceedings of the 2nd Annual Macarthur Interpreting and Translation Conference "Research, Training and Practice",* Milperra: UWS Macarthur/LARC, 37-45.
------ and J. Gibbons (1999) 'Varying realities: Patterned changes in the interpreter's representation of courtroom and external realities', *Applied Linguistics* 20(1): 203-220.
Halliday, M.A.K and R. Hasan (1985) *Language, Context, and Text. Aspects of language in a social-semiotic perspective*, Victoria: Deakin University.
Harris, S. (1984) 'Questions as a mode of control in magistrates' courts', *International Journal of the Sociology of Language* 49: 5-27.
Loftus, E. (1979) *Eyewitness Testimony,* Cambridge, MA: Harvard University Press.
Maley, Y. and R. Fahey (1991) 'Presenting the evidence: constructions of reality in court', *International Journal for the Semiotics of Law* V(1): 3-17.
Pórtoles, L. (1988) 'La respuesta sí/no a interrogativas generales', *Español actual* 49: 65-83.
Quirk, R., S. Greenbaum, G. Leech, J. Svartik (1985) *A comprehensive grammar of the English language*, London & New York: Longman.
Real Academia Española (1981) *Esbozo de una nueva gramática de la lengua española,* Madrid: Espasa-Calpe.

---

[5] This is part of the author's PhD research carried out through Macquarie University under the supervision of Professor Christopher Candlin.

Rigney, A. C. (1997) 'The Pragmatics of question/answer structures in a bilingual courtroom', paper presented at the Conference of the National Association of Judiciary Interpreters and Translators, Seattle, USA.

------ (1999) 'Questioning in interpreted testimony', *Forensic Linguistics* 6(1): 83-108.

Schegloff, E. and H. Sacks (1973) 'Opening up closings', *Semiotica* 8: 289-327.

Thomson, A.J. and A.V. Martinet (1983) *A Practical English Grammar,* Oxford: Oxford University Press.

Walker, A. G. (1987) 'Linguistic manipulation, power and the legal setting', in L. Kedar (ed) *Power through discourse*, Norwood, N.J.: Ablex Publishing Corporation, 57-80.

Woodbury, H. (1984) 'The strategic use of questions in court', *Semiotica* 48(3/4): 197-228.

Interactional Pragmatics, Face and the Dialogue Interpreter

IAN MASON AND MIRANDA STEWART

The aim of this paper[1] is to hypothesize that issues of politeness and other interactional pragmatic variables are crucial to an understanding of what is involved in dialogue interpreting events; and to illustrate what is at stake by reference to an instance of courtroom interpreting (during the OJ Simpson trial) and instances of immigration service interviews. In these triadic speech events, which inherently contain a degree of threat to face, it is found that face-threatening acts are frequently modified in the act of translating, irrespective of the style of interpreting adopted.

1. Introduction

In previous studies of dialogue interpreting, relatively little attention has been paid to issues of politeness, face and other pragmatic constraints on interaction. Yet it has been apparent from an early stage that, in this mode of translating above all others, the immediacy of the event and the physical presence of all the participants exert a determining influence on the way the meanings are exchanged and negotiated. For example, Lang (1976, 1978) observed interpreter behaviour in traditional courtroom settings in Papua-New Guinea. He noted the importance of gaze, posture and gesture in the behaviour of each participant and how these features signalled inclusiveness or exclusiveness of the interpreter in the exchange. His findings pointed to issues we would now describe in terms of participation framework, power, distance, footing and so on. It seems plausible to suggest, therefore, that linguistic politeness, as the means whereby interlocutors negotiate interpersonal relations in speech exchanges, will feature prominently in dialogue interpreting events.

Despite the lack of studies exclusively focused on politeness and related issues,[2] it has surfaced in works primarily concerned with other issues. An early example would be Harris and Sherwood (1978), whose study of 'natural' – i.e. untrained bilingual – interpreters revealed intuitive awareness on the part of the latter of the need to pay attention to face. An instance is quoted of a business

---

[1] Our thanks are due to Robin Warner and Magda Montgomery for their insightful comments on an earlier version of the paper and to Magda Montgomery for transcription and translation of the Polish data.

[2] See however Hale (1997a) on politeness in courtroom settings and more generally, Hale (1997b) on the importance of pragmatics to the analysis of courtroom interpreting.

negotiation between an Italian immigrant to Canada and a monolingual Canadian. The Italian employs his daughter as interpreter. At a crucial juncture, the following exchange takes place (Harris and Sherwood 1978: 157):

Father:	*Digli che è un imbecille!*
Daughter (to 3rd. party):	My father won't accept your offer.

What can have motivated such a translational shift? In the absence of access to the interpreter and the actual event, no definite pronouncements can be made. Nevertheless, it seems plausible to suggest that a translation which relays the intended illocutionary force (rejecting an offer) but deliberately omits its face-threatening potential (as an insult) is a response to two perceptions: (1) accepted ways of rejecting an offer without closing down the channel of communication differ between traditional Italian and modern Canadian cultures; (2) a literal translation of what is uttered in Italian would constitute a three-way threat to face: to the addressee, who is being insulted; to the speaker, whose positive face would be under threat, were he aware of the impact of his words in a different cultural setting; and to the interpreter, who might appear to be assuming responsibility for the words uttered.[3]

Knapp-Potthof and Knapp (1987), studying some exchanges between German academics and Korean visitors to Germany, also attest to the untrained (Korean) interpreter's tendency both to attenuate the threat to face of certain utterances and to protect her own face in doing so by clearly dissociating herself from these utterances. For example, when relaying a direct enquiry 'How old are you?', she adopts framing devices such as 'what interests him is...' and 'what he wants to know is...', thus making explicit her non-responsibility for the potentially face-threatening request. It is significant that these devices are not characteristic of the rest of the interpreter's output. The analysts consequently regard these devices as evidence of politeness strategies which "strongly suggest that [the interpreter] is very much concerned with saving her own face" (Knapp-Potthof and Knapp 1987: 198).

The work of the court interpreter is far-removed from the circumstances of the unregulated exchanges quoted above. In United States courtrooms, for example, interpreters, specifically trained for the purpose, are enjoined to translate

---

[3] See Wadensjö (1998: 88) who, following Goffman (1981: 226), distinguishes between different production roles: the animator (who takes no responsibility for words uttered and is merely a 'sounding box' for others' speech); the author (who drafts and utters the text without 'owning' it); and the principal (who assumes full ownership of and responsibility for the words uttered). What the interpreter in this case may not have considered is how such a move can backfire. In this case, the father, whose English is apparently good enough for him to monitor his daughter's performance, immediately interjects (in Italian): 'Why didn't you tell him what I told you?'.

exactly and only what is said.[4] Despite this, there is evidence both of subtle shifts of politeness in interpreting and of the actual effects such shifts may have. Berk-Seligson (1990: 142) notes that interpreters may either delete hedges and other particles or, conversely, add them. She concludes:

> these linguistic categories are not salient enough for court interpreters to include them in their interpretations when they ought to be included, and to exclude them when they should be omitted.

In other words, they are "not perceived as being sufficiently important for attention to be paid to them" (idem: 143), an explanation remarkably similar to that offered *à propos* of the same phenomena by Knapp-Potthof and Knapp.

Berk-Seligson (1988) describes a related phenomenon. Noting that the use of honorifics such as *Señor*, *Señora* is more commonplace in Latin American Spanish than are 'Sir' or 'Madam' in North American English, she observes a tendency to omit these forms of polite address in interpreters' output from Spanish into English (particularly when a witness has inappropriately addressed the interpreter – *Señorita* – instead of the attorney). In an experiment to gauge the effects of such omissions, she found that witnesses who were interpreted as using these honorifics were perceived by jurors to be more trustworthy and convincing than those who were interpreted without using them. This suggests that failure to reflect markers of politeness in interpreting in a courtroom setting can have serious consequences. Moreover, we are here considering only a very superficial feature of conventional politeness, rather than the vast array of linguistic resources noted by Brown and Levinson (1987) as being indices of the interpersonal negotiation of face.

Studies by Brennan (1999) and Tebble (1999), inter alia, reported in the special issue of *The Translator* devoted to dialogue interpreting (Mason ed., 1999), bear witness to the kinds of issues that may be at stake. For example, when a doctor has relatively bad news to convey to his patient, it is significant that, instead of addressing her directly, he addresses the interpreter and adopts third person style ('she/her' instead of 'you') to refer to the patient. He also hedges ('we can't do a lot to treat her') (Tebble 1999: 190). Interpreting from signed language, an interpreter in court turns the sign meaning 'Again?' into 'I'm sorry, what do you mean?' (Brennan 1999: 242), thus employing a conventional

---

[4] Assumptions such as these appear to be based on a faulty paradigm of language use, favouring propositional content over interpersonal meaning and considering languages as isomorphic. Other unexamined notions about language use held by the legal profession are mentioned by Pym (1999: 277), who reports the Court (the judge) in the same case as asserting authoritatively that 'there are 60 major dialects of the Spanish language', an assertion which would be questioned by linguists.

apology as a means of redressive action.

In order to study face-work in dialogue interpreting, there is a clear need to understand the 'participation framework' (Goffman 1981) in which such events take place. In this respect, Wadensjö (e.g. 1998) and Roy (2000) have done much to improve understanding of the interpreter's role as a manager of the exchange (shifts of footing, gate-keeping, etc.). No study of interpreted exchanges can afford to overlook these factors. Moreover, as the incidental examples cited above demonstrate, they are closely involved in the negotiation of face and other pragmatic variables. Thus, the approach we propose to adopt is one which, rather than comparing the propositional meaning of utterances and their interpretation, seeks to describe the behaviour of all parties in terms of the set of factors governing the exchange.

Courtroom interpreting and immigration interviews are instances of what Kang (1998) refers to as triadic exchanges. That is, a speaker seeks to reach a target addressee via an intermediary, thus:

Speaker → Mediator → Target

Kang's interest is in monolingual exchanges in which a speaker addresses to another participant remarks about a third party, also present, as a means of calling on the latter to "actively participate in the communicative act that is being performed". The triadic exchange is thus seen as a "strategy of inclusion" (Kang 1998: 383). Kang's use of the term 'mediator' is not necessarily intended to imply an active role on the part of the middle party. Rather, the mediator is the medium through which the speaker reaches the target. At a primary level, what is going on in a particular courtroom exchange may be described in similar terms, thus:

Witness → Attorney (direct addressee) → Judge and jury (auditors)
Members of public in court (overhearers)

That is, a witness, in responding to an attorney's question in cross-examination, is aware that the judge and jury are participants in the event (as auditors) and that it is the effect on them (as 'Target') of what he/she says that is crucial to the outcome of the event.[5] Although not an invitation to the Target to participate actively, witnesses' responses may still be described as part of an inclusion strategy in the sense that they are directed towards influencing the Target's behaviour or way of thinking. Now, in an interpreted cross-examination, there is a second-

---

[5] Cf. Rigney (1999: 84), who suggests that the interaction is designed for a "non-speaking audience, the jury and/or the judge".

ary triad, which we may represent thus:

Witness → Interpreter → Attorney → Interpreter → Witness

In this triad, the witness's response reaches its direct addressee (the attorney) only via the interpreter (or 'intermediary', to use Kang's term).

The importance of such distinctions will be seen when the courtroom cross-examination is contrasted to the typical format of the immigration interview. There are two essential differences. Firstly, the initial triad identified above, whereby the speaker seeks to reach a target other than the direct addressee, does not normally exist in such encounters: the immigration officer, the interviewee and the interpreter are normally alone in the interview room. These are not multi-party events in the same way as are courtroom hearings.

Secondly, the nature of the triad formed by both interlocutors and the interpreter is perceived differently by those involved. Whereas the courtroom interpreter is trained and expected to act as a non-party, almost a translating machine (see Berk-Seligson 1990; Morris 1995), the immigration interview interpreter is manifestly a full party to the exchange, recognized as such by all participants. For example, when an officer asks an interviewee for the spelling of his name, the interpreter takes this task upon herself without referring it to the interviewee. Neither of the other parties objects to this intervention on the part of the interpreter. In this way, participants' perceptions of the participation framework exert a determining influence on the dynamics of the whole exchange. The analyses presented below must be seen in the light of the particular triadic relations governing each case.

2. The data

The data used in this study are taken from televized broadcasts of dialogue interpreting; the O.J. Simpson trial in the United States and a Channel Four *Cutting Edge* documentary about immigration to Britain. The languages involved are Spanish/English and Polish/English.

In section 3 below, we focus on one particular section of the 1995 televized proceedings of the O.J. Simpson case, the pre-trial cross-examination of the witness Rosa López, given that this witness, of Hispanic origin, had chosen to avail herself of the interpreting facilities of the court. The transcripts are compiled from those provided by Walraven (n.d.) of the English language input and our own transcription of elements of the Spanish output of both witness and interpreter, supplemented by transcripts provided by Miguel (1998). However, in many places these are incomplete for a variety of reasons. Principally, the interpreter uses simultaneous mode when interpreting for the witness and consequently her output is obscured by that of the deputy district attorney; there is considerable overlap between participants; the faces of interpreter and witness are often obscured when they are interacting in Spanish; the microphones frequently favour English-language output. Consequently transcription of interaction in Spanish is partial.

In the case of the immigration interviews, transcripts were commissioned in addition to a literal translation of the original Polish.

3. Face and politeness in a courtroom setting: the Rosa López tapes

We have chosen to confine our analysis to the pre-trial cross-examination of the potential witness for O.J. Simpson, Rosa López, an event previously analysed from different perspectives by Pym (1999) and Rigney (1999). Within the framework of Brown and Levinson's (1987) politeness theory, this particular speech event is inherently threatening for the positive face of the witness as the cross-examination is designed to demonstrate to the court that the witness is unreliable, that is to destroy the "public self image" (1987: 61) that the witness has of him or herself.

We already mentioned Berk-Seligson's finding that court interpreters, despite the injunction to provide a literal word-for-word translation of what is said, may add or delete hedges or particles, possibly unaware of their potential significance. Here, we would like to focus on an instance where the interpreter tends to abide by the above injunction and generally translates literally; yet the inclusion or deletion of hedges or particles may be necessary to preserve the functional if not the literal meaning of the utterance. A literal translation may alter the illocutionary force of the utterance (cf. Hale 1997) and consequently affect its face-threatening or face-protective potential. We are going to examine an extended sequence of cross-examination which is maximally face-threatening for the positive face of the witness, Rosa López, who is being accused of 'material misrepresentation', in this instance of having claimed that she had already reserved a flight back to El Salvador when she had not in fact done so.

Extract 1
Att: Miss López, we just called the airline. They don't show a reservation for you. Can you explain to the court why it is that you just told us you have a reservation?
Int: +++
W: Porque yo lo voy a reservar, señor. Inmediatamente que salga de aquí. Yo compro mi ticket y me voy. (etc)
Because I am going to reserve it, sir. Immediately after I leave here. I buy my ticket and I go.
Int: Because I am going to reserve it, sir. As soon as I leave here, I will buy my ticket and I will leave. If you want to, the cameras can follow me.

Att: So you have not made a reservation?
Int: +++
W: No pero voy a hacerlo no más salir de aquí (xxx) tiempo para salir. (waves arm) No voy a hablar a las diez/ a la una de la mañana...(xxx)
No but I am going to do it as soon as I leave here (xxx) *time to leave. I am not going to speak at ten/ at one in the morning...* (xxx)
Int: But I will make it as soon as I leave here.
Att: Okay.
You have not made a/
Int: I can't call at 1:00 in the morning because the airlines are closed at that time. I have to wait.
Att: You just told us that you already made a reservation.
Int: +++
W: Pero voy a hacer la reservación y me voy, señor (xxx)
But I am going to make the reservation and I am going, sir (xxx)
Int: But I will make the reservation, sir, and I will leave, that is for sure, today.
Att: Okay.
So when you told us you already made a reservation, you were lying?
Int: +++
W: No, porque la voy a hacer, señor.
No, because I am going to make it, sir.
Int: No. Because I will make it, sir.
Att: You told us you made a reservation prior to coming to court this morning, Miss López.

W: = witness (Rosa López), Att: = attorney (Mr. Darden), Int: = interpreter (Doris Weitz)

In line 7 the attorney asks what Hale (this volume) refers to as a confirmation-seeking question with a constant polarity tag 'so'. His yes/no question is weighted to the preferred response 'no'. Conversationally López's face is doubly threatened. If she adopts the preferred response, she incriminates herself. If she does not, she may have to engage in some interactional face-work to preface a dispreferred response. As it is, she briefly admits guilt ('no') and quickly proceeds to refocus discussion onto her future intentions. Her interpreted reply 'But...', without the 'no', could be seen as uncooperative in Gricean terms, flouting the maxims of Quantity and Quality. Had this 'no' been interpreted, it is conceivable that the attorney would have abandoned his face threatening line of enquiry seeking to establish that López has deceived the court. López, as we have seen, proceeds to refocus the discussion onto her intentions to leave thereby protecting her own positive face. At this point her irritation, possibly with the position she feels she has been placed in, becomes apparent and she shows this through a dismissive hand gesture and the following utterance: *No voy a hablar a las diez/ a la una de la mañana...* Here both the kinesics (the hand gesture) and the intonation used clearly implicate her rejection of the attorney's line of questioning. The illocutionary force of her response is that it is unreasonable of the attorney to have expected her to make a reservation, given that the only time she had available to do so was during the night. López, in attempting to protect her own face, goes on the offensive and attacks the face of the attorney by implicating that he has asked an inappropriate and unreasonable question: *no voy a...* Pragmatically her utterance could be argued to require in English the strengthening hedge 'hardly' as in 'I'm hardly going to phone at one in the morning...'. Yet the requirement to translate literally tends to dissuade interpreters from adding, for example, hedges or particles to convey pragmatic implicature. Nonetheless, it is noticeable that the interpreter does deviate from a literal translation by translating *no voy a...* as 'I can't' rather than 'I am not going to' (I won't), choosing to place ability over willingness and using conventional indirectness, a standard politeness strategy. Thus she reduces the face-threatening force of López's response in two ways. Firstly, López is presented as being unable rather than unwilling to phone the agency at 1 a.m. Secondly, and more importantly, in the absence of any indicator that the illocutionary force of the response is to reject the line of questioning (Don't ask stupid questions), it is reduced to a mere justification of why she has not made a reservation and consequently an implicated admission of guilt. This is not an isolated instance. At a later point López is put under increasing pressure in cross-examination to be precise in her recollections of past events; her inability to recall a precise time may suggest that she is unable to provide a reliable recollection in general.

Extract 2
Att: OK. What time did you return home on Sunday morning June twelfth?
Int: ¿A qué hora regresó a casa el domingo por la mañana, el doce de junio?
What time did you return home on Sunday morning June twelfth?
W: Uh, Uh (.) como a las diez y media o las once.
Uh, Uh at about ten thirty or eleven.
Int: At about ten thirty or eleven.
Att: You are not sure of the time?
Int: ¿No está segura de la hora?
Are you not sure of the time?
W: Eso más o menos.
That more or less.
Int: That is more or less.
Att: You were not watching the clock?
Int: ¿No estaba viendo el reloj?
You were not watching the clock?
W: Claro que no.
Of course not.

Int: Of course not.
Att: You don't always watch the clock throughout the day. Correct?
Int: Usted no siempre está viendo el reloj durante el día. ¿Correcto?
      You are not always watching the clock during the day. Correct?
W: No, señor. No voy a estar sentada mirando el reloj todo el día, señor.
      No, sir. I am not going to be seated watching the clock all day, sir.
Int: No, sir. I am not going to be sitting just watching the clock, sir
                         (in Miguel, 1998: 111, back translation our own)

López's response to a straightforward Wh- question leads to a series of yes/no questions to which the preferred response is 'no'. Crucially, if López responds 'no' to *¿No está segura de la hora?* her response may be taken to implicate that she is equally unsure of other facts relating to the case. So when she is asked 'You were not watching the clock?' she may be unsure what the preferred 'no' response might potentially implicate. Here, as in the sequence discussed above, López starts to attack the face of her interlocutor in a bid to protect her own. Her response 'Of course not' is face-threatening insofar as it implicates that the questioner should already know the answer and that consequently, she views this to be an inappropriate question. As the attorney continues to probe, López, while putting on record deference towards the attorney through the repeat use of the honorific *señor*, again rejects the line of questioning in *No voy a estar sentada mirando el reloj todo el día* (I'm hardly going to sit about watching the clock all day). Again, the requirement for literal translation means that the illocutionary force of this statement is attenuated although the interpreter again deviates from a strictly literal translation by including the particle 'just', which implicates that López has other (better) things to do than watch the clock.

In both these instances, it appears from the fact that the interpreter partially addresses the issue of illocutionary force ('can't', 'just'), that she is aware that there is a translation difficulty. However, the constraints under which she is working – both physical (the demand for an immediate response) and regulatory (the injunction to translate literally) – appear to militate against transfer of pragmatic meaning. In both instances, it is the power relationship between the interrogator and the interrogated which is at stake and in both instances it is the interrogated party who is disempowered through this particular interpreting process.

It is also possible for the injunction to translate literally to strengthen the illocutionary force of an utterance. In Extract 3, the cross-examining attorney is seeking to establish that López had told a newsreporter that she did not want to return to El Salvador (some of the witness's interventions have been omitted for reasons of economy).

Extract 3
Att: Didn't you tell her that you didn't want to go back to El Salvador?
Int: +++

W: +++
Int: Why not? That's my country. I love it very much.
Att: Well, are you a U.S. citizen?
Int: +++
W: +++
Int: No. I'm a legal resident.
Att: Okay.
     And you've been here 27 years, correct?
Int: +++
W: Haga la cuen/ Vine en 69. Haga la cuenta.
     Calcula/ I came in 69. Calculate.
Int: I came in '69. YOU figure it out. (laughter in courtroom)
Att: Okay.
     Why don't YOU tell me, how long you've been here.
Int: +++
W: Póngale 34 años.
     Put it at 34 years.
Int: Let's say 34 years.

When López is invited to confirm that she has been in the US for 27 years, she is undoubtedly aware that the attorney is conforming to standard legal practice of never asking a question to which he does not already have the answer (Hale, this volume). However, she may not have the answer and (being semi-literate) may also doubt her numeracy skills. She offers him the fact that she is sure of, i.e. that she came in 1969 and invites him to calculate how long she has been there. In Spanish she uses the imperative *haga* (used more frequently than in English) and, while she is using the formal V form, she omits the personal subject pronoun *Vd.*; were it included, its presence would specify that it was the attorney's responsibility to engage in this mental arithmetic. Her utterance and intonation clearly implicate that this is an invitation rather than a challenge; the fact that it is in the attorney's interest to arrive at the correct figure further justifies the bald-on-record imperative. Here the translation provided by the interpreter does nothing to mitigate the threat to face inherent in the use of the imperative and the second person subject pronoun. Her intonational stress on the pronoun 'you' in 'YOU figure it out', the choice of the colloquial verb 'to figure out' (implicating a difficult task) rather than the more neutral and consequently more deferential 'to calculate' make the pragmatic force conveyed something like 'If you really want to know, work it out for yourself'. It is clear that this is the implicature understood by the courtroom, who laugh, and by the attorney since the perlocutionary effect of the translation is to turn the discussion onto who is responsible for providing the information rather than onto the information itself. The attorney's rhetorical question 'Why don't YOU tell me, how long you've been here?' is non-standard in terms of the cross-examination, ostensibly calling on López to provide reasons for not providing this information. López's reply, *Póngale 34 años*, using the imperative form *ponga* addressed to her interlocutor and inviting the attorney to 'call it' 34 years, might be construed within the terms of the powerplay now in force as a confrontational response, disclaiming all responsibility for the accuracy of the information provided (incidentally inaccurate). It is translated by the interpreter as the inclusive 'Let's say', a positive politeness device possibly designed to defuse the confrontation which has inadvertently been generated by her previous intervention. This may indeed be an instance of repair by the interpreter, who is aware of the impact of her previous translation of an imperative in Spanish by an imperative in English. Miguel (1998: 88) notes that later in the trial a similar, potentially face-threatening, use of the imperative *Ponga a las diez y media, señor* (Put it at ten thirty, sir) by the witness is attenuated by the interpreter 'JUST say ten thirty, sir'. Here the interpreter uses the hedge 'just', this time a negative politeness strategy.

In these two instances there appears to be evidence that the requirement to translate literally conflicts with the fact that languages do not encode politeness in strictly equivalent ways. The inclusion in Extract 3 of the attention to face conventional for the English language (possibly, in the case of *haga la cuenta*, 'Could you work it out for me?') might have avoided a cross-cultural misunderstanding of this nature.

Let us now turn to broader questions of modality, for here again it is our contention that modality is conveyed by a range of devices in different languages, which may or may not coincide. Consequently, the degree of commitment by a speaker to a given proposition is not necessarily conveyed by the same structural means in each language. We return to our examination of Extract 1, where López is being accused of having lied about making an airline reservation. As Extract 4, we reproduce her defence and the interpreter's versions (the attorney's interventions have been removed).

Extract 4

W: Porque yo lo voy a reservar, señor. Inmediatamente que salga de aquí. Yo compro mi ticket y me voy (xxx)
Because I am going to reserve it, sir. Immediately after I leave here. I buy my ticket and I go (xxx)

Int: Because I am going to reserve it, sir. As soon as I leave here, I will buy my ticket and I will leave. If you want to, the cameras can follow me.

W: No pero voy a hacerlo no más salir de aquí (xxx) tiempo para salir. No voy a hablar a las diez/ a la una de la mañana...(xxx)
No but I am going to do it as soon as I leave here (xxx) *time to leave. I am not going to speak at ten/ at one in the morning...*(xxx)

Int: But I will make it as soon as I leave here. I can't call at 1:00 in the morning because the airlines are closed at that time. I have to wait.

W: Pero voy a hacer la reservación y me voy, señor (xxx)
But I am going to make the reservation and I am going, sir (xxx)

Int: But I will make the reservation, sir, and I will leave, that is for sure, today.
W: No, porque la voy a hacer, señor.
No, because I am going to make it, sir.
Int: No. Because I will make it, sir.

Leech and Svartvik (1975: 141) distinguish between four types of volition: willingness, wish, intention and insistence and note that 'will' (with different degrees of intonational stress) can cover all of these. The form 'going to' expresses intention and contains an element of prediction which makes it more definite than, for example, 'to intend to'. In Spanish *ir a* (lit. 'to be going to') can express intention but also, and in particular in Latin American varieties of the language, is increasingly used to replace the morphological future, allowing this to be used for other functions, e.g. prediction. Consequently, unlike the English 'going to', *ir a* can merely replace the future tense without intentionality necessarily being a component. Indeed, in all occurrences bar the first the interpreter chooses to translate *ir a* by the future tense in English, marking commitment to the proposition through stress. The present tense in Spanish can also be used for prediction, to refer to future events which are taken as given, and is known as the *presente de anticipación* (Alarcos 1994: 157). Consequently, when López uses the present tense (*yo compro, me voy, me voy*) to follow her *ir a* statements, she is marking absolute commitment to the proposition.[6] This use of the present, however, is interpreted into English by the future tense, lessening the speaker's commitment to the proposition. Finally, like a number of Romance languages, Spanish is a pro-drop language which means that person tends to be encoded in the verb ending. Pronominal absence is the norm. Consequently pronominal presence is the marked form and tends to be pragmatically significant, frequently acting as a strengthening or weakening hedge (see Stewart 2000). In this extract, López's first two utterances (***yo** lo voy a reservar,* ***yo** compro*) significantly include this pronoun and strengthen the speaker's commitment to the proposition that she intends to purchase the ticket, again marking insistence. López is presenting this issue less as one of what she might have done prior to the moment of speech (as opposed to the future) and more in terms of her own personal integrity. She is implicating that her intention to purchase the ticket is more important than the fact of whether or not she has actually done so. Given that this pragmatic dimension is largely absent from the interpretation, López does not benefit from its face-protective potential in the course of this particular bout of interrogation.

The pragmatic effect of the inclusion of the first person subject pronoun in

---

[6] Note that the use of the present tense in a question or a negation may acquire a different pragmatic value (cf. *no voy a estar sentada* – 'I'm not going to be sitting') to that of an assertion in that it expresses counterfactuality or factual remoteness.

marking the speaker's commitment to a proposition is clear; Stewart (forthcoming) argues that the commitment is equivalent to the perceived credibility of the speaker. In Extract 5, López clearly marks her commitment to her belief that a given clock told the right time:

Extract 5
Att: If any of that, you don't know if the clock was right or wrong. Correct?
Int: De todas formas, usted no sabe si el reloj dice la hora correcta o la hora inco/ o la hora/ dice/ dice la hora correcta o la hora incorrecta. ¿Es eso así?
In any case, you do not know if the clock says the correct time or the incorr/ or the incorrect/ he says/ he says the correct time or the incorrect time. Is that so?
W: Yo creo que el reloj estaba correcto, porque yo creo que éstos están correctos. ¿Verdad?
I believe that the clock was correct, because I believe that these are correct. True?
Int: I think the clock was [saying
W: [¿Qué?
What?
Int: the right time because I think these clocks are telling the right time. All right? OK?

Here the addition of the pronoun *yo* to the verbal form *creo* implicates a degree of commitment, whether weak or strong, to the proposition of belief: 'I (firmly) believe'. It is also a rejection of the face-threatening implicature that López does not know (*saber*) whether the clock tells the right time. What is striking about verbs of cognition used in the first person singular is that they are what Palmer (1965) in Weber and Bentivoglio (1991: 194) called private verbs because they refer to activities available for perception by the speaker only and are therefore not open to challenge by other speakers. Consequently, López's response is protective of her positive face in that her beliefs (*creo*) cannot be challenged although her knowledge (her *saber*) could. This implicature is conveyed by the translator's use of 'I think'. What is not conveyed is the degree of commitment to this proposition implicated by the presence of the marked form, the personal subject pronoun. 'I think' implicates a lesser degree of commitment than *yo creo* (indeed, it could more easily allow an inference of doubt) and here it is again possible that the witness is presented as less sure of her facts in the English interpretation.

In this brief analysis we have examined hedging and modality, which combine to provide the speaker with resources with which to negotiate face (and crucially to protect his or her own face) in what is essentially a highly face-threatening speech event. In the data the interpreter appears, through her inclusion within her largely literal translation of certain hedges or particles, to be aware of the non-correspondence between the source and target language of the linguistic resources used to negotiate face. Yet the injunction to translate literally and to leave the interpretation to the court has meant that the illocutionary force of witness statements has been frequently modified in translation, in this instance possibly resulting in presenting the witness as speaking with less confidence, expertise or knowledge than she actually does.

4. Face and politeness in an Immigration Office setting: Polish illegal immigrants

Bearing in mind the different participant perceptions of the triadic relationship involved in the exchange, we now turn to the immigration interview data. These interviews also present a threat to the positive face of the interviewee insofar as they are designed to elicit a confession that the interviewee has lied to the immigration services on entry to Britain. There is a secondary purpose, that is, to track down the agents who organize the illegal immigration. In the case of these interviews the interpreter is under no injunction to translate literally and indeed there is ample evidence in the text of free and frequently amplified or truncated translation; both clients, the immigration officer (IO) and the interviewees (a Polish woman (PW) and a Polish man (PM)), are in all probability fully aware of this. In addition to her role as animator (see endnote 3), the interpreter (Int) on occasion, and no doubt drawing on the experience of many previous interviews of very similar format, expands on the IO's questions and takes on the role of principal, asking further supplementaries of her own. For example, in one interview the IO wishes to find out what an agency in Poland had promised their client, the interviewee.

Extract 6
IO: What did they say?
I: I co oni powiedzieli?
And what did they say?
PM: Że pojedziemy do pracy do Anglii.
That we'll travel to work to England
I: Co znaczy pojedziemy? Bo bylo więcej?
What does it mean 'we'll travel'? Because there were more?
PM: Tak
Yes
I: Yes they said they'd go and work in England because apparently he wasn't the only one, there were several people involved.

Given the highly participative role of the interpreter within the triad, and a willingness to anticipate and modify the communicative needs of her clients, it might be anticipated that the interpreter would not only be sensitive to face wants but also, unlike her colleague in a courtroom setting, be better placed to address them. However, analysis of the data appears to point to two areas where there is a pragmatic mismatch between the source and target texts.

The interviews with the immigrants are a formality prior to their speedy deportation to Warsaw. Probably as a result of this, the interpersonal tenor adopted by the IO is not formal and distant but rather ranges between neutral and casual/solidary. For example, in Extract 7 below, the IO uses modality ('would ask') to soften the potentially face-threatening thrust of his line of argument, i.e. seeking to establish that the immigrant lied to the immigration officer in charge.

Extract 7
IO: That immigration officer would ask you some questions.
I: Urzędnik zadał ci dwa pytania. Coś ty jemu powiedział a? Dlaczego tutaj przyjechałaś?
The official asked you two questions. What did you say to him? Why did you come here?

The use of the modal form, suggesting that an interview with an immigration officer is normal procedure but not alleging that it has taken place in this particular instance, rather than the direct assertion ('asked') gives the addressee an 'out'; she can always deny having spoken with the immigration officer and thus avoid further questioning. A similar strategy is employed in another interview when the IO chooses to ask 'Do you remember seeing an immigration officer...?' allowing PM again the opportunity to exploit, if he wishes, the 'out' provided by faulty memory, e.g. 'no, I don't remember' (another instance of the use of a private verb).

However, the interpreter does not convey the modality of the source into Polish but rather presupposes that the PW has been interrogated by the immigration officer. Indeed, by choosing, on her own initiative, to add two further wh- questions (the content of which is predictable within the genre of the speech event), she increases rather than decreases the degree of face-threat involved in the interview, e.g. by turning this sequence into one of interrogation, forcing the interviewee to admit precisely what claims she had made to the immigration officer.

The relatively informal tenor adopted by the immigration officer is for the most part relayed into a similar tenor in Polish with a degree of sensitivity to pragmatic norms in both cultures. For example, the conventional indirectness of the IO's request 'Can you write her name down for me? (referring to the name of an agent who arranged the employment) is relayed in Polish by the more culturally appropriate imperative form 'Napisz jak ona się nazywa' *(Write down her name)*. However, there is evidence that the interpreter on a number of occasions adopts a more formal tenor in interpreting into English for the interviewee. Extracts 8 and 9 are examples of this.

Extract 8

PW: Bo chciałam iść tutaj do szkoły, do tej pory udało mi sie, musiałam zarobić pieniądze żeby iść do szkoły bo szoła jest dosyć droga.
Because I wanted to go to school here, till now I've managed to. I had to earn money to go to school because school is quite expensive.

I: I had to, my intention was to attend an English course here and I didn't have enough money so I had to earn the money in order to pay for the course.

PW: I do tej pory chodzę do szkoły, chodziłam raz w tygodniu, niestety.
And I still go to school, I did go to school once a week unfortunately.

I: And I have been attending an English course once a week.

+++

PW: Bo sie bałam że nie zostanę wpuszczona, bo słyszałam wiele historii, że mimo wszystko że ktoś miał szkołę kupioną nie został wpuszczony, a nawet znam takie osoby
Because I was afraid that I wouldn't be allowed in because I heard many stories that even if someone had school paid for, they weren't allowed in, I even know such persons.

I: Because I knew people who having said to the immigration officer on entry that they had already paid for a course of English lessons had been turned away.

+++

PW: Tak
yes

I: That's correct.

The use of a more formal register can be seen in lexical and syntactic choices such as 'My intention was to...' for 'I wanted to' and 'attend an English course' for 'go to school', 'That's correct' for 'yes' and the inclusion of supplementary information specific to this particular setting such as 'having said to the immigration officer on entry'. This tendency on the part of the interpreter to adopt a formalese judged to be appropriate to the context of interpretation has been observed in the case of court interpreting by Berk-Seligson (1990) and Hale (1997). It has the effect of modifying the socio-cultural personae of the participants as presented in the speech exchange as well as affecting their interpretation of the appropriate level of formality of the speech genre. It relates to face insofar as it alters power relations in favour of the discourse of the institution and subtly alters the relationship between the immigration officer and the interviewee to the disempowerment of the latter. In this extract, the interpreter's interventions also alter the tenor adopted by the participants at a more pragmatic level; the omission of a series of attitudinal markers ('I wanted to', 'unfortunately', 'I was afraid') used by the interviewee serves to downplay her strategy of presenting acceptable reasons for being in Britain, i.e. a genuine desire to study, and to make more prominent the unacceptable face of her conduct, i.e the need to earn money to pay for this activity.

The other area where there appears to be a pragmatic mismatch between speaker and interpreter output concerns a series of questions seeking to establish the culpability of the interviewee. In Extract 9, IO goes 'off-record' (Brown and Levinson 1987) and uses repetition and irony to implicate that the interviewee (PW) has lied to the immigration officer at Dover. After establishing that she entered the country ostensibly for a period of one week with two hundred pounds in her pocket, IO interrupts the question sequence with what appears to be a statement, the implicature of which is that PW cannot possibly have survived in Britain as a tourist for two months on £200. A further implicature is that the immigrant must have acquired an alternative source of income during this period and consequently violated the terms of her entry permit. The statement effectively threatens the positive face of the interviewee as it constitutes an indirect accusation of illegal entry.

Extract 9
IO: Two hundred pounds. OK, that was certainly more than a week ago. That was over two months ago.

The interpreter omits the off-record face-threatening implicature of this statement and reverts to the question-and-answer format, inquiring about the precise period for which PW has been in Britain.

I: Dwa miesiące temu, prawda?
Two months ago, is that right?

The answer 'Tak' (*yes*) paves the way for a follow-up question which is designed to lead the interviewee gently into admitting that the only way that she has been able to stay in the country has been by working illegally.

IO: How is it that you're still in this country?

Again the off-record face-threatening implicature (i.e. an indirect accusation of having worked illegally) is replaced by a bald on-record wh-question.

I: Dlaczego tutaj dalej jesteś ?
Why are you still here?

The interpreter's question is an invitation to provide reasons for staying and is considerably less coercive than the initial formulation 'How is it...', which inquires more precisely about the circumstances which have enabled the immigrant to stay.

What is striking about these particular triadic exchanges is the degree to which the intervention of the interpreter subtly affects the pragmatics of the interventions of the other two speakers and thus modifies the unfolding relationship between the principal participants.

5. Conclusion

In the analysis of these two distinct speech events we have looked at hedging, modality, register and off-record speech acts, all of which are linguistic devices used differently in different languages and cultures to encode attention to face. For example, the marked use of the present tense in Spanish may find its pragmatic equivalent in hedging in English; the use of the conventional politeness device 'Can you...' in English may be appropriately relayed by the imperative in Polish. We have not, however, focussed our study on conventional politeness (e.g. the mitigation of threat to the face of the other through devices such as conventional indirectness 'could you...' or the use or non-use of honorifics). Rather we have looked primarily at instances where the speaker, while frequently protecting his or her own face, actively seeks to threaten the face of the interlocutor or, conversely, to offer it some protection. What is interesting about the analysis of speech events which inherently contain a degree of threat to the face of the interviewee or the interviewer is the extent to which face-threatening acts are frequently modified in the course of the interpreting, regardless of the style of interpreting adopted. While an initial hypothesis might have led one to believe that the more formally literal style of interpreting would prove a barrier to the transfer of interpersonal rather than propositional meaning, it is possible to suggest, from the evidence above, that this style of interpreting may do as much to preserve interpersonal meaning as it does to destroy it. In fact, our admittedly limited evidence suggests that while the literal style of interpreting does not necessarily suppress interpersonal meaning, the freer, less regulated style does not necessarily preserve it. It is clear that this is an area of face-to-face interpreting which has been largely neglected in most previous research. More investigation is needed both into cross-cultural equivalence of pragmatic meaning and into the effects of a failure to relay face-related effects on, say, witness credibility, or the future direction of the talk exchange.

References

Alarcos Llorach, E. (1994) *Gramática de la lengua española*, Madrid: Espasa Calpe.
Berk-Seligson, S. (1988) 'The Impact of Politeness in Witness Testimony: The Influence of the Court Interpreter', *Multilingua* 7(4): 411-439.
------ (1990) *The Bilingual Courtroom: Court Interpreters in the Judicial Process*, Chicago: The University of Chicago Press.
Brennan, M. (1999) 'Signs of Injustice', *The Translator* 5(2): 221-246.

Brown P. and S. Levinson (1987) *Politeness*, Cambridge: Cambridge University Press.
Goffman, E. (1981) *Forms of Talk*, Philadelphia: University of Pennsylvania Press.
Hale, S. (1997a) 'Interpreting Politeness in Court. A Study of Spanish-English Interpreted Proceedings', in S. Campbell and S. Hale (eds) *Proceedings of the 2nd annual Macarthur Interpreting and Translation Conference 'Research, Training and Practice*, Milperra: UWS Macarthur/LARC, 37-45.
------ (1997b) 'The Interpreter on Trial: Pragmatics in Court Interpreting', in S. Carr et al. (eds) *The Critical Link: Interpreters in the Community*, Amsterdam & Philadelphia: John Benjamins, 201-211.
Harris, B. and B. Sherwood (1978) 'Translating as an Innate Skill', in D. Gerver and H. W. Sinaiko (eds), *Language Interpretation and Communication*, New York & London: Plenum Press, 155-170.
Kang, M. A. (1998) 'Strategies of inclusion: Addressee(s) in triadic exchanges', *Text* 18(3): 383-416.
Knapp-Pothoff, Annelie and Karlfried Knapp (1987) 'The Man (or Woman) in the Middle: Discoursal Aspects of Non-professional Interpreting', in K. Knapp, W. Enninger and A. Knapp-Potthoff (eds) *Analyzing Intercultural Communication*, Berlin: de Gruyter, 181-211.
Lang, R. (1976) 'Interpreters in Local Courts in Papua New Guinea', in W. M. O'Barr and J. F. O'Barr (eds) *Language and Politics*, The Hague & Paris: Mouton, 327-365.
------ (1978) 'Behavioural Aspects of Liaison Interpreters in Papua New Guinea: Some Preliminary Observations', in D. Gerver and H. W. Sinaiko (eds) *Language Interpretation and Communication*, New York & London: Plenum Press, 231-244.
Leech, G. and J. Svartvik (1975) *A Communicative Grammar of English*, Harlow: Longman.
Mason, I. (ed) (1999) *Dialogue Interpreting*, special issue of *The Translator* 5(2).
Miguel, M. A. (1998) *Witness Testimony in the Bilingual Coutroom: The Interpreting of Politeness*, Unpublished MSc dissertation, Heriot-Watt University, Edinburgh.
Morris, R. (1995) 'The Moral Dilemmas of Court Interpreting', *The Translator* 1(1): 25-46.
Palmer, F.R. (1965) *A Linguistic Study of the English Verb*, London: Longman.
Pym, A. (1999) '"Nicole slapped Michelle": Interpreters and Theories of Interpreting at the O. J. Simpson Trial', *The Translator* 5(2): 265-283.
Rigney, A. (1999) 'Questioning in Interpreted Testimony', *Forensic Linguistics: The International Journal of Speech, Language and the Law* 6 (1): 83-108.
Roy, C. (2000) *Interpreting as a Discourse Process*, Oxford: Oxford University Press.
Stewart, M. (2000) 'Pronouns of power and solidarity: the case of Spanish first person plural '*nosotros*'', *Web Journal of Modern Language Linguistics* 4.
------ (2001) 'Hedging your bets – the use of *yo* in face-to-face interaction', *Multilingua* 20.
Tebble, H. (1999) 'The Tenor of Consultant Physicians: Implications for Medical Interpreting', *The Translator* 5(2): 179-200.

Wadensjö, C. (1998) *Interpreting as Interaction,* London: Longman.
Walraven, J. (n.d.) *Simpson Trial Site.* www3.islandnet.com/~walraven/simpson.html.
Weber, E. and Bentivoglio, P. (1991) 'Verbs of cognition in spoken Spanish: a discourse profile', in S. Fleischman and L. Waugh (eds) *Discourse Pragmatics and the Verb: the Evidence from Romance*, London: Routledge, 194-213.

Interpreting in Crisis
The Interpreter's Position in Therapeutic Encounters

CECILIA WADENSJÖ

The present paper[1] explores interaction in two interpreter-assisted therapeutic encounters. The analysis suggests that the physical position of the interpreter may be decisive for the kind of care-providing the encounter can bring about. More precisely, I claim that the position of the interpreter can potentially facilitate as well as obstruct the participants' synchronization of talk. This in turn may have an impact on their experience of spiritual affinity, of 'being with' one another, and hence on the refugee-patient's willingness and ability to re-tell traumatic memories. The paper points to the placement of the interpreter in relation to the primary parties as one of the factors that could be further explored, not only for a better understanding of the role of the dialogue interpreter, but also for the development of interpreter-mediated encounters as a specific form of mental healthcare.

1. Introduction

Is it at all possible to provide mental health care to a patient you can't talk to? Can traumatized patients really come to trust psychiatrists who talk to them in a foreign, obscure language? Can psychotherapy really be carried out with the assistance of interpreters? Some people might want to argue that all of this is simply impossible. Others still – and certainly care providers involved in the treatment of traumatized refugees – would argue instead that there is simply no other choice. During the late 20th century, millions of people have been forced to leave their homes and become refugees, due to wars and political or religious persecution. Their experiences of violence, terror and forced migration sometimes lead to urgent need for mental health care, a care which in many cases cannot take place without the assistance of interpreters.

Within the field of psychiatry and social medicine, in the literature on migration and mental health generally, and on post-traumatic stress-disorder (PTSD) in particular, the issue of interpreting is often mentioned. Practitioners naturally need to understand the impact of interpreters on their working relationship with the patients and on the content and the structure of the psychotherapy session.

---

[1] A version of this paper was read at the 2nd International Conference on Interpreting in Legal, Health, Educational and Social Services Settings, Vancouver, Canada, May 1998. A German version was published in Birgit Apfelbaum and Hermann Müller (eds. 1998), *Fremde im Gespräch – Gesprächsanalytische Untersuchungen zu Dolmetschinteraktionen, interkultureller Kommunikation und institutionalisierten Interaktionsformen*, Frankfurt: IKO – Verlag für Interkulturelle Kommunikation, 47-62.

However, to my knowledge, there are few efforts made to explore interpreting on its own conditions, one exception being a chapter in a handbook for interpreters by Gentile and his colleagues (1996). In the medical literature, I have found interpreters and interpreting sometimes mentioned, and then basically as a methodological *problem* in the practice of the medical expert (at times also as a methodological problem for researchers, applying interviews or questionnaires as research methods). An alternative approach, suggested in this paper, is to explore the potential of interpreter-mediated therapeutic care, the *possibilities* provided by the interpreter-mediated mode of communication. One way of doing this would be to describe and explore the communicative tasks carried out in interpreter-mediated mental health care encounters, and try to distinguish more precisely what duties interpreters tend to undertake, why, and with which possible effects. Of course, this implies a need to problematize the (at one level self-evident) task of translating. In a more fine-graded analysis, translating could be seen as consisting of a range of activities, which, if labelled more sensitively in terms of the work mental health care encounters are designed for, would contribute to generating knowledge about the specific conditions of interpreter-mediated therapeutic care.

2. Analytical focus: the interpreter's placement in joint narrative activity

The data analysed in this paper are drawn from a corpus of eight video-recorded encounters involving three parties – a patient, a mental healthcare provider and an interpreter. All the patients originated from the former Yugoslavia, had recently arrived in Sweden and had no knowledge of Swedish, the language in which they were being treated.

As my point of departure I take an issue which was first brought to my attention by an interpreter, during an interview for the above-mentioned project. She expressed a very strong opinion about how to sit in relation to the others during therapy sessions. She recalled a particular encounter where the therapist had insisted on placing her beside the patient, in order to remove her from the patient's direct line of sight, which he thought would be a way of minimising the risk of her getting involved in processes of transference and counter-transference. In the interpreter's opinion, the therapist had promoted exactly the opposite of what he intended. She had felt caught in an undesired relationship with the patient, sitting physically close to her. This story inspired me to reflect upon the impact of the interpreter's position with regard to the core activity taking place in therapeutic encounters, namely narrative activity.

In her book *Trauma and Recovery,* Herman (1992) convincingly argues in favour of an idea which today is widely shared within the field of psychotherapy. She has found that the very activity of re-telling a traumatic experience in the safety of a protected relationship can make patients change their view of the memory of this experience (1992:183). Remembering is also forgetting, as Milan Kundera (1981) has it. Hence, when this very activity, the re-telling, is performed in interpreter-mediated interaction, what does it mean for the patient-storyteller, for the practitioner providing care and for the interpreter enabling communication between them to take place?

Summarising a great range of work on narrative and its role in human interaction, Ochs and Capps (1996), two American anthropological linguists, note that narrative is a fundamental means of making sense of experience. "Personal narrative simultaneously is born out of experience and gives shape to experience. In this sense, narrative and self are inseparable" (1996:20).

What is the role of the interpreter in the shaping of orderliness and in the reconstruction of selves? What about the interpreters' own safety? What does the re-telling of others' traumatic memories demand from them? How can interpreters avoid burnout and vicarious traumatization, consequences of working with refugees found among therapists (e.g. McCann and Pearlman 1990; van der Veer 1992: 241-8). A recent interview study among interpreters (Plimer and Candlin 1996) indicates that interpreters may indeed suffer burnout resulting from their work, and may need to unburden themselves of their anxieties in confidence. Elsewhere (Wadensjö 1998: 239-74), I discuss the marking, in interaction, of a distinction between the speaking self and the meaning other as something belonging to what can be seen as an interpreter's normal needs while on duty in face-to-face interaction. This need would seem all the more understandable in conversations where narrators' selves "open themselves to reconstrual" (Ochs and Capps 1996:37).

Focusing on *communication*, I have found it useful to think of interpreter-mediated talk in terms of a communicative *pas de trois* (Wadensjö 1997, 1998). Taking an interactional approach and applying a dialogic view of language and mind, I foreground and describe the intimate interdependence between the participants involved and their respective communicative projects and goals. The dialogical perspective treats all participants in a communicative event as doing interpretative work. In making sense, people may bring all kinds of rationalities to interaction. Hence, the primary parties – as well as the interpreter – may occasionally mobilize various levels of understanding, i.e. understanding of the situation, of the participants as individuals and as group members, of what information and emotions are currently relevant, to whom and why.

Working with narrative activity, I am interested in how people construct versions of past events within the joint practices of the conversation. The discourse-analytic approach leads me to look at the particular communicative circumstances present in the encounter at various levels; peoples' background assumptions about the situation as a whole and about each other, peoples' communicative behaviour as they develop interaction on a turn-by-turn basis. Scrutinising video-recorded interpreter-mediated interaction between patients and practitioners I can observe remembering as a social, joint activity, in line with psychologists like Middleton and Edwards (1990). I will use two excerpts – drawn from two encounters – to point to some factors which are potentially important in the social organization of remembering, and discuss how they link to the issue of interpreters' placement in relation to the primary participants.

3. One patient – two encounters, two stories, two interpreters

A male patient, who has spent two and a half years in concentration camps in the former Yugoslavia, visits a Swedish Medical Centre for Refugees, where psychiatric, psychosocial and medical care is provided. The patient is treated for various physical injuries and he is also offered therapeutic talks. In the extracts reproduced below he meets a doctor who is ultimately in charge of the whole treatment. They meet on several occasions. I video-recorded two of these. In the excerpts selected, the patient makes essentially opposing statements about remembering. The doctor had planned both talks partly as opportunities for the patient to tell some of his war experiences, but while this did occur in the second talk, in the first it did not.

The first extract starts where the doctor follows up on a question concerning the patient's eating problems. The patient's stomach was severely injured by torture in the camp. He had a spoon stuck down his throat, and it remained in his body for four years. This is known to the doctor as a fact but he has no details about the event. The parties are assisted by an interpreter, here called Irina. Five minutes after the beginning of the talk, the doctor asks the patient about the torture with the spoon.

Extract 1: 'I don't remember that well'

		ORIGINAL CONVERSATION	AUTHOR'S TRANSLATION
1	Doctor	hur gick de till?	*how did it happen?*
2	Irina	°kako se to desilo°?	*°how did that happen°?*
3	Patient	pa ne sećam se dobro bio sam u komi	*er I don't remember that well I was in coma*
4	Irina	de kommer ja [inte ihåg-	*I don't rem[ember that*
5	Patient	[tokom bio- ne u: da kažem u nesvesčenom tuću	*[during I was- no in: to say I was beaten unconscious*
6	Irina	a var i koma har har något så när kan man säga att ja var medvetslös av allt stryk ja fått	*I was in coma I have in a sense one can say that I was unconscious because of all the beating I got*
7	Doctor	°mm°	*°mm°*
		(3s)	(3s)

(Four turns excluded: Pat., Irina, Pat., Irina. The patient mentions a visit to the doctor – some years after he had been released from the camp – in which he learned that he had a spoon inside his body).

		(11s)	(11s)
14	Doctor	hur mycke kommer du ihåg eh fram tills att du var (.) medvetslös?	how much do you remember er before the point that you became (.) unconscious?
15	Irina	Koliko se sećaš dok nisi se unesvestio?	how much do you remember before that you became unconscious?
16	Patient	pa sećam se ovo kad su (mi) dali tu porciju (.) pa sam počeo nekaku čorbu da jedem °i ništa više°	er I remember that when they gave me this portion (.) er I began to eat some kind of stew °and nothing more°
17	Irina	ja kommer ihåg tills dess dom kom fram me en sån portion me nåt slags flytande soppa me skeden i så ja skulle äta °å inget mer sen dess°	I remember before the point when they came forward with this portion with some kind of liquid soup with the spoon in it so I was supposed to eat °and nothing more after that°
18	Patient	tek eh su- eh sutra dan pa sam tek počeo da se-	not until er mo- er the next morning I eventually began to-
19	Irina	inte förrän dan därpå så har ja vaknat till	not before the next day I did come round
20	Patient	(coughs) (7s)	(coughs) (7s)
21	Doctor	va de i samband me de som du också fick eh (touches his chin) slag mot (.) käkarna?	was it in connection with this that you also got er (touches his chin) blows on (.) your jaws?
22	Irina	jel isto uz tu priliku (touches her chin) (xx) kad si dobio udarci prema vilicama?	was this in that connection (touches her chin) (xx) when you got blows on your jaws?

This whole sequence, including the four missing lines in the middle, takes two minutes and five seconds. To give an idea of how the setting looked, I have provided a stylized picture on the basis of the video recording.

The second extract is from an encounter recorded a month later. The doctor and the patient had met in between, assisted by Irina and another interpreter, the one who was present for my second recording. Here I call him Izmet. In this second extract, the patient is apparently more prepared to tell of his experiences in the concentration camp and the war. The doctor asks about his sleep, and the patient starts mentioning his bad dreams. Asked to be more specific regarding what he dreams about, the patient tells about a series of traumatic experiences and starts reflecting upon how this might have changed him as a person.

Figure 1: The patient in the middle leans back while saying
'I don't remember that well I was in coma' (1:3).

The actual sequence reproduced in Extract 2 took 58 seconds. During the following 20 minutes or so the patient tells a number of personal stories about horrifying war experiences. He has survived not only the torture with the spoon, briefly touched upon in the first talk, but also harsh imprisonment, being selected to act as a living shield and being selected to be executed. Moreover, he mentions the loss of several close relatives.

Exploring the transcriptions as texts, comparing primary interlocutors' utterances with the interpreters' renditions of them, the second excerpt can be seen to contain inconsistencies of translation (cf. utterance 2:3 and 2:4, 2:5 and 2:6). Irina's renditions match in greater detail the preceding originals. Comparing the transcriptions of the whole encounters, the general impression remains of Izmet producing fewer 'close' renditions and Irina more. Moreover, while Izmet keeps his hands together on his lap practically all the time, Irina performs accompanying gestures, reminiscent of the gestures performed by the primary parties (see utterances 1:21 and 1:22). Occasionally, she varies between higher and lower pitch as the preceding speaker did in the corresponding original (see 1:16 and 1:17). Her performance gives a relaxed impression. Izmet, in turn, does not make any effort of the kind described above to 'replay' (cf. Wadensjö 1998: 246-7) prosodic and other features of the preceding utterance. He speaks in the same even pitch throughout the encounter, in a rather monotonous voice. Later, when the interpreter and I looked at the video recording together, he commented spontaneously, somewhat surprised and slightly disappointed, that he found himself sounding quite strained. Apparently, there is no simple correlation between 'closeness' and scrupulousness of interpreting of spoken 'texts',

Extract 2: 'dates and days and minutes'

		ORIGINAL CONVERSATION	AUTHOR'S TRANSLATION
1	Doc	vad är det för bilder som kommer tillbaka?	what kind of pictures are coming back?
2	Izmet	a koje ti se slike to vraćaju?	and which are the pictures coming back to you?
3	Pat	pa recimo isto ta sila koja se desila na	well let's say also these the violence that took place on
4	Izmet	våldtäckter som ägt rum	rapes that took place
5	Pat	ubijanje tih ljudi civila što ja znam to su- pokupio sam tih	the killing of these people civilians what do I know they are- I gathered these
6	Izmet	dödandet av dessa civila människor jag har ju själv fått gräv- begrava många av dom	the killing of these civil people I had to dig- bury many of them myself didn't I
7	Pat	izvadio isto iz vode °i tako°	I dragged these out of water °and so°
8	Izmet	molim?	sorry?
9	Pat	izvadio iz vode isto	I dragged out of water these
10	Izmet	jag har dragit upp dom ur vatten	I have dragged them out of water
11	Pat	i tako °da se to° vraća mi se sve film unutra (iz početka i tako)	and so °it is like° the whole film is played inside of me (from the beginning and forth)
12	Izmet	så allt detta °alltså° filmen rullas tillbaka å de börjar från början åter igen	so all of this °that is° the film is played back and it starts all over again
13	Pat	ali recimo od sve to vreme ja sam presisovao i datum °i dana i minute°	but let's say of all that time I have specifications of both dates °and days and minutes°
14	Izmet	ja kan minnas allting ... eh kronologiskt både dag och timmar och minuter (2s)	I can remember everything... er chronologically both day hours and minutes (2s)
15	Pat	i šta ja znam i sam sebe nekad pitam odkud baš to kad ne mora ustvari uop- uopšte kako kako sam normalan °uopšte°	and what do I know I even ask myself at times from where just that when it doesn't have to in fact real-really how how I can be normal °really°
16	Izmet	ibland frågar jag mig varifrån ja får (har) ett sånt minne va eller hur hur ja överhuvudtaget (.) har förstånd kvar	sometimes I ask myself from where I get (have) such a memory where or how how I really (.) have [my] reason left

and adequacy of the situation for narrative activity. In any case, equivalence between 'texts' in interpreter-mediated interaction does not in itself constitute a necessary condition of successful interpreting. The actions and interactions performed in a social encounter, depend not only on the participating individuals' individual capacities, but also on how personal preferences and individual skills fit together in the given constellation of people and the situation at the time.

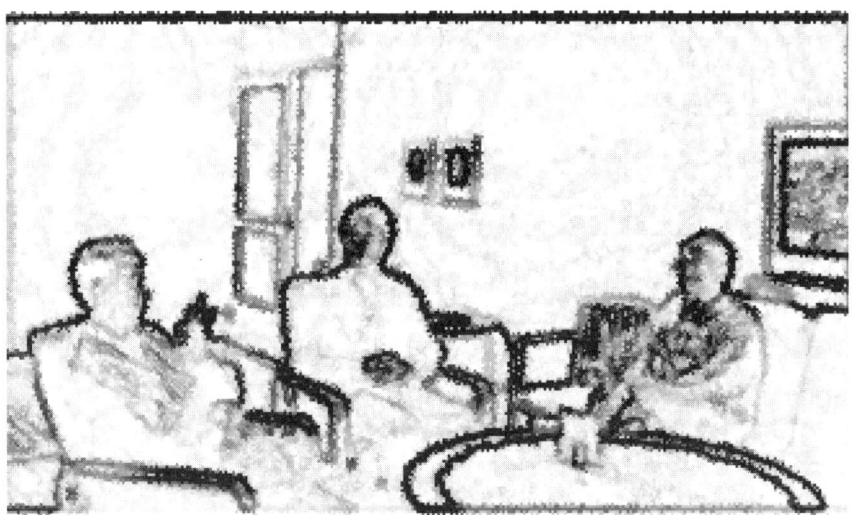

Figure 2: The patient to the left says
'I have specifications of both dates °and days and minutes°' (2:13).

After the first encounter, the doctor said spontaneously that talk had developed in a direction he had not counted on. He had felt as if being tested and, in a sense, not approved of as a listener. At the beginning of the encounter he made several efforts to frame the conversation as a 'remembering-wartime-experiences' situation. Fairly soon, however, he dropped these initiatives, when the patient switched over – in the midst of mentioning war experiences – to more recent experiences of practical problems and frustrations. The second encounter, in contrast, mainly consisted of the patient's telling of his experiences from the recent war. The three persons came out from it noticeably affected. I was waiting in a room nearby when it took place. My impression from meeting them was confirmed by what I saw and heard on the videotape.

4. Differences between the situations

If we compare the two sequences, some features can be identified quite obviously as being linked to remembering as a joint activity. To start with, one could compare the situations 'globally', i.e. taking the conversation as a whole, including some general assumptions brought to them by the participants. Obviously, factors like the time, place and relationships between the participating individuals could increase or reduce the chance of talk developing into the telling of personal stories.

		Extract 1	**Extract 2**
G	TIME	The participants meet in this situation for the first time.	The participants have met in a similar situation before.
L			
O	PLACE	Relatively new place for the patient.	Relatively well-known environment.
B		Video-recording – a new experience.	Video-recording: already experienced
A	RELA-	Patient – doctor: newly acquainted.	Patient – doctor: better acquainted.
L	TION-		
L	SHIP	Male patient, female interpreter, noticeably differing linguistic background (at level of dialect) between interpreter and patient.	Male patient, male interpreter, slightly differing linguistic background (at level of sociolect) between interpreter and patient.
Y			

Figure 3: Situational differences between the encounters

By the time of the second encounter, the patient has arguably had more time to get used to the idea of speaking to the doctor, of doing so through an interpreter, and of talking while being video-recorded. Indeed, what is presented here as extract 2 is in fact the third recording I made with the same patient. In between the two encounters exemplified above, I recorded a meeting between the patient and another care-provider, a woman psychologist. The interpreter present on this occasion was Irina, as in the first encounter. Meeting the psychologist, the patient talked very openly about various personal matters. However, his experiences from the war were not touched upon.

The value of gender differences between participants in social interaction should not be understated, yet I would argue that there is no need to overplay either this difference or differences in linguistic or ethnic background. Obviously, features of social identity are mobilized as communicative resources when people come together and talk, but precisely which features, and how, can be hard to predict. However, to judge from the interview with the interpreter Irina, her gender appears indeed to have influenced the interaction in encounters involving her and this particular patient. She reports that she occasionally felt somewhat disturbed by his flattering comments on her appearance – delivered off-the-record as it were – while she was on duty interpreting. He might have disliked the idea of being seen by her as pitiful and weak. He might also have wanted to protect her from hearing about his horrible experiences.

Elsewhere (Wadensjö 1992,1998), I have discussed the interpreter's skill as a mastery of controlling various modes of listening and speaking. Interpreters' listening behaviours constitute one of their main resources for demonstrating their particular status of being excluded from the exchange but included in the exchanging. One of the therapists I interviewed mentioned that feelings of strong affection during a therapy session were not more strange or uncommon than feelings of strong antagonism and anger. "All patients have the right to fall in love with their therapist", to use her words. While therapists are trained not to take patients' emotions to heart, but rather to make them work for the patients' recovery, interpreters do not normally receive such training. While therapists are trained to listen attentively and respond, interpreters are trained mainly to mobilize another mode of listening: to listen attentively, render what they have heard in a new version and avoid direct response. They might be trained in distancing themselves from others' emotions, concentrating as they are on the verbal means by which emotions are expressed. Yet, as Watzlawick and his colleagues already argued in their studies of human interaction in the 1960s, when present in an interactional situation, "no matter how one may try, one cannot *not* communicate" (Watzlawick *et al.* 1967:49). A person who pays attention to someone will interpret the mere appearance of this person and his or her behaviour (whether verbal or non-verbal). Hence, each time the patient looked at Irina, it must have put an additional strain on her need to mark the distinction between her own speaking self and the meaning other, given she felt that he was interested in *her* reactions to what he said.

5. Differences in the organization of interaction

To judge from the talk it was evident that the second encounter was a much more focused communicative event, in which all participants present seemed to share involvement and focus, while the first one had much fewer such moments. Comparing the two encounters, in search for 'locally'-manifested differences – in the turn-by-turn organization of talk – I found that certain features vary in a significant way. Potentially, I would venture, they make a difference to the joint activity of remembering. These features may again be seen as involving time, place and personal relations, as outlined in Figure 4.
The method of analysing at the 'local' level includes comparing impressions from repeated, concentrated listening to the two recordings. In the first recording, I noted that the participants talked at their own pace, quite stable at the personal level, but different from one another. The doctor's speech was noticeably slow. The interpreter talked faster and in quite a modulated voice, with changing pitch, while the patient talked relatively faster still, with an even, more monotonous pitch. In the first encounter, there were quite a few long silences, like those seen in the transcription (3, 11 and 7 seconds long). In the second

		Extract 1	Extract 2
L O C A L L Y	TIMING	The participants' talk seems less synchronized.	The participants' talk seems more synchronized.
	POSITION-ING	The interpreter is outside of the communicative radius formed between patient and doctor.	The interpreter – placed centrally between the parties – forms part of a communicative radius shared by all those present.
	RELATION-SHIP	The interpreter avoids exchanging gaze with the patient and does not engage in any direct verbal exchange with him.	The interpreter occasionally allocates turns at talk using gaze and head movements. He also engages in clarification sequences with the patient.

Figure 4: Local differences between the encounters

encounter the participants talked at quite a similar pace. Moreover, the interpreter and the patient talked with a similar, fairly monotonous voice pitch throughout the encounter. There were few long silences. Like the example in the transcription, these were relatively shorter than in the first encounter. During these silences, the primary parties exchanged gaze and nods. In the first encounter some of the pauses were too long to be filled only with exchanges of gaze, nods or smiles.

In the second extract, the interpreter addressed the patient with a question of clarification (*molim?*, 2:8). This is one of 22 occasions he does so during the 45 minute encounter. In the first encounter, it is possible that the primary parties talked more clearly, and/or the interpreter listened more attentively. Irina did not once ask back to check a term or a formulation.

From the point of view of the patient, Izmet's questions were concrete reminders of the communicative conditions obtaining at the time. The patient was thereby urged to repeat what he had just said, in order to make the interpreter grasp it as an auxiliary listener and provide a second version of it for the doctor. These temporary mini-exchanges between the interpreter and the patient became a resource by means of which Izmet demarcated himself as a speaker of others' words. Irina had to rely on other ways of marking her particular mode of listening and speaking only on others' behalf. The non-standard direction of her gaze and talk was one way of signalling non-involvement. She avoided answering directly when she was addressed directly by the patient. Moreover, she was probably counting on a clear contrast between her own voice and the words she voiced.

In the second encounter, on no occasion did the patient ask back to check anything with the interpreter whereas in the first he did. When from time to time the patient looked in Irina's direction – to check the content of talk, or its current state of progress, or to see how she reacted to a given piece of information – he had to turn his head away from the doctor (see Figure 5). One could say that the participants did not share the same *communicative radius*.

Figure 5: The patient from time to time glances at Irina but has to look away from the doctor.

In the second encounter both primary parties could see the interpreter in the corner of their eye, without changing their main orientation towards one another. In the first, they were seated in a less immediately available way in relation to one another.

6. Preliminary conclusions and further questions

In their book *The Counselor as Gatekeeper*, Erickson and Schultz (1982) examined the temporal complementarity between speaking and listening behaviour in face-to-face institutional encounters. They observe that rhythmic regularity, for example, nods, body positioning and prosodic pattern of speech, more than the substance of talk, made the participants (students meeting with student counsellors) perceive each other as "being *with*" one another. In contrast, while jointly performing in "interactional arhythmia", they were revealing themselves as not sharing an adequate interpretative framework (Erickson and Schultz 1982:143). This remains to be explored further in the context of interpreter-mediated encounters. The present investigation suggests, however, that – in interpreter-mediated encounters – rhythmic regularity, which plays a constitutive role in the social organization of interaction, is intimately connected to how the participants are positioned in relation to one another; that is, whether or not they share the same 'communicative radius'. This observation is in line with what Apfelbaum (1998) has witnessed in video-recorded interpreter-mediated instruction data (French and German). Analysing in detail ten hours of interpreter-mediated interaction, she notices that the synchronization of interaction is highly dependent on *the interpreter's* anticipation of turn-taking and turn allocations. Only when they are within a shared communicative radius can interpreters – when they feel the need for it – mark their anticipation of the current participation framework, i.e. the distribution of responsibility for turns at talk, some milliseconds ahead of time and with non-verbal means, while talking. Thereby they can potentially promote the primary participants' experience of "being *with*" one another.

The eight interpreters I have interviewed so far within my present study all mentioned that they preferred to look straight ahead of themselves and to avoid exchanging gazes with the primary parties in the process of therapeutic encounters. Three interpreters mentioned that they had been specifically instructed by the therapist to avoid looking at the patient and to avoid moving their head back and forth between the parties to mark the anticipated exchange of turns. Maintaining this as a general bearing, some experienced interpreters mentioned, however, that they had found occasional eye-contact with the patient to be a way to handle temporary tension; to help 'normalize' the situation, as it were. Once in a while, primary parties may feel a need to check on their understanding of the substance and progression of current talk, which means that they will take a rapid glance at the interpreter. The patient, in contrast to the therapist, may lack a theory of what the encounter is generally designed for, and what kind of brief the institution has predefined for the interpreter.

No doubt, interpreters do indeed have a role to play in the framing of encounters as opportunities for remembering personal traumatic experiences. A preliminary observation, which is more a research issue than a clear finding of my present project, is that interpreters seem to be more 'out of the way' when they are present in a communicative radius, than if they are present in the room but without access to, and not immediately available in a common, triadic, focused interaction.

To my mind, the seemingly simple issue of the interpreter's placement in relation to the primary parties in therapeutic encounters is worth considering in theory and in practice. The following are what I believe to be the main reasons for this view.

– Given a shared communicative radius in the encounter, the interpreter's coordination of interaction – performed by his or her taking every second turn at talk – is immediately and simultaneously available to both primary

parties. This potentially facilitates the participants' synchronization of talk.
- Given a shared communicative radius, the interpreter's marking of the necessary distinction between the speaking self (him- or herself) and the meaning other (the primary participants) can be conveyed immediately by both verbal and non-verbal means.
- Moreover, given a shared focus of interaction including the interpreter, he or she can support the necessary spiritual affinity between the patient and the care-provider (provided, of course, that the patient finds it relationally relevant to recall traumatic experiences in the presence of the current care-provider and the current interpreter).

Working with traumatized refugees puts specific demands on all professionals involved. The presence of interpreters puts additional demands on the care-providers at the same time as adding to the potential of the therapeutic encounter and to the chances of traumatized patients remembering – and forgetting – the past. Exactly how this happens and how responsibility for it is distributed remain to be further explored.

References

Apfelbaum, B. (1998) Instruktionsdiskurse mit Dolmetscher-beteiligung. Aspekte der Turnkonstruktion und Turnzuweisung, in A. Brock and M. Hartung (eds) *Neuere Entwicklungen in der Gesprächsforschung*, (Vorträge der 3. Arbeitstagung des Pragmatischen Kolloquiums, Freiburg 1997), Tübingen: Narr, 11-36.

Erickson, F. and J. Shultz (1982) *The Counselor as a Gatekeeper. Social interaction in interviews*, New York: Academic Press.

Gentile, A., U. Ozolins and M. Vasilakakos (1996) *Liaison Interpreting: a Handbook*, Victoria: Melbourne University Press.

Herman, J. L. (1992) *Trauma and Recovery*, New York: Basic Books.

Kundera, M. (1981) *The Book of Laughter and Forgetting*, Harmondsworth, UK: Penguin.

McCann, L. and L. A. Pearlman (1990) 'Vicarious Traumatization: A Framework for Understanding the Psychological Effects of Working with Victims', *Journal of Traumatic Stress* 3(1): 131-149.

Middleton, D. and D. Edwards (eds) (1990) *Collective Remembering*, London, New Park & New Delhi: Sage Publication.

Ochs, E. and L. Capps (1996) 'Narrating the Self', *Annual Review of Anthropology* 25: 19-43.

Plimer, D. and N. Ch. Candlin (1996) *Language Services for Non-English-speaking-background Women*, Canberra: Bureau of Immigration, Multicultural and Population Research, Australian Government Publishing Service.

van der Veer, G. (1992) *Counselling and Therapy with Refugees, Psychological Problems in Victims of War, Torture and Repression*, New York: John Wiley and Sons.

Wadensjö, C. (1992) *Interpreting as Interaction. On Dialogue Interpreting in Immi-*

gration Hearings and Medical Encounters, Linköping Studies in Art and Science 83.

------ (1997) Recycled Information as a Questioning Strategy – Pitfalls in Interpreter-Mediated talk, in S.E. Carr, R. Roberts, A. Dufour and D. Steyn (eds) *The Critical Link: Interpreting in the Community*, Amsterdam & Philadelphia: John Benjamins Publishing, 35-52.

------ (1998) *Interpreting as Interaction*, London & New York: Addison Wesley Longman.

Watzlawick, P., J. Helmick Beavin and D.D. Jackson (1967) *Pragmatics of Human Communication – A Study of Interactional Patterns, Pathologies, and Paradoxes*, New York: Norton & Company.

How Untrained Interpreters Handle Medical Terms

BERND MEYER

This article[1] addresses and discusses situations in which untrained interpreters deal with medical terms. I will show that the different ways in which this is done can be seen in relation to the particular speech situation, the pre-existing action systems between the interpreter and the primary interlocutors, and the organization of the source discourse. After a general introduction and some considerations of the pragmatic function of medical terms, three authentic cases will be discussed. The article finishes with a discussion of the data and my conclusions.

1. General aspects of interpreting in health care settings

German medical institutions mostly make use of staff members or patients' relatives to serve as interpreters in doctor-patient communication. These persons usually have limited or no experience of the interpreting task. Their capacity to communicate in both languages is important, but the language barrier is not the only problem when doctors speak with their patients (native or non-native speakers). Difficulties can also arise from the fact that medical professionals have knowledge of medical issues and medical communication which differs from that of the patients. Medical communication is, as many studies show (see Cicourel 1981; Löning and Rehbein 1993; Lalouschek 1995), a type of discourse which is guided by institutional purposes and professional knowledge structures. These in turn lead to the use of a certain vocabulary, formulaic syntactic structures and a certain organization of discourse. All this can affect the process of mutual understanding – especially when lay persons are drafted in to work as interpreters.

Differences in knowledge structures may lead interpreters to modify the use of certain terms, as the following example from Fredericks (1998) shows. In this case an English-speaking doctor (DOC) communicates with a Cantonese-speaking patient via a bilingual nurse (INT):

    DOC   She can loose weight a little bit also because I think she can be a little overweight.
    INT   Yee san gew nay gam sik. Um moy um moy sik gum daw.
                The doctor asks you to reduce your food intake. Not to not to eat so much.

---

[1] I am very grateful to Ian Mason and to two anonymous referees for helpful comments on an earlier version of this article.

As Fredericks (personal communication) explains, the avoidance by the interpreter of the terms 'weight' and 'overweight' in the doctor's utterance may come from the fact that calling somebody *guo shong* ('overweight') is considered to be face-threatening. Moreover, the idea of a connection between obesity and physical illness is not common in Chinese culture, whereas it is obviously presupposed in the doctor's utterance. The finding then is that the primary interlocutors hold conflicting assumptions concerning this connection and that the interpreter tries to regulate this imminent conflict.

The fact that interpreters become full participants in three-way interaction seems to be a general feature of dialogue interpreting. Although empirical studies are still rare, the existing literature attributes a wide range of activities to the performers of this task, confirming Keith's statement about liaison interpreting: "the interpreter bears responsibility for the entire discourse, of which each text (utterance) is only one element" (Keith 1984: 312). The empirical cases discussed in Rehbein (1985) and Knapp and Knapp-Potthoff (1986) show that community interpreters may switch into a participant role by, for example, adding their personal advice to the discourse of doctors or legal advisers. These findings have led Knapp-Potthoff (1987) to come to the conclusion that activities like 'condensing', 'deleting', or 'expanding' the source discourse are typical features of non-professional interpreting in general. Wadensjö (1998) has shown that trained professional dialogue interpreters in medical encounters and immigration hearings also play an active role in the communication process. She distinguishes 'coordinating' activities (such as turn organization or clarifying) on the one hand, and different types of 'relaying' on the other. In section 4, I shall relate some of her findings to my data. In addition to these linguistic or sociolinguistic studies, Pöchhacker's (1998) survey shows that, in the view of both the interpreters and the providers, activities such as 'simplifying technical language for the clients' or 'explaining technical terms' seem to belong to the interpreting task.

The present article picks up the discussion about the 'addition' or 'omission' of propositional elements by focussing on interpreters' use of medical terms. I shall try to show that the speech situation, the pre-existing action systems between the primary interlocutors and the interpreter, and the linguistic organization of the source discourse play an important part in determining how the interpreters handle these linguistic forms. Other important aspects, such as the contrast between the languages involved, will also be considered, though to a lesser extent.

The second claim is that the modifications of propositional elements observable in the data cannot be adequately accounted for by descriptive, sign-centred categories like 'adding' or 'condensing'. Rather, the functional quality of linguistic forms and their relation to the interactional process should be taken into account when identifying what has been modified and why this has been done. The next section discusses what is meant by 'functional quality' and presents some considerations concerning German *medizinische Fachsprache* (specialized language for medical purposes).

2. The pragmatic function of medical terms

One main characteristic of language is that it enables us to transfer knowledge: a speaker can evoke mental representations of reality in the mental sphere of a listener by using certain linguistic forms. One could call this the propositional dimension of language. Whereas Speech Act Theory (e.g. Searle 1969: 16-19) views the propositional act as a sentence-based realization of reference and predication, scholars within the framework of Functional Pragmatics reconstruct the propositional content (*propositionaler Gehalt*) of utterances as the verbalization of knowledge associated with features which indicate illocutionary forces or 'actional quality' (*Handlungsqualität*) (cf. Ehlich 1991/1996; Bührig 1996; Rehbein 1998).

According to Ehlich (1991/1996), the propositional content of utterances is composed mainly of speech actions, which are considered to be smaller than Searle's speech acts. He calls them *nennende Prozeduren* ('appellative procedures'), with critical reference to Bühler (1934). Appellative procedures are speech actions carried out by means of lexical aspects of nouns, verbs or adjectives (Grießhaber and Rehbein 1992). These linguistic forms do not refer directly to elements of the real world, but rather to knowledge structures in the mental sphere of speaker and listener. This pragmatic concept of the relationship between the world (P), knowledge about the world in the mental spheres of speaker and listener (Π S and Π L) and verbalization of knowledge about the world (p) in the utterance act (Ehlich and Rehbein 1986:96), is presented in Figure 1.

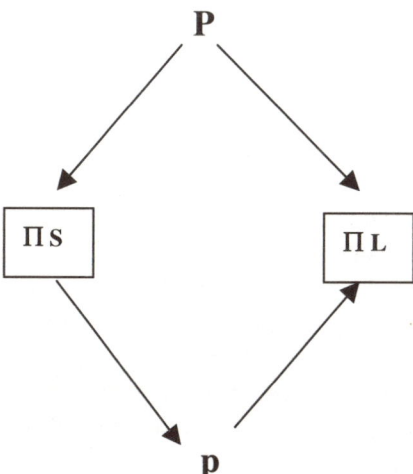

Figure 1: The relationship between world, knowledge and propositional content

The model in Figure 1 is based on the assumption that there is a difference between the three components: world, knowledge about the world and verbalization of knowledge about the world. From this perspective words like *haematoma* or *bruise* do not refer directly to a certain physical phenomenon. Rather, they are related to different mental representations of this phenomenon. The link between linguistic forms and knowledge elements then depends on and evolves from the social practice of the participants. As the reality P is not necessarily equally represented in Π S and Π L, the processing and verbalization of knowledge in the propositional content (p) of the utterance may differ for speaker and listener. Different social practices lead to the evolution of different linguistic forms and to different links between these forms and knowledge structures in the mental spheres of the actors. This (briefly outlined) approach may be seen as belonging to the field of communicative/functional approaches, which have been applied in translation studies (for surveys see Hatim 1998; Mason 1998).

The fact that participants in different social institutions, professions, scientific communities, and, generally speaking, social groups develop linguistic forms (from single elements to larger *chains of actions* like speech action patterns – Ehlich and Rehbein 1979 – or even styles) conforming to the specific purposes of their social practice has been analyzed as deriving from and being a prerequisite for their cooperation in 'action systems' or 'systems of actions' (Ehlich and Rehbein 1972; Rehbein 1994):

> Daily communication within any social group functions by reason of the familiarity of the participants with the different forms of communication being used (one can refer to this as a 'system of actions'). The forms have been handed down over the years, have become routine, prefabricated and provide the actors with common communicative action plans. (Rehbein 1994:84)

Rehbein states further that, when participants of different action systems need to communicate with each other, "a common basis for communication must first be established by the participants" (ibid.).

Within the action system of the German medical *Fachsprache* (language for specific purpose) there are many nouns and verbs compounded of German lexical stems, which at first glance seem to be more comprehensible for lay persons than the alternative expressions of Latin-Greek origin. According to Wiese (1998) there is a coexistence of Latin-Greek-based expressions and German or hybrid expressions. On the other hand, the lexical items in medical English or Portuguese seem to be more Latin- or Greek-based with accessibility obviously restricted to experts. Löning and Rehbein (1995) call the hybrid or purely German forms 'semi-professional expressions'. They found that in doctor-patient interactions the doctors tend to prefer these semi-professional or common-language terms when talking to a patient, because, although related to specific medical purposes, they seem to be more comprehensible for lay persons.

One English example of a choice between a Graeco-Latin based expression and a native language term is a word such as *bruise*: a doctor might use *bruise* instead of *haematoma*. This does not mean that doctors do not refer to their professional knowledge built up in relation to their professional practice. Rather, it means that the expert tries to speak in a manner which is (semi-) comprehensible for the lay person. For the expert it is the medical purpose which functions as a frame for the interpretation of a term like *bruise* (cf. Rehbein 1998). For the lay person, there is no such frame, but only the everyday experience of what bruises look like, and what usually causes them.

The pragmatic function of medical terms should thus be seen as being based on specific communicative needs of the actors, who are familiar enough with an action system to realize the specific purposes of medical institutions. Doctors, medical researchers, and to some extent all medical personnel have at their disposal specific linguistic forms for participating in this action system. They might use semi-professional terms to accommodate their discourse to the patient's knowledge, but this only simulates a common basis for interaction on the lexical level. The patients as clients of medical institutions are usually lay persons: they have no frame for the correct interpretation of semi-professional terms.

In interpreter-mediated communication, the unequal distribution of knowledge and linguistic means is even more complex because the interpreters may or may not know anything about a certain issue, and they may or may not be able to use an adequate linguistic form of the target language to evoke a representation of knowledge in the mental sphere of the listener. The fact that an interpreter knows what one of the primary interlocutors is talking about does not necessarily mean that he/she is able to use the adequate expressions. The nurses, who serve as interpreters at their workplaces, have knowledge about the medical issues being discussed. However, they acquired their professional and linguistic skills in German, and not in their mother tongue. They can talk about medical issues in German, but not necessarily in other languages.

In the next section, three cases will be discussed in which untrained community interpreters have to handle medical terms. In the first case (section 3.1), the interpreter (a lay person and relative) has difficulty interpreting semi-professional terms used by the doctor, although she obviously has some knowledge about the issue being discussed. In the second case (section 3.2), a nurse explains a semi-professional term used by the doctor. In the third case (section 3.3), a nurse uses a professional medical term although the patient has used a common language term.

Whereas in all three cases the interpreters seem to know about the issues discussed, the verbalization of knowledge differs with respect to the interactional process. In the case presented in section 3.1, the interpreter understands the semi-professional term used by the doctor, but has no adequate expression at hand to express the same knowledge in the target language, her mother tongue. Similarly, the interpretations in sections 3.2 and 3.3 are cases where the interpreters know about the issues discussed and the medical terms in the source and target languages. However, in these cases it is the organization of the doctor's discourse (3.2) or the complex role of the interpreter (3.3), rather than lexical problems, which leads to the different choices.

3. Three case studies

The sequences discussed below are taken from a sample of thirteen authentic interactions in German hospitals, which have been audiotaped and transcribed. Two examples deal with internal medicine, one with surgery. The first two cases are taken from pre-operative explanatory talks between doctor and patient, which are required by law before certain operations or types of diagnosis. The third is taken from a kind of interview in which the doctor wants to find out details about the patient's medical past. In all cases the patients are Portuguese migrants with some knowledge of German. None of the doctors has any knowledge of Portuguese.

In all transcriptions, the participants are represented by acronyms: DOC for the doctor, PAT for the patient, and INT for the person who is performing the interpreting task.

The transcription format is akin to that of a musical score, which makes the synchronicity of actions visible. The languages involved are German and Portuguese. A code switch (Portuguese to German or vice-versa) is indicated by brace brackets: { }. For other transcription conventions, see the introduction to this volume.[2]

3.1. 'It is what you call the rabbit's poison'

In this case, a 55-year old woman with an aching stomach is informed about the doctor's plan to carry out a certain type of diagnosis, which includes a gastroscopy. The aim of the diagnosis is to find out whether she still has gallstones in her bile ducts or not. The patient has been living in Germany for more than 20 years and some of the staff members of the hospital had the impression that her German was relatively good. Nevertheless, that afternoon her 17-year old daughter is there and acts as an interpreter during some parts of the conversation, which as a whole lasts 11 minutes. The three persons are alone in the room and the doctor has just started his explanations. He has brought an information sheet

---

[2] For further details concerning HIAT transcription conventions, see Ehlich (1993) or Meyer (1998).

with him, which shows a graph of the inner organs (Bartels and Rönsch 1994). They all look at the picture; the doctor is about to elucidate the position of the gallbladder and the way the bile passes into the duodenum. The example is taken from the very beginning of the interaction.

Extract 1

1	DOC	Das ist die Leber. (1.2) Das ist die
		That is the liver That is the gallbladder.
	PAT	(...) Hm ⟩hm⟨
2	DOC	Gallenblase. (1.3) Da sitzen die Steine drin, (.) nech? (.)
		The stones are in there, right?
3	DOC	Und (.) das is (.) ein Speicher für die Galle und de/ (...) die
		And it is a reservoir for the bile and th/ the bile
4	DOC	Galle wird (.) über den Gallengang (..) in den Darm
		is passed via the bile duct into theIntestine
5	DOC	Abgegeben (xxx)
	INT	{Also} vai pra ... Äh (.) aqui é o coisu, {ja}? Tu
		So it moves to...Er here is the thingy, right? It is
6	INT	dizes que é o veneno dos coelhos. Vai, e depois vai para os
		what you call the rabbit's poison. It moves, and then it moves to
	PAT	Bom
		Okay
7	DOC	Und wenn jetzt ein Stein dort
		and if there is a stone there
	INT	Intestinos
		the intestines

DOC begins with 'That is the liver' (score 1), which is followed by an affirmative listener signal of PAT and a pause of slightly more than a second. He then points to the gallbladder and says 'That is the gallbladder'. The action of pointing can be deduced from the fact that the graph is in the perception space of all three actors and that DOC refers to it with the double use of the deictic expression *das* ('that'). This deictic expression only makes sense in combination with a gesture towards objects in the perception space of the actors; since the utterances are not integrated in larger portions of discourse, *das* ('that') cannot refer to previously established knowledge. After another pause DOC elucidates that '(gall-) stones' are found in the gallbladder and explains the function of the gallbladder as a reservoir for the bile (score 2-3). He then explains that the bile moves from the gallbladder through the bile ducts to the intestine (score 3-5). This information is new and important because it serves as a basis for the further explanation (not in the transcript) that gallstones can follow the bile on its way to the duodenum, which can then cause pain in the stomach area. DOC's turn follows consequently a 'given-new'-format (Chafe 1976): he first names the elements which are given because they are on the sheet, and then he provides the listener with new information. DOC names both given and new pieces of knowledge by using semi-professional terms like *Galle* ('gall'), *Gallenblase* ('gallbladder'), *Gallengang* ('bile duct'), etc.

INT begins with the German complex connector *also* ('so'), which initiates an aborted utterance ('So it moves to...'), where the incomplete predicate 'moves to' picks up one propositional element from DOC's last turn, the movement of the bile via the bile duct towards the duodenum (score 5). DOC has referred to this movement by using the verb *abgeben* ('to pass into') in a passive construction (*wird ... abgegeben*). The reference of the anaphoric third person singular features on the verb *vai* (translated as 'it moves') is not really clear at that point. INT then hesitates and states *Aqui é o coisu, ja?* ('Here is the thingy, right?'). Again one can presume that the deictic *aqui* ('here') is combined with a gesture of pointing at the sheet. The Portuguese *coisu* ('thingy') (derived from *coisa*, 'thing') has no specific meaning: the colloquial, oral expression is not directly linked to specific knowledge, but rather indicates a mental search procedure by the speaker, similar to saying: 'There is a word for it, but I cannot find it yet'.

Her next utterance (score 5-6), 'It is what you call the rabbits' poison', is an attempt to characterize the knowledge element that she cannot name. The characterization refers to a common experience of both women: preparing a rabbit for cooking. When the dead rabbit's intestines are removed from the body, one must be careful with the gallbladder because if the gall is splashed over the flesh, the rabbit is inedible. 'It' (i.e. the gallbladder's content, the bile or gall) is therefore referred to as 'rabbit's poison'. This characterization is understood by the mother. She reacts with an affirmative *Bom* ('Okay', score 6). Then INT picks up her original utterance: she reproduces the second part of DOC's contribution, i. e. the movement of the bile via the bile duct to the intestine(s) (score 6-7). There are three reasons for her to do so:

1. The doctor has structured his turn exactly in the 'given-new'-format, where important information is verbalized at the end of the utterance.
2. All other elements mentioned by DOC ('liver', 'gallbladder', 'bile ducts', 'intestine') are visible on the sheet. The patient thus has access to them, they are in her perception space and they have been indicated by the doctor. This does not hold true for the information that the gallstones are in the gallbladder. However, this information is not new to the patient because it has been mentioned before and PAT has previously been treated in another hospital for the same reason. This information, therefore, can be analyzed as already established knowledge. The only element of DOC's contribution that is not present in the perception space of the three actors is the liquid and its movement. And this is exactly what INT chooses for interpretation.
3. PAT has some command of German. She does not need a full interpretation,

only the important or difficult parts of the doctor's discourse. For such cases, Müller (1989: 716) talks of 'transparency' and 'opacity' as properties of bilingual interactions, which depend "on how far linguistic repertoires of participants are mutually exclusive". According to this dichotomy the interaction is relatively transparent.

INT's contribution is separated into three steps: She first tries to interpret the important and less accessible part of the doctor's contribution. Then she aborts this plan and tries to establish a theme to which the predicate refers. This necessity also comes from the fact that in Portuguese the use of pronouns is limited. INT's contribution (after *also*) starts with an inflected verb *vai* ('goes, moves'; third person singular, present tense). The anaphoric relationship of these morphological features is not clear. INT has difficulty finding an adequate thematic expression and aborts the utterance. Then she overcomes these difficulties by characterizing the thematic knowledge element ('rabbit's poison'). The characterization is adequate for PAT because both women share knowledge and experience concerning the preparation of rabbits for cooking. It is based on an existing action system. Finally, INT picks up her original plan by saying that 'it (i. e. the 'rabbit's poison') moves to the intestines'.

In summary, one can say that the reduced propositional content of INT's utterances as a whole depends on the transparency of discourse and the availability of the graph in the perception space of the actors. Her solution to the problem of transferring the word *Galle* ('bile') into her mother tongue is triggered by the contradiction between her knowledge about what is meant by the doctor, and on the other hand her lack of an adequate expression to verbalize this knowledge. She overcomes this problem by using the idiomatic form *veneno dos coelhos* ('rabbits' poison'), which originated in the mother-daughter action system for the preparation of food.

3.2. 'The fixation is made of cement'

In this case a young surgeon is about to prepare a seventy-year-old Portuguese male pensioner for a hip joint replacement. The old man came to Germany in the early seventies, but lived most of his life in the Portuguese community of a big city. His German is fairly weak. The interpreter is a Portuguese nurse in her fifties, who has worked for more than 20 years in German hospitals. She is relatively experienced in assuming the interpreter role during her work.

In the sequence discussed here, the surgeon names what type of (artificial) joint will replace the damaged one. There are three possibilities: cemented and partly cemented hip joints, and replacements which do not need any cement. The medical terms used by DOC are semi-professional ones. He organizes his utterance in a characteristic way, which is not easily processed by the interpreter, although the contrary is actually intended by the speaker. Interpreter and patient get into a short discussion to clarify what DOC meant. The source of trouble in this case is not the medical term itself, but the syntactic construction used by the doctor.

Extract 2

1	DOC	(l) Und zwar wird das ein () kompletter
		And that will be a complete substitute of the hip joint -
2	DOC	Hüftgelenksersatz-
	INT	(1.2) Ähm vai ser (…) do lado direito (.)
		Uhm it will be on the right side
3	INT	uma renovação(.) de/completa do seu/(…)d/äh da rótula, não
		a complete renewal of your/ er of the joint, right?
4	DOC	(1.7) aller Wahrschinkliet (l) zementiert.
		most probably cemented
	INT	é?
	PAT	Hm ⟩
5	INT	(l) Ähm (1.5) directamente (.) deve ser (.) um/acimentada
		Uhm directly it may be a/ cemented then/afterwards
6	INT	{dann}/(.)depois. Sim, põem assim cimento
		Yes, they put cement to fix it
	PAT	Sim? Ahn depois
		Yes? Oh afterwards
7	DOC	Hm ⟩hm⟨ (…) Es gibt da
		There are two
	INT	para fixar. (raises voice) A fixação é cimento
		The fixation is made of cement
	PAT	Sim. Um e, (..) um e o outro.
		Right. One end, one and the other
8	DOC	noch zwei andere Möglichkeiten ohne Zement und teilweise
		other possibilities without cement and partly cemented
9	DOC	zementiert. Das entscheidet der Oberarzt während der
		This decision will be up to the senior physician

The first part of the surgeon's utterance starts in score 1 and ends in score 2 without sentence final punctuation. The transcription thus indicates that the intonation continues until the end of the word *Hüftgelenksersatz* ('substitute of the hip joint') and that the following utterance of DOC (score 4), *aller Wahrscheinlickeit (1s) zementiert* ('most probably cemented'), belongs to the same syntactic construction. This way of separating utterances has been called 'dissociate processing' (Rehbein *et al.* 1993; Meyer 1998): the speaker verbalizes a larger syntactic construction in portions, giving the interpreter time to interpret each portion, while at the same time indicating that the utterance still has not been concluded.

Reasons for this type of discourse organization in the present case might be that the doctor is trying to avoid an informational overload in the rhematic part of the utterance, and the fact that his contributions are pre-structured by the information sheet, which he is holding in his hands. These sheets usually guide the doctors through pre-operative explanatory talks. In this case, the sheet (Pförringer 1997) names the operation under discussion by a professional name (*Totalendoprothese*), by a hybrid term (*Hüftgelenkendoprothese*), and by an analytic, common language form (*Ersatz des Hüftgelenks*, 'substitute of the hip joint'). The doctor uses none of these terms, but he does follow the text structure on the sheet insofar as he first names the type of operation in general and then adds the specification 'cemented'.

The interpreter reproduces the first portion in scores 2-4: 'Uhm it will be on the right side a complete renewal of your/ er of the joint, right?'. She avoids creating a Portuguese version of the semi-professional term *Hüftgelenksersatz* or substituting it by a Graeco-Latin technical term. She rather tries to characterize what is meant by the doctor ('renewal' instead of 'substitute'), and deletes evident information ('joint' instead of 'hip joint'). I will not speculate about her reasons for doing so. The two indications of planning ('Uhm', 'Er'), the pause at the beginning, the four shorter and longer hesitations and the three instances of self-repair clearly show that the doctor's utterance is not easy for her to process. PAT ratifies the reproduction with a listener signal (score 4), which is not really affirmative because the intonation falls.

After the doctor has verbalized the separate constituent 'most probably cemented' (score 4), the interpreter continues only after a pause, an indication of planning and another pause (score 5). She then says in Portuguese 'directly it may be a/ cemented then/ afterwards', interrupted by short hesitations. Again the pauses, indications of planning, and the switch into German (*dann*/'then', score 6) show that she has difficulty in processing the doctor's turn. Obviously she tries to integrate the participle *acimentada* ('cemented') into a syntactic structure. Her attempt to do so becomes clear within the explanations in score 6, 'They put cement to fix it', and in score 7, 'The fixation is made of cement'. With these syntactic structures the interpreter emphasizes in both explanations the process, and not the result. She also adds professional knowledge concerning *why* cement is used ('to fix it') and *what* is made of cement ('the fixation').

The integration of the participle into a complete construction is one way of making it accessible to the listener. Another possibility would have been the integration of the participle into a noun phrase ('a complete, cemented substitute of the hip joint'). However, this possibility is not available because she has already talked of 'renewal' instead of 'substitute', and renewals can hardly be cemented, either in English or in Portuguese. The agreement between *renovaçao* ('renewal') and *acimentada* ('cemented') – both are feminine singular forms – might be one reason why the first attempt of the interpreter to integrate the participle into a syntactic structure does not satisfy her.

In summary, one can state that the additional speech actions of the interpreter are triggered by the fact that the separate constituent is not transferable. These speech actions do not result from a deficit of knowledge or terminology on the part of the interpreter, but rather derive from her problems in transferring the doctor's discourse. By explaining the term *zementiert* ('cemented'), which the doctor has not explained, the nurse departs from her role as relayer of the doctor's words – apparently unavoidably in this case.

3.3. 'She had a haematoma then'

The actors in the third interaction are the patient, a 72-year old Portuguese woman who has lived in Germany for a long time and has some command of German, a Portuguese nurse, who grew up in Germany and has worked for several years in this hospital, and a German doctor of internal medicine. The nurse sometimes serves as an interpreter in interactions with Portuguese-speaking patients.

When the patient came to hospital several days before, she had suffered a light stroke. She has now been treated and is about to leave. The doctor would like one last conversation with her because he needs to determine whether it is possible to give her a certain medicine. This medicine reduces the coagulation of the blood and requires strict cooperation between patient and doctor. As the course of the conversation before and after the section of discourse reproduced here shows, the doctor has already decided that the best solution would be to apply this medication. However, he is not yet sure because of the age of the patient and because of the fact that the family doctor had taken her off the medicine some time before the patient came to the hospital. For the doctor, the conversation is a preparation for the conversation he will have later that day with the family doctor concerning his therapy proposal. At the point where the transcript starts, the hospital doctor is about to recall that one reason why the family doctor took her off the medicine was the fact that the patient bled once when she had injured herself.

Extract 3

```
1   DOC   Ähm (.) sei hat ja mal so eine, eine verLETZung am Bein
             Uhm she once had an, injury on her leg and that bled and then
             Dr Müller took
2   DOC   gehabt und das hat geBLUTet und daraufhin hat Dr Müller
             her off the medicine because of that.
3   DOC   Das abgesetzt.  Sie hat also eine kleine (…) am Bein
                           She had after all a small (…) on her leg
    INT              Hm ⟩⟨              Ja
                                        Yes
                    (Telephone rings)
4   DOC   Gehabt.
```

	INT	Você teve um ähm… Si:m,
		You had a uhm…. *Ye:s,*
	PAT	Eu tomei o, (..) o reMÉdio, (.)
		I took the, the medicine
		(Telephone rings)
5	DOC	(speaks on the phone)
	INT	e depois você aleijou-se aí (…) e depois ….
		And then you injured yourself there and then ….
	PAT	depois…. Não, (..) não me aleijei. Estas
		then … *No, I did not injure myself. These*
6	DOC	(speaks on phone)
	INT	Apareceram. E
		They appeared. *And*
	PAT	nódoas negras apareceram. Aparecerem.
		buises appeared. *Yes, they appeared.*
7	DOC	(speaks on phone)
	INT	depois/ e äh..
		then/and er….
	PAT	Und nun Doktor {que} sagt "{Tu}, Frau Aleida, nu
		And then doctor who says "You, Miss Aleida, now no
8	DOC	(speaks on phone)
	INT	{Genau}, e depois ele (..) tirou äh o remédio. É
		Right, and then he took you off the medicine. Yes
	PAT	Nix mehr."
		More
9	INT	Isso é que está a dizer, hm ⟩⌊. Ele também sabe (..) que depois
		That is what he says, hm. He also knows that he took
	PAT	Sabe.
		He knows it.
10	INT	Tirou o remédio, depois dequela nódoa. Você também botou
		you off the medicine, after this bruise. Did you bleed too or
		was it
11	INT	sangue ou era só uma nódoa negra?
		just a bruise?
	PAT	Não, era só nódoa negra.
		No, it was just a bruise.
12	INT	A outra (xxx) por alto. {Hämatom hat sie n gehabt dann}
		The other (xxx) on top. She had an haematoma then
	PAT	Era só (..) (xxx) Ja
		It was just (..) (xxx) *Yes*
13	DOC	Hm ⟩hm⌊
	PAT	Assim/disse "Só sò."
		So/he said "So,so"

The participants are alone in the doctor's office. While the doctor is completing his turn, the telephone rings. The interpreter starts to interpret, the patient starts to react to what the doctor has said, and the doctor picks up the phone and speaks (score 5). While the doctor is on the phone, INT and PAT get into a conversation of their own. In the course of this conversation PAT clarifies that she was not injured, but that *nódoas negras* ('bruises') appeared and that that was the reason why she was taken off the medicine. INT first confirms this version. Then, in score 10-11, she asks a question, 'Did you bleed or was it just a bruise?' The patient confirms (score 11) that it was 'just a bruise'. Then (score 12), the interpreter addresses the doctor and reports, 'She had a haematoma then', thus switching to the use of a professional medical term.

The pre-history of this switch is relatively complex. First, one has to consider that PAT interrupts INT's interpretation (score 4). PAT has seemingly understood enough to react directly and present her own version of the story. Then, she herself (PAT) is interrupted by INT, who tries to finish the interpretation. Again, PAT interrupts INT emphasizing that 'I did not injure myself' (score 5). This is where the mutual interrupting stops and PAT has time to tell (partly in German) her version of the story (scores 5-8). During this, the doctor is out of the conversation because he is answering the phone. The nurse then confirms PAT's version and asks the question about the bruise (scores 8-11), which in turn leads to a professional categorization of the bruise as a *Hämatom* ('haematoma').

From the first interruption of her interpretation, INT is treated by PAT as a primary interlocutor. Although the doctor is not listening, PAT tells her the whole story and receives several reactions from INT. While these reactions in the beginning are restricted to the attempt to reproduce the doctor's turn, later INT gradually assumes the role of a listener (score 6). In score 8-9 she compares the story of PAT with the version the doctor has given: 'That is what he says, hm' and confirms that the doctor's story is not different from that of PAT: 'He also knows that he took you off the medicine, after this bruise'. Her following question (scores 10-11) can still be analyzed as a clarification turn, although it already presupposes that the difference between 'bruise' and 'bleeding' is relevant for DOC.

Contrary to this, the following use of the professional medical term 'haematoma' in her utterance addressed to the doctor is a speech action which is based on professional knowledge and presupposes communication between two medical professionals. The whole utterance addressed to DOC is a short report given from one expert to the other about the talk INT has had with PAT during DOC's phone call. In this report INT extracts (from her point of view) the relevant piece of knowledge from her conversation with PAT and verbalizes it by using a medical term. Although there is an act of transfer from the Portuguese *nódoa negra* to *Hämatom* as a professional term in medical German, this action has nothing to do with interpreting in the strict sense of the word, in which the interpreter is perceived as an actor who assumes communicative functions in *support* of the interaction of the primary interlocutors (Bührig and Rehbein 1996).

The choice of the professional term, instead of the common language term *blauer Fleck*/ 'bruise', and the extraction of an isolated knowledge element without referring to the discussion which had taken place, indicate that the nurse is stepping out of her supportive role. In her conversation with PAT and the following report for DOC, INT is no longer just a supporter, who helps others to communicate, but rather embodies a professional of the medical institution.

INT gradually shifts her interpreter role after PAT has talked to her while the doctor as the real addressee is not listening. As INT is a nurse, it is not surprising that the patient talks to her as she would to a medical professional and that INT finally acts as such. INT's entrance into the professional role is the result of the fact that PAT treats her constantly as a primary interlocutor. Moreover, her question concerning 'bruise' or 'bleeding' shows that the contradictions between the two versions of the story seem to be relevant to her from a professional point of view.

4. Discussion

In all cases a switch between professional or semi-professional and common language terms can be observed. In the first case, the lay person uses a term of the 'mother-daughter'-action system ('rabbit's poison'), while in the source language a semi-professional term (*Galle*/'bile') has been used by the doctor. In the second case, the interpreter, a nurse, explains one part of a semi-professional noun phrase, the participle *zementiert* ('cemented'). In the third case, the interpreter, also a nurse, uses a professional term instead of the common language term she had used while talking to the patient in her (and the patient's) native language.

The use of the expression 'rabbit's poison' has been analyzed as an attempt to characterize a propositional element of the source discourse by using linguistic items from a pre-existing action system between mother and daughter. It is not lack of comprehension, but rather lack of an adequate term which leads the daughter to use this term. She integrates the important linguistic element ('rabbit's poison') into an utterance which differs from the doctor's utterance, with its explicit elucidations characteristic of the written mode of discourse. Due to the relatively high transparency of the interaction, this interpreter feels the need to act only on a few occasions. When she does so, she does not try to reproduce the doctor's discourse as a whole, but rather tries to help her mother to understand chosen parts of it. On this phenomenon see also Wadensjö (1992:102).

In the second case, the discourse is obviously expanded by the nurse's explanations concerning the participle *acimentada* ('cemented'), which is literally translated from the German *zementiert*. Her short interaction with the patient is not transferred into German. The actional quality of the interpretation differs insofar as the doctor has not explained what 'cemented' means. So an important reason for carrying out the explanations seems to be the organization of the source discourse. As in the first case, the doctor's discourse is accommodated to the patient's by the interpreter, this time by creating a syntactic surrounding for the problematic constituent.

In the third case, it is the nurse who uses the professional term, not as part of her task as interpreter but rather by assuming the role of a medical professional who gives a report to her colleague (the doctor) on what she has discussed with the patient while her colleague was on the phone. By reporting the relevant outcome of her conversation with the patient, she coordinates the interaction. The use of a professional term ('haematoma') corresponds to the actional quality of the report. The type of accommodation to the listener (the doctor) differs from the other cases, as it has nothing to do with a knowledge deficit or a processing problem: the interpreter speaks to the doctor as a colleague in their common language for medical purposes.

Thus, this case shows similarities to one discussed by Knapp and Knapp-Potthoff (1986), in which the interpreter in an encounter between a Turkish client and a German legal adviser starts to give advice to the client and later on in the interaction has to inform the legal adviser about this. As in this case, the drifting apart of the interaction (the actors carry out different activities at the same time) needs to be corrected, and the only person able to do this is the interpreter. Another similarity is that the interpreters in both cases introduce their own opinions into the interaction – in the case of the advisory talk by adding advice, in the case of the medical interview by asking professional questions.

The cases discussed here confirm the active role that the interpreters assume within the interaction. In this sense, Wadensjö (1992) has talked of *coordinating* and *relaying* as the 'two activities in one' which dialogue interpreters carry out. Especially in the last example the nurse's continuation of the conversation and the adding of a report to inform the doctor about the relevant outcome are examples of coordinating activities. This is because she brings the activities of both actors together after they had been drifting apart while the doctor was on the phone.

This discussion also relates to Wadensjö's second concept, the notion of *relaying* and her taxonomy of renditions, which refer to the propositional relationship between source and target discourse. This relationship is also relevant for the analysis of the way medical terms are transferred. Wadensjö discusses 'close', 'expanded', 'reduced', 'substituting', 'summarizing' renditions (= acts of relaying), as well as 'lack of rendition' or 'non-rendition' (1992: 70ff). This taxonomy is sign-centred because the decision to call an act of relaying, for instance, a 'reduced rendition' depends on the amount of information that has been uttered in target and source discourse. Although it is not explicitly stated that information is represented by lexical items, one can presume this is Wadensjö's point of view. Therefore, the first four types of renditions (close, expanded, reduced and substituting) finally depend on the number of words used by the interpreter in comparison to the primary interlocutors.

From this perspective a case like the one discussed in section 3.1 (the 'rabbit's poison') may – for the most part – be called a reduced rendition: only a fragment of the doctor's turn has been relayed into Portuguese. But within this fragment, the medical term *Galle* ('gall') has been substituted by an idiomatic expression. At the same time, there is also lack of rendition as some parts of the doctor's discourse have been omitted. The rendition, or rather renditions, discussed in section 3.1 thus cover a range of possibilities.

Although these quantitative categories may lead to an adequate description of the linguistic surface, such analysis does not grasp the actional quality of what the interpreter has done, i. e. the extent to which modifications of the source discourse discussed above reflect shifts or switches within the interactional process. The discussion has shown that different uses of medical terms lead not just to differences in the informational structure, but also indicate which roles the interpreters are assuming and how imperceptibly the switches from one role to the other may occur. The frequent switches between interactional functions may be a result of the conflicting demands which are made on the interpreters: they are expected to relay or reproduce what has been said, but as nurses or relatives they can hardly avoid introducing their own experiences into the conversation.

5. Conclusions

The cases discussed in this article are examples of authentic dialogue interpreting in medical institutions performed by untrained subjects – one might call this an archetype of community interpreting. In the analysis, I tried to show that the rendition of medical terms is not just a problem of knowing the correct terminology. Rather, it is influenced by the particular speech situation. The pre-existing action systems, the fact that the clients in cases 1 and 3 have some command of the source language, German, the access to visual representations in their perception space (case 1), and the organization of the source discourse (cases 1 and 2) all play an important role.

A general answer to the question of how untrained community interpreters handle medical terms is that they may use common language instead of professional terms and vice versa, or that they may introduce professional knowledge to explain single words. In the cases presented here, these modifications are not just carried out because of the responsibility the interpreters bear for the entire interaction. They also indicate another level of participation in the interaction:

participating as a colleague or relative of one of the primary interlocutors. As the examples have shown, this participation may in some cases be helpful for the mutual understanding of the primary interlocutors. Nevertheless, it also leads to defamiliarization in the interactional process since such switches are usually not apparent to the other actors.

There is no attempt here to generalize these findings, by making a quantitative claim such as: 'in all occasions similar to these, the subjects will perform in the same way'. The claim is that certain factors may influence the performance of the interpreters, not that these factors always have the same effect. Moreover, the cases discussed here are rather eccentric ones in the sense that the interpreters do something that differs considerably from what the primary parties have done, or that they step out of their role as supporters of the primary participants' interaction. Of course one can find sections of discourse in the sample, where the interpreters' performance is more straightforward. I have chosen some of the problematic cases in order to show what the performance of untrained interpreters may reveal about the three-way interaction of dialogue interpreting.

References

Bartels, O. and W. Rösch (1994) *Darstellung des Bauchspeicheldrüsen- und/oder des Gallenganges (ERCP)*, Erlangen: Perimed Compliance Verlag.

Bühler, Karl (1934/1982) *Sprachtheorie. Die Darstellungsfunktion der Sprache*, Stuttgart: Fischer.

Bührig, Kristin (1996) *Reformulierende Handlungen*, Tübingen: Narr.

------ and J. Rehbein (2000) *Reproduzierendes Handeln – Übersetzen, simultanes und konsekutives Dolmetschen im diskursanalytischen Vergleich*, Arbeiten zur Mehrsprachigkeit/Working Papers on Multilingualism (Folge B/Series B), No. 7. Universität Hamburg: SFB Mehrsprachigkeit.

Chafe, Wallace (1976) 'Givenness, Contrastiveness, Definiteness, Subjects, Topics and Point of View', in C. Li (ed) *Subject and Topic*, London & New York: Academic Press, 27-55.

Cicourel, Aaron V. (1981) 'Language and Medicine', in C. A. Ferguson and S. B. Heath (eds) *Language in the USA*, Cambridge: Cambridge University Press, 407-429.

Ehlich, Konrad (1991/1996) 'Funktional-pragmatische Kommunikationsanalyse – Ziele und Verfahren', in L. Hoffmann (ed) (1996) *Sprachwissenschaft – Ein Reader*, Berlin & New York: de Gruyter, 183-203.

------ (1993) 'HIAT: A Transcription System for Discourse Data', in J. Edwards and M. D. Lampert (eds) *Talking Data. Transcription and Coding in Discourse Research*, Hove & London: Lawrence Erlbaum, 123-149.

------ and J. Rehbein (1972) 'Erwarten', in D. Wunderlich (ed) *Linguistische Pragmatik*, Frankfurt/Main: Athenäum, 99-115.

------ and J. Rehbein (1979) 'Sprachliche Handlungsmuster', in H. G. Soeffner (ed) *Interpretative Verfahren in den Sozial- und Textwissenschaften*, Stuttgart: Metzler, 243-274.

------ and J. Rehbein (1986) *Muster und Institution. Untersuchungen zur schulischen Kommunikation*, Tübingen: Narr.

Fredericks, Cecilia (1998) 'Using Non-Professional Interpreters in a Multiethnic Primary Care Clinic', paper presented at the *Critical Link II – Interpreters in the Community* Conference held in Vancouver, Canada, May 19 - 23.

Grießhaber, Wilhelm and J. Rehbein (1992) *Kontextualisierte Wortschatzanalyse (KWA). Ziele, Probleme und Verfahren*, Arbeitspapier Nr. 1 des DFG-Projektes 'ENDFAS', Universität Hamburg: Germanisches Seminar.

Hatim, Basil (1998) 'Discourse Analysis and Translation', in M. Baker (ed) *Encyclopedia of Translation Studies*, London & New York: Routledge, 67-71.

Keith, Hugh A. (1984) 'Liaison Interpreting: An Exercise in Linguistic Interaction', in Wolfram Wilss and Gisela Thome (eds.) *Die Theorie des Übersetzens und ihr Aufschlusswert für die Übersetzungs- und Dolmetschdidaktik*, Tübingen: Gunter Narr, 308-317.

Knapp-Potthoff, Annelie (1987) 'Speaking for Others – On a neglected Aspect of using a Foreign Language', in W. Lörscher and R. Schulze (eds) *Perspectives on Language in Performance*, Tübingen: Narr, 1125-1142.

Knapp, Karlfried and A. Knapp-Potthoff (1986) 'Interweaving two Discourses – the difficult task of the non-professional Interpreter', in J. House and S. Blum-Kulka (eds) *Interlingual and Intercultural Communication. Discourse and Cognition in Translation and Second Language Acquisition Studies*, Tübingen: Narr, 151-168.

Lalouschek, Johanna (1995) *Ärztliche Gesprächsausbildung. Eine diskursanalytische Studie zu Formen des Ärztlichen Gesprächs*, Opladen: Westdeutscher Verlag.

Löning, Petra and J. Rehbein (1993) (eds) *Arzt-Patienten-Kommunikation. Analysen zu interdisziplinären Problemen des medizinischen Diskurses*, Berlin & New York: de Gruyter.

------ (1995) 'Sprachliche Verständigungsprozesse in der Arzt-Patienten-Kommunikation. Linguistische Untersuchungen von Gesprächen in der Facharzt-Praxis', in *Arbeiten zur Mehrsprachigkeit* 54, Universität Hamburg: Germanisches Seminar.

Mason, Ian (1998) 'Communicative/functional Approaches', in M. Baker (ed) *Encyclopedia of Translation Studies*, London & New York: Routledge, 29-33.

Meyer, Bernd (1998) 'What Transcripts of Authentic Discourse Can Reveal about Interpreting', in *Interpreting* 3(1): 65-83.

Müller, Frank (1989) 'Translation and Bilingual Conversation: Pragmatic Aspects of Translatory Interaction', in *Journal of Pragmatics* 13: 713-739.

Pförringer, W. (ed) (1997) *Basisinformationen zum Aufklärungsgespräch über Hüftgelenkendoprothese*, Erlangen: Perimed Compliance Verlag

Pöchhacker, Franz (1998) 'The Community Interpreter's Task: Self-Perception and Provider Views', paper presented at the *Critical Link II – Interpreters in the Community* Conference held in Vancouver, Canada, May 19-23.

Rehbein, Jochen (1985) 'Ein ungleiches Paar – Verfahren des Sprachmittelns in der medizinischen Beratung', in J. Rehbein (ed) *Interkulturelle Kommunikation*, Tübingen: Narr, 420-447.

------ (1994) 'Rejective Proposals: Semi-professional Speech and Clients' Varieties in Intercultural Doctor-Patient Communication', *Multilingua* 13(1/2): 83-130.

------ (1998) 'Austauschprozesse zwischen unterschiedlichen fachlichen Kommunikationsbereichen', in L. Hoffmann, H. Kalverkämper and H. E. Wiegand (eds) *Fachsprachen. Handbücher zur Sprach- und Kommunikationswissenschaft* 14.1, Berlin & New York: de Gruyter, 689-710.

------ W. Griesshaber, P. Löning, M. Hartung and K. Bührig (1993) *Manual für das computergestützte Transkribieren mit dem Programm syncWRITER nach dem Verfahren der Halbinterpretativen Arbeitstranskriptionen HIAT*, Universität Hamburg: mimeo.

Searle, John (1969) *Speech Acts: An Essay in the Philosophy of Language*, Cambridge: University Press.

Wadensjö, Cecilia (1992) *Interpreting as Interaction. On Dialogue Interpreting in Immigration Hearings and Medical Encounters*, Linköping Studies in Art and Science 83.

Wadensjö, Cecilia (1998) *Interpreting as Interaction*. London: Longman.

Wiese, Ingrid (1998) 'Die neuere Fachsprache der Medizin seit der Mitte des 19. Jahrhunderts unter besonderer Berücksichtigung der Inneren Medizin', in L. Hoffmann, H. Kalverkämper and H. E. Wiegand (eds) *Fachsprachen. Handbücher zur Sprach- und Kommunikationswissenschaft* 14.1, Berlin & New York: de Gruyter, 1278-1285.

Part II

Traditions

The Rebirth of the King's Linguist

PIERRE KOURAOGO

> *Oral translation from French into the native languages assumes a particular importance in Burkina Faso, a francophone African country, because of the language diversity, the high illiteracy rate and the urgency of development tasks requiring effective modes of communication. After noting the poor state and status of translation into Burkinabè languages, this article[1] argues that a closer look at instances of effective performances by outstanding untrained interpreters can give interesting insights into the role and practices of interpreting in similar contexts. Of particular interest is the innovative use of the skills and strategies deployed by interpreters in traditional Africa referred to in the literature as the **king's linguists** (Bandia 1998). The samples analysed show that although what is involved can be rightly categorized as consecutive translation of speeches, this activity shares many features with dialogue interpreting because it is carried out face-to-face with an audience (the interpreter's handling of interpersonal communication, his facial expressions, gestures and interjections, direct forms of address, etc). These aspects key in with previous studies on the interpreter's footing, face, power, distance. The paper then considers some methodological issues to be solved in an in-depth study of this mode of interpreting.*

1. Introduction

The complexity of the language situation in Africa constitutes one of the many factors impeding development efforts on the continent. Most African states were indeed carved out by former colonial rulers with little consideration for language or ethnic entities. This resulted in a wide variety of language situations in post-colonial Sub-Saharan African states, which Alexandre (1968: 88-91) groups into six categories ranging from tiny "linguistically homogenous states" such as Rwanda, Burundi, Botswana and Lesotho, to states with "great linguistic heterogeneity" such as Liberia, Côte-d'Ivoire, and Cameroon. In between, a few

---

[1] Most of the inspiration for this paper came from a short training course I attended with a NUFFIC scholarship in the translation studies programme of the University of Manchester Institute of Science and Technology in 1998. I should like to express my deepest thanks to Professor Mona Baker and Professor Ian Mason who encouraged me to pursue these ideas. My thanks also go to Professor Norbert Nikiema and Dr Pierre Malgoubri of the Linguistics department of the University of Ouagadougou who read the first draft and checked the Moore transcriptions. My gratitude finally goes to the organizers, the speakers and interpreters who kindly allowed me to use their tape recordings. All errors remain of course mine.

countries have one or several dominant African languages that could be used regionally or nation-wide for education and the administration. This is for instance the case of Hausa, Yoruba and Ibo in Nigeria and Swahili in Tanzania.

The language question has in fact been a battlefield in which African intellectuals have made claims and counterclaims, often reflecting their subjective or political attitudes rather than empirical evidence. Research into the exact number, the geographical distribution and actual use of African languages is still embryonic because continental or regional studies require resources and a political will is rarely available. Within each State, the work of academics and national research centres has however been clearing the ground for a better understanding of some language issues such as the status of African languages and the function they should have in the educational and administrative systems.

The present paper contributes to this much needed language debate by focusing on the role of translation – and more specifically consecutive dialogue interpreting – in social mobilization schemes. The limits of this study must be acknowledged at the outset. The objective is not to make an exhaustive analysis of the history and practices of translation in Burkina Faso but rather to provide an exploratory description of the ways a traditional mode of oral translation is being used to advantage to meet present-day communication needs. It is hoped that this will be followed up by more in-depth studies of the phenomenon with more refined methodological approaches and tools. The paper will also draw attention to the importance in plurilingual developing countries of this mode of interpreting, which is understandably of limited use in more developed countries.

2. The linguistic situation in Burkina Faso and the need for interpreting into the national languages

The linguistic make-up of Burkina Faso is typical of most West African Francophone countries. With 105,811 sq. miles and a population estimated at about ten million inhabitants, the country has some sixty distinct languages officially referred to as 'national languages', French being the 'official language'. One of these, Moore is spoken by half of the population and it is estimated that four or five of the largest national languages cover about 80% of the territory. This does not solve the language planning problems as all languages, regardless of their size, must be taken into account in the delicate exercise of 'nation building' (Das Gupta 1968). It partly explains why Alexandre (1968) quoted above, classifies Burkina with the group of African countries with no 'immediately useful language or languages', even though this classification can only be understood when placed within the context of Francophone African countries generally unfavourable to local languages.

French typically remains the only language of the administration and the exclusive vehicle for education from day one at school, despite pedagogical arguments showing the advantage of using the children's mother tongues in early schooling (see Cummins 1980; Kouraogo 1995). The current language policy is also bound to widen and perpetuate the socio-economic gap between the tiny privileged elite and the remaining illiterate and often monolingual 80% of the population.

National languages are felt to have a low status. Although one-third of them are used for mass literacy programmes by the National Institute for Literacy (*Institut National d'Alphabétisation*) and many are heard in the audio-visual media, they are still absent from the formal education syllabus. The only serious attempt to introduce three national languages (Moore, Jula and Fulfulde) in primary schools as part of an experimental scheme in the 1970s was met with some hostility (see Sanou F. 1989) and ended in confusion in 1983 (IRAP 1984a and 1984b; Sanou B. 1993). And yet there is an increasing awareness that national languages must play a role, not only in reducing illiteracy but also in boosting access to basic education as the current primary school enrolment rates are still below 40%. This explains why both the country's constitution and the official education policy guideline (*Loi d'Orientation Scolaire*) allow for the use of national languages in schools. Some studies and experiments which replicate somehow the Nigerian experiments (Afoloyan 1976; Bamgbose 1984) actually tend to show that even the learning of French, which is believed to account for a good part of high school drop out, can be significantly improved by the use of the children's mother tongues in the early years at school (Nikiema forthcoming).

A long-term solution to the language problems in the country would appear to be bilingualism in French and at least one national language. In the meantime, the urgency of development tasks requiring efficient modes of communication between the elites and the masses calls for an immediate resolution of the language question. This is where translation and more specifically oral translation is bound to play a key role.

Burkina draws most of its resources from agriculture and livestock, which constitute the main activity of 85% of the population. Most development targets therefore profess to give a priority to the rural world where French, the official language, is hardly spoken. Yet any development schemes in these rural contexts must usually include a good battery of sensitization and popularization messages, conceived of in the official language and then conveyed to the population in their local languages. Resident village extension agents who work with the peasants on a daily basis to show them how to use new farming techniques are required to speak the local language but translation is frequently needed, particularly when top civil servants or NGO officials visit villages. A small-scale market research project carried out prior to setting up the translation section of the University of Ouagadougou (FLASHS 1995) has revealed an acute need for translation from and into national languages.

3. The provision of translation into the national languages

In Burkina Faso written translation and professional interpreting are relatively new activities that tend to focus on European languages even though consecutive interpreting has existed since pre-colonial times. This reflects the general picture in many Sub-Saharan African countries as reviewed by Bandia (1998) and Nama (1993). (See however Anyaehie 1993 and Okpewho 1992 concerning the place of African languages in translation).

The few Burkinabè trained professional translators and conference interpreters work almost exclusively with French and other international languages (English, Spanish, Portuguese, and Arabic). This is also true for the occasional free-lance translation performed by language specialists. The absence of a translators' association makes it difficult to organize the profession and improve working conditions but on the whole the best professionals make a comfortable living, selling their services full-time or part-time to the administration, international organizations and the private sector. Moreover, the relative stability of the country has made Ouagadougou, the capital, a popular venue for inter-African gatherings. The Panafrican Film Festival (FESPACO)[2], the international craft show (SIAO), and the national cultural week (SNC) attract huge multilingual crowds requiring translation and various forms of interpreting between French and the major international languages. Other recent international events which kept translators busy were the 1996 Franco-African Summit, the 1998 African football cup and the summits of the Organisation of African Unity held in Ouagadougou in June and December 1998.

On the other hand, translation and interpreting involving national languages unsurprisingly have low status despite the needs mentioned earlier. Trained professional translators and interpreters hardly ever translate into or from these languages. Some improvements are expected as a result of the action of a dynamic association of linguists (*ELAN-Développement*) and the recently opened translation programme of the University of Ouagadougou which devotes a department to national languages. But the current situation is characterized by amateurism and improvisation. It is wrongly believed that anyone who speaks French and the local language can be used on the spot to translate or interpret.

Written translation involving the major national languages is growing but remains much less important than oral translation or, to glamorize it, interpreting, which has been widely used for a long time. The following typical situations illustrate the actual use of consecutive interpreting in development schemes.

---

[2] FESPACO: Festival Panafricain du Cinéma et de la Télévision de Ouagadougou
SIAO: Salon International de l'Artisanat de Ouagadougou
SNC: Semaine Nationale de la Culture.

The rural radio team arrives in a village to sensitize the population to the problem of bush fires. The programme to be recorded and broadcast later nation-wide takes the form of a contest involving a few local peasants to see who will produce the best arguments on how to prevent bush fires. The instructions of the panel of judges are translated from French into the local language and the contestants' answers are translated into French by a primary school teacher or an agriculture extension agent. Another example might be a delegation of foreign donors visiting a dam or a school built with their assistance in a remote village. A high-ranking civil servant native of the village, who serves as guide and interpreter, will often accompany them. Finally, a third example that comes closer to those discussed later in this paper is a public ceremony, with officials speaking in French and the would-be interpreter conveying their messages for the audience in the local language.

After listening to radio broadcasts of a good number of interpreted speeches from and into the Moore language and observing several live interpreting performances, we are left with the general impression that interpreting into national languages, despite its indispensable role and its frequent use, is often of dubious quality, resulting from the use of non-professional low-ranking local agents who hardly receive any remuneration in return for the task. The latter's low motivation and lack of translation skills are often compounded with poor oral skills in the use of their mother tongues. The cruel reality is that few Burkinabè who have completed secondary school can deliver a flawless speech in their mother tongue without interspersing it with French words and phrases. A light-hearted illustration of this situation is provided by a contest on a private radio station in Ouagadougou that rewards anyone who can sustain a short conversation with the presenter in Moore without uttering a French word. Significantly most contestants fail. Code-switching and reverse interference from French would deserve a full separate study. They are of particular relevance here because they contribute to lowering the effectiveness of the translated message in a context of oral tradition such as ours, where speaking skills are highly valued and the way the message is rendered largely determines how it is received. Most of the translated sequences are at best too literal and dull and at worst hilariously wrong or unintelligible because of the intrusion of French. An area of particular difficulties, besides that of technical concepts requiring new terms in the local language, concerns the translation of cohesive devices. For instance many interpreters' Moore sentences are full of French conjunctions such as *parce que* ('because'), or *c'est-à-dire* ('that is to say') and the Moore word *wala* ('such as') is used with confusing frequency to replace a whole range of conjunctions and prepositions and even as a dummy filler.

Fortunately not everything is bleak. Some instances of public consecutive interpreting do constitute signs of hope for improvement in the field. The extracts given in Appendix 1 show that, with the right background, some individuals can provide high quality interpreting even when we use the classical criteria of accuracy and faithfulness. This performance took place during the opening ceremony of a village savings bank known as people's bank (*caisse populaire*) built with the support of a Swiss non-governmental organisation, the OSEO.[3] The 'interpreter' was a trained linguist and an excellent speaker of both French and Moore. In addition he was the Burkinabè OSEO representative and a native of the village where the ceremony was taking place. Interpreting his Swiss guest into Moore, the local language, he was therefore in a privileged position to convey the contents and the cultural context of the message delivered to him in French. For instance, unlike the interpreter in Appendix 2, he translates the actual sentences of the speaker, making use of translation techniques such as compensation (Delisle 1993). For example, he renders the contents of *en tant que responsable d'une ONG suisse* ('as the official of a Swiss NGO') in three sentences: 'He comes from Switzerland. He is the representative of a Swiss organisation. He would therefore like to tell you...'. He uses implicitation when he omits *l'Oeuvre Suisse d'Entraide Ouvrière (OSEO)*, which is inferrable from the context because it was the only Swiss NGO known in the village and also the focus of the ceremony. We can also find a few instances of explicitation, for instance when he adds 'cotton' to specify the meaning of 'industrialization', a clarification for listeners whose only experience of industrialization is the country's textile factory. He even uses explanation *(explication* in Delisle's terms*)* when he inserts a long stretch after the translation of *douze à quatorze heures de travail par jour* to give the working hours in the Burkinabè civil service as a point of comparison for the audience. Stylistic improvements were also brought to the text by the use of rhetorical *questions* with *tˋ bõe* (why). This case, however ideal, is unfortunately rather rare.

4. The rebirth of the king's linguist

Much more impressive was a less orthodox performance on which we shall focus the rest of our discussion. It is illustrated by the transcripts in Appendix 2 of the performance of another untrained interpreter at the same ceremony. It displays some innovative features, which we have observed on three other occasions and which offer insights into the interpreting process and inspiration for improving local practices through pre- and in-service training. The first of these was the closing ceremony of the annual meeting of the above-mentioned Swiss NGO, unusually held in a small Burkinabè village in February 1998. The second was the opening on the outskirts of Ouagadougou of a tile factory which uses local materials. The third was the official launch in August 1998 of the national campaign to promote breast-feeding.[4] The quality of the

---

[3] OSEO: Oeuvre Suisse d'Entraide Ouvrière (Swiss Labour Assistance).
[4] Unfortunately when we borrowed the videotapes of these other three ceremonies, we

non-professional interpreting displayed on these occasions differed markedly from the usual dull and laborious renditions into the national languages.

The key features of these performances lead us to believe that the amateur interpreters were reviving the skills of the pre-colonial traditional public interpreter referred to in the literature in English as 'the king's linguist' and in French as *griots*. These are well summarized by Danquah, quoted in Bandia (1998:295):

> Referring to the Ashanti 'linguists', Danquah (1928:42) points out that 'not only were they charged with repeating the words of their patron after him, acting as a herald to make it clear to all his audience and to add to his utterances the extra authority of remoteness, but they were also expected to 'perfect' the speech of a chief who was not sufficiently eloquent, and to elaborate his theme for him'. However, the 'linguist' was not expected to 'add any new subject-matter, but... he may extend the phrases and reconstruct the sentences and intersperse the speech with some of the celebrated witty and philosophical reflections for which they are justly celebrated to the credit of both himself and his chief.

The character depicted by Danquah has been an important member of the king's court throughout West Africa for centuries. In the Francophone literature this role is subsumed under that of the *griot*. We prefer however to use the term *king's linguist* because it focuses on the role of consecutive intra- or interlingual interpreter, while the *griot* refers more to the bard, and guardian of the kingdom's oral history. Even though traditional *griots* are still held in high esteem, the term has taken on a negative connotation. It is used disparagingly in contemporary political phraseology to refer to sycophants who sing the praises of undeserving patrons for fees or advantages. More research into the make up of Mossi king's courts[5] may actually reveal that the official griot is in fact different from the language specialist with the more down-to-earth skills of *no-rɛ̃ ɛ̃ sa*, literally *voice relay* of the king. In one instance witnessed recently by the author, the king's linguist during the traditional ceremony was in fact the *raag-naaba* (*market-chief*), the minister in charge of collecting taxes and making public announcements in markets, a role which is markedly different from

---

were dismayed to discover that the Moore versions of the speeches had been edited out to shorten the reports, further evidence of the neglect of national languages.

[5] The Mossi are believed to have migrated from northern Ghana in the 15th century to the central area of Burkina Faso where they founded a powerful empire, the expansion of which was only halted by French colonization a century ago. The basic structure and organization of the traditional Mossi kingdom has however survived and is still flourishing today. The Moro Naaba, the emperor of the Mossi who lives in a palace at the heart of Ouagadougou, is still revered by his subjects and the appointments of village chiefs often result in deadly feuds sometimes involving intellectuals.

that of the *griots* called yʋ ʋmba in Moore. We also suspect that in cases involving a foreign language, other actors on the scene may be called upon to act as interpreters. We were told that the Moore word *bademda* refers to the interpreter even though it was more commonly used for those who translated drummed language into spoken words. These points and more generally the question of how traditional Africa coped with cross-lingual communication deserve a more thorough investigation. But to return to our main theme, we shall use the term king's linguist to focus on the language and interpreting skills he had and still has to deploy, while acknowledging that this is probably just the tip of the *griot* iceberg.

The interpreter's translation of the speeches in all these instances shared many features with those of the king's linguists in the quotation from Danquah above. We shall summarize them under two umbrella headings: the constraints and pressures of context and the interpersonal dimension of the traditional mode of consecutive interpreting.

Concerning the context of the interpretation, the traditional interpreter had to perform in public under considerable pressure, having to translate quickly and well under the constant monitoring of a powerful patron. He could serve as a scapegoat or a fuse, should the communication break down or the message backfire.

As suggested above, an important function of this mode of interpreting is not just cosmetic but above all interpersonal. Unlike the classical interpreter who strives to be neutral and 'invisible', here we notice a clear engagement with the audience. In the king's court, the linguist is often not translating between two languages, but rephrasing and reformulating the king's speech within the same language to improve its communicative effectiveness by:
- improving the acoustic qualities (loudness and voice quality);
- ensuring the clarity of the message through lexical, terminological or syntactic modulation (see Delisle 1993:36);
- improving the stylistic features by the use of metaphors, proverbs, sayings;
- using non verbal resources (posture, gestures).

A brief description of the setting of the ceremonies will illustrate the contextual pressures, while specific examples from the interpreter's performance in Appendix 2 will exemplify the search for efficiency which often brings the interpreter away from the wording of the source speech. We shall then mention some of the methodological problems that need to be tackled for a more thorough analysis of the phenomenon.

5. Contextual pressures

These ceremonies took place in the open-air with officials neatly seated in the front rows surrounded by delegates of various peasants' organizations and a huge crowd of local villagers. The interpreter had to climb onto a podium or stand in the middle of the crowd to translate after each speaker. In the case of the launch of the breast-feeding campaign, heavy rain obliged the organizers to move the meeting at the last minute (wasting almost two hours in the process) to the Head of State's private village residence. All the participants had to squeeze into a hall, which brought the interpreter even more uncomfortably close to the personalities and the crowd.

The audiences included high-ranking officials such as ministers, Members of Parliament, diplomats, top civil servants and in one case the First Lady. Other participants were delegates of women's organizations and non-governmental agencies in uniform. The illiterate villagers, the normal target audience of the interpreting, typically had to stand for hours under a scorching sun throughout the ceremonies.

Everything was audio- and video-recorded by the organizers and the national press agencies. About 80% of the particular audience could understand both the French and the Moore versions, which means that the accuracy of the interpretation was monitored not only by the organizers but also by the rather august audience. One can guess the pressure put on the interpreter who, in the case of the extract in Appendix 2, was a primary school teacher on secondment as the local correspondent of the Burkinabè News Agency. He had no formal training for the trade, but was keen to preserve his emerging reputation as a good public speaker and performer.

6. Translation procedures and interpersonal devices used

The most striking feature of this performance is that the untrained interpreter has spontaneously opted for free translation, applying the slogan expressed in the title of Seleskovitch's (1977) paper 'Take care of the sense and the sounds will take care of themselves'. No attempt is made to translate term-for-term or even sentence-for-sentence. Instead, he has extracted the key information or 'units of meaning' (to borrow a term used by Mackintosh 1998) from the source speech; he has then rearranged them into natural wording. These units can be identified in the source and translated speech as in Table 1.

Table 1: Units of Meaning in Source and Target Speech

- The people's banks are open to anyone rich or poor.
- You are encouraged to save your spare cash by depositing it at the bank.
- Members can get loans.
- Specific amounts of the loans for individuals or village association.
- Administrative formalities to open an account.
- The banks promote solidarity and democratic management.
- If you succeed you will be a proud model for others.

The interpersonal and cosmetic nature of the interpreting is also obvious.

In a sense, the interpreter substitutes himself for the speaker and subsumes the role of 'principal' (Mason 1999:152) to achieve better interpersonal communication. Even though he distances himself from the speaker by referring to him in the third person (*a rat n yeelame* – 'he means'), this actually helps him to signal his solidarity with the audience and make them feel he is just one of them. He appeals more directly to their own experience, which he claims to share: 'if you make a mat and sell it for 500 CFA francs... you want to pay a visit to Geneba (where you are likely to spend your money)...'. He also avoids conveying some face-threatening statements made by the speaker, as illustrated in Table 2. These statements are simply omitted in translation.

Table 2: Face Threatening Acts in Source Speech

- Certains d'entre vous ignorent ce que c'est qu'une caisse populaire
  Some of you do not know what a people's bank is
- Vous avez la possibilité de demander le crédit qui vous convient sans en abuser ou tenter de tricher
  You can apply for a loan without over-indulging or trying to cheat
- Toute tentative de récupération ou de manipulation ne sera pas tolérée
  No political scheming or attempt to hijack the project will be tolerated.

The interpreter also changes the tenor of the source speech, making it more informal to accommodate to the level and taste of the audience and substituting humorous allegories for some flat narration of facts in the source speech. The video-tape shows that the interpreter speaks louder than the original speaker, smiles constantly and uses ample gestures and keeps some form of eye-contact with the crowd. The original speaker, on the other hand, stood still, sternly reading his text throughout. The interpreter uses interjections such as *haya!* or *e!!* which usually denote exhortation. All in all, the way he expressed the information unit follows the hard-sell advertising style while the source speech was rather of the soft-sell style.

It is also worth noting how the interpreter's awareness of the listeners' level of information pushes him to elaborate on how to obtain the two photographs and what they will be used for. Similarly, when he uses the term *milyõ*, a loan word from French, along with the native equivalent sum of money in Moore (*tus k ma* – literally 'big thousands'), he seems to be trying to teach the audience how to convert huge figures.

At the same time, we can mention some idiolectal features such as the empty *woto wã* ('like this'), which recurs as a refrain in the interpreting. His strong northern accent also earns him laughter from the crowd when he uses *talg bio* for what the audience would call *talg biiga*, literally 'son of a proletarian' or poor person.

The whole approach is functional and the performance appears to have been geared to the *skopos* (Nord 1997) or aim of the organisers of the ceremony. There are signs that the audience were enjoying and following more carefully the brilliant summary interpretation in Moore than the original speech in French. On the videotape the French version was at times inaudible because of the noise level showing that the monolingual listeners had 'switched off'. Only the Moore translation was not disrupted by noise except for some approvingly cheerful laughter.

Given that translation has to fulfil the specific goals or *skopos* set by the client, it is appropriate to ask whether this was achieved in the cases under analysis. We were not able to carry out a follow-up questionnaire to measure the impact of the ceremonies on the attitudes and behaviour of the target population. We can however infer from the reaction during the interpreting and from informal discussions with some participants after one of the events that many of the arguments were indeed aptly driven home. In the case of the people's bank we actually had a chance to visit it some six years later. It is indeed flourishing, with members holding bilingual Moore-French savings booklets.

A more interesting case is the launch of the breast-feeding campaign. The objective of the organizers was to encourage women to breast-feed their babies by stressing the weaknesses and dangers of imported artificial baby foods. The Moore translation gave most participants a vivid portrayal of the cost and dangers of artificial baby food. Even though no tape-recording of the Moore translation of the speech is available (see explanation above and endnote 4), we attended the event and remember the hilarious anecdotes the interpreter gave to show the physical superiority of breast-fed babies in former times over the weaklings we now produce with artificial milk. From informal discussion with some participants after the ceremony, it appeared that the interpreter's praise of the nutritive and protective values of mother's milk fell on favourable ears. However, the translation seems to have failed to rid listeners of their scepticism about the recommendation that the baby need not drink any water during the first few weeks of its life. More time for elaboration would have been needed to develop the technical justification of this innovation and to soften the repulsion and slight embarrassment raised by the suggestion that mothers should extract their milk and store it up for feeding the baby while they are away to work. Of course we must not blame translation for such failings, which, after all, highlight the difficulties of trying to change people's attitudes and behaviour by means of a fine speech.

7. Methodological aspects

This brief discussion of the sample translation in Appendix 2 and mention of other interpreting events not reproduced here should suffice to give the reader an idea of the kind of findings that could be obtained by extensive analysis of instances of this kind of interpreting. We need however to outline some methodological problems which are likely to arise in the process.

First of all, based on the experience of this exploratory study, we cannot overlook the practical difficulty of transcribing and translating the spontaneous Moore oral translations in such a way that a reader with no familiarity with Mossi culture can grasp the cosmetic aspects of the interpretation. To show evidence of some of the crucial non-verbal features, video recording is necessary. This however raises problems of cost, copyright and practicability.

More fundamental methodological issues include the sampling procedures for choosing which translations to tape. Even a larger scale study will be more of a 'case study' type than a representative 'sample' type (Stenhouse 1980). It will probably have to use purposeful or even convenient sampling based on clients' and participants' judgements about 'outstanding untrained interpreting'. This will bear some similarities with early studies of second language learning strategies (see Rubin 1975; Naiman *et al.* 1996; O'Malley and Chamot 1990; Kouraogo 1993; Oxford and Burry-Stock 1995). We could actually further borrow from strategy studies to try to identify a set of translation procedures, techniques or even gimmicks used by the new king's linguists. These could then be validated against other observations and interviews with practitioners and when some stable results are obtained, they could be used for training or retraining consecutive interpreters in similar contexts.

A more in-depth study would require a multidisciplinary team, with translation and language specialists working on a more refined analysis of the translation procedures used and their effects on the audience. A team of specialists in mass communication could jointly study other non-linguistic aspects of the communication event. A carefully designed and implemented interview protocol would tap the views and attitudes of the translator, the client and target audience. A descriptive approach would avoid being judgmental and respect research ethics.

Finally, to return to the theme of this volume, it would be interesting to apply the formal tools that would be developed to the many instances of spontaneous dialogue interpreting taking place daily in development schemes, in the courts, in medical interviews and other service encounters involving French and Burkinabè languages.

8. Conclusion

The description we have given of the language situation and the need for oral translation into local languages in contexts like those prevailing in Burkina Faso has highlighted the urgent need to find ways of promoting high quality interpreting. Rather than review the literature on consecutive interpreting for insights, we have taken a different direction that consists trying to detect and use endogenous solutions more likely to suit the context. The cursory analysis made of the strategies and skills deployed by the outstanding untrained interpreters which remind us of those of the king's linguist shows that this area of investigation is quite promising and deserves further investigation, using a more careful design and more formal research tools. The results can then be used for initial professional training in consecutive and dialogue interpreting into national languages and for planning short in-service training programmes to improve the quality of the performance of the many untrained practitioners so as to maximize their contribution to social mobilization for development.

References

Afoloyan, Adebisi (1976) 'The Six-Year Primary Project in Nigeria', in Ayo Bamgbose (ed) *Mother Tongue Education: The West African Experience,* London & Paris: Hodder & Stoughton/Unesco, 113-134.
Alexandre, Pierre (1968) 'Some linguistic problems of nation-building in Negro Africa', in Joshua Fishman, C. A. Ferguson and J. D. Das Gupta (eds) *Language Problems of Developing Nations,* New York & London: John Wiley and Sons, 119-127.
Anyaehie, Evaristus O. (1993) 'Language status and translation studies: a Nigerian perspective', in Cay Dollerup and Annette Lindegaard (eds) *Teaching Translation and Interpreting 2,* Amsterdam: John Benjamins, 9-46.
Bamgbose, Ayo (1984) 'Mother-tongue medium and scholastic attainment in Nigeria', *Prospects Quarterly Review of Education,* Paris: Unesco, 87-93.
Bandia, Paul (1998) 'African tradition', in Mona Baker (ed) *Routledge Encyclopaedia of Translation Studies,* London & New York: Routledge, 295-304.
Cummins, Jim (1980) 'The Cross-lingual Dimensions of Language Proficiency: Implications for Bilingual Education and the Optimal Age Question', *TESOL Quarterly* 14(2): 175-187.
Danquah, J.B. (1928) *Gold Coast: Akan Laws and Customs,* Oxford: Oxford University Press.
Das Gupta, Jyotirinda (1968) 'Language diversity and national development', in Joshua Fishman, C. A. Ferguson and J. D. Das Gupta (eds) *Language Problems of Developing Nations,* New York & London: John Wiley and Sons, 17- 26.
Delisle, Jean (1993) *La Traduction Raisonnée,* Ottawa: Presses de l'Université d'Ottawa.
FLASHS [Faculty of Languages, Letters, Arts and Humanities] (1995) *Rapport de l'Etude de Marché sur les besoins en journalistes, communicateurs, traducteurs et Interprètes.* Unpublished report, University of Ouagadougou.
IRAP (Institut de la Réforme et de l'Action Pédagogique) (1984a) *Résultats de l'Evaluation Approfondie des EB3 et EB4 de l'Année Scolaire 1982-83,* Ouagadougou: Ministère de l'Education Nationale.
------ (1984b) *Résultats de l'Evaluation comparée des EB5 et CM1 de l'Année Scolaire 1983-84,* Ouagadougou: Ministère de l'Education Nationale.

Kouraogo, Pierre (1993) 'Language learning strategies in input-poor environments', *System* 28(2): 65-173.

------ (1995) 'Problématique de l'utilisation des langues africaines à l'école: Recentrer le débat sur les arguments pédagogiques', *Annales de l'Université de Ouagadougou*, Séries Lettres N° VII.

Mackintosh, Jennifer (1998) 'Message integrity in Relay Interpreting', unpublished lecture delivered on 14 December 1998, UMIST Translation Studies Seminar Series.

Mason, Ian (1999) 'Introduction', in Ian Mason (ed) *Dialogue Interpreting*, special issue of *The Translator* 5(2): 147-160.

Naiman N., M., Frohlich, H.H. Stern and A. Todesco (1996) *The Good Language Learner*, Clevedon: Multilingua Matters.

Nama, Charles A. (1993) 'Historical, theoretical and terminological perspectives of translation in Africa', *Meta* 38(3): 414-425.

Nikiema, Norbert (forthcoming) 'A la recherche de formules alternatives d'éducation dans la perspective d'un développement durable au profit du plus grand nombre', paper presented at the National Research Forum (FRSIT), Ouagadougou, March 1998.

Nord, Christiane (1997) *Translating as a Purposeful Activity. Functionalist Approaches Explained*, Manchester: St. Jerome.

Okpewho, I. (1992) *African Oral Literature: Background, Character and Continuity*, Bloomington: Indiana University Press.

O'Malley, Michael J. and Anna Uhl Chamot (1990) *Learning Strategies in Second Language Acquisition*, New York: Cambridge University Press.

Oxford, Rebecca L. (1989) 'Use of language learning strategies: a synthesis of studies with implications for strategy training', *System* 17(2): 235-247.

------ and Judith A. Burry-Stock (1995) 'Assessing the use of language learning strategies worldwide with the ESL/EFL version of the strategy inventory for language learning (SILL)', *System* 23(1): 1-23.

Rubin, Joan (1975) 'What the good language learner can teach us', *TESOL Quarterly* 9: 41-51.

Sanou, Bernadette (1993) 'Réforme de l'éducation: Bilan d'une expérience d'utilisation des langues nationales à l'école', *Actes du Colloque sur les Langues Nationales dans les Systèmes Educatifs du Burkina Faso*, Ouagadougou, 2-5 March 1993.

Sanou, Fernand (1989) 'Qui a peur des langues nationales comme véhicules d'enseignement?', in Unesco-Unicef (ed) *Propos Africains sur l'Education pour Tous*, Dakar: UNESCO-UNICEF, 85-111.

Seleskovitch, Danica (1977) 'Take care of the sense and the sounds will take care of themselves or Why Interpreting is not tantamount to Translating Languages', *The Incorporated Linguist* 16: 27-33

Stenhouse, Lawrence (1980) 'The study of samples and the study of cases', *British Educational Research Journal* 6(1): 1-7.

Appendix 1

En tant que responsable d'une ONG suisse, l'Oeuvre Suisse d'Entraide Ouvrière (l'OSEO), permettez-moi, mesdames et messieurs de présenter une expérience suisse.

Il y a à peu près 150 ans la Suisse était encore un pays pauvre, certes il y avait quelques familles riches et quelques villes riches, mais la population en général était pauvre. La misère régnait, on connaissait la famine, même la mort. Il y a 150 ans, c'était l'époque de l'industrialisation, de la révolution industrielle. La Suisse était l'un des premiers pays à se lancer dans l'industrialisation. C'était misérable. Douze à quatorze heures de travail par jour du lundi au samedi, et puis un salaire qui ne suffisait pas pour nourrir une famille. Il fallait que les femmes et les enfants aussi aillent travailler dans les bas...

La situation à la campagne n'était pas meilleure. Le climat suisse est dur. Souvent les produits plantés étaient détruits par le gel, une maladie de plantes ou des parasites. Dans cette situation de misère générale, les paysans et les ouvriers ont commencé à s'organiser. C'est ainsi que les syndicats et les associations paysannes sont nés.

Interpreter's version
(With English glosses provided by the author)

M na n lebga a gomdã bilfu tɩ sẽn pa wʋmdb nasaarenda me wʋme.
I am going to provide a quick translation for those who do not understand French.

Yaa yõensg bala.
I shall just select a few passages.

A wilgame tɩ yẽnda yii Swis. Yẽnda yaa sull taoor soab Swis.
He has said that he comes from Switzerland. He is the representative of a Swiss organization.

Rẽ la a kot n na n wilg Swis me sẽn da ya bũmbg ninga.
He would therefore like to tell you what Switzerland used to be like.

A yeelame tɩ pipi, sẽ zems yʋʋm koabg la pis nu tɩ Swis me yaa nãong tẽnga,
He said first that, some 150 years ago Switzerlands was also a poor country,

yaa nimbãanega, yaa pɛta... Yaa sɩd tɩ rakãagb kẽer da bee be, tẽms kẽer me ra
characterized by misery and suffering... Although there were a few rich people and a few rich

são sãoome. La tẽngã zãnga nin-buiidã rag n bee pɛtê, tɩ ya nin-bãanega, tɩ yaa
cities. But on the whole the people was miserable and suffered from poverty and

kom, tɩ kẽer meng tolg n kiidẽ. Sɛgame tɩ wakat kãnga, rat n yet tɩ sê ta yʋʋm
famine, some people even died of starvation. At the time, that is to say 150 years ago,

koabg la pis-nu wã, rẽ tɩ tʋʋm bed la b siginda. Swis yɩɩ pipi tẽnga, sẽn na n
some important development projects [industrialization] were being launched. Switzerland was

tʋm tʋʋm kãnga, la yɩɩ wala lamdã tʋʋm bed siglg la b sɩng yã.
the first country to be involved in this, particularly in the cotton industry.

Tɩ b rɩk tʋmtʋmdba tɩ b be be n tʋmdẽ. La yellã rag n pa naana ye.
Workers were hired to do the work. But it was really difficult.

Tɩ bõe? A wilgame tɩ tʋmtʋmdbã sã n yik yibeoog n kẽng tʋʋmdã,
Why? He has explained that the worker went to work in the morning

a tɩgd n tʋma wakat piig la a yiibu, nina wakat piig la a naase.
he had to work for twelve hours, sometimes even forteen hours.

Sẽn na yɩlẽ tɩ y wʋm võore, rũndã Burkina ka, nebã tʋmda wakat a nii
To give you an idea, today here in Burkina people only work eight hours

raar pʋgẽ bala, la pĩnd beenẽ wã wakat piig la yiib n tall n tɩ ta wakat
a day, but in those days people there worked twelve to forteen hours.

piig la naas la b tʋmda. Tɩ kiuugã yaood me pa sek baa fɩ, pa tõe n dɩlg
And yet the monthly salary was insufficient, and could not feed

zakã rãmb ye. Rẽ n so tɩ raowã kiuug ligd sẽn pa sekdã, tɩ pagã me ne kambã
the family properly. Because the husbands' salary was inadequate his wife and

fãa yita tɩ b naagd taaba n kẽngd tʋʋmde, rẽnd kambã me tʋmdame, pagabã,
children would all go to work, so that the children and the women

nebã fãa naage, sẽn na yɩlẽ tɩ sek zakã zãabo. La baasgo, sɩd pa sekd ye.
everyone had to contribute to the family income. But it was still insufficient

Rẽnda yaa b galẽ teẽnsẽ wã.
That's what happened in their cities.

La sã n ya wa ne b tẽn-bãoonesẽ wã rag n yaa koaadb tẽnga. La be wã me koaadbã
In small villages they practised agriculture. There too, farmers

rag n namsdame, b ra namsdame tɩ bõe? Swis tên-gãongã zĩigã
suffered, why? Because the soil was affected by the extreme

ni n maagda wʊsgo, tɩ koodã sãamdẽ. Sã n pa zĩigã n mãagd tɩ koodã sãamdẽ
cold and and the crops were damaged. Besides the cold weather that destroyed the crops

yaa wala bõn-yood n dɩt koodã tɩ sãamdẽ. Kɩtame tɩ rɩɩ bã pa sekdẽ tɩ yaa nimbãanega.
some pests would attack the crops. As a result there was not enough food and it was misery.

Tɩ nebã sɩd namsdẽ. Rẽ n so tɩ koaadbã, tʊmtʊmdbã fãa yik n maan
People really suffered. That is what pushed the farmers and all the workers to

sula sẽn na n yɩlẽ n zabe, tɩ yellã maneg.
form associations [unions] to fight and solve the problem.

Appendix 2

Monsieur le Haut Commissaire de l'Oubritenga,
Monsieur le Député
Monsieur le Préfet de Loumbila
Monsieur le Représentant de l'Oeuvre Suisse d'Entraide Ouvrière
Monsieur le coordonnateur national des caisses populaires
Honorables invités

C'est pour moi un grand honneur de prendre la parole au nom du Conseil d'Administration des Caisses Populaires, des 138 membres des Caisses Populaires pour vous souhaiter la bienvenue à l'ouverture de la Caisse Populaire de Loumbila qui est la 20 ème du Plateau et la 63 ème du réseau national.

Certains d'entre vous ignorent ce que c'est qu'une caisse populaire. C'est un regroupement de plusieurs personnes qui décident de mettre leurs épargnes en commun et de se faire du crédit au besoin. Ce qui veut dire, en même temps que les membres de la caisse populaire sont aussi les propriétaires et les gestionnaires contrairement à certaines institutions de la place. C'est en 1900 au Canada que l'idée de créer des caisses populaires est venue d'un homme dénommé Alphonse Dejardins qui s'est totalement engagé à combattre les usuriers de son pays qui spoluaient les braves citoyens. Avec l'aide du clergé d'antan, il a multiplié les caisses populaires qui sont devenues aujourd'hui les premières banques du Canada.

Monsieur le Haut Commissaire
Monsieur le Député
Monsieur le Coordonnateur National des Caisses Populaires
Honorables invités

Comme dans tout pays, il y a des patriotes. En 1972 de braves concitoyens ont pris la résolution de sortir les populations laborieuses les plus démunies du marasme et de la dépendance économique en implantant la première caisse populaire. Quelques années plus tard, comme une trainée de poudre, les caisses populaires ont envahi les provinces du Yatenga, du Passoré, du Kadiogo, du Mouhoun, de la Comoé, du Bazèga, de l'Oubritenga, du Boulgou, du Nememtenga, du Sanmatenga, etc. pour enfin aujourd'hui voir le jour à Loumbila, noble ville de la province d'Oubritenga.

Mesdames et messieurs,

Les caisses populaires vous ouvrent grandement leurs portes sans distinction aucune, de la dolotière à la bergère, du mécanicien à l'électricien, du pêcheur au laboureur, de la vendeuse de soumbala au commerçant grossiste, du tablier au boutiquier, du maraîcher à l'instituteur en passant par les groupements villageois, les caisses populaires peuvent vous donner un crédit allant de 5 000 à 3 000 000 de francs pour les personnes physiques et de 5 000 à 10 000 000 de francs pour les personnes morales. Il vous suffit seulement d'être membre de la caisse populaire en ouvrant votre compte avec deux photos d'identité plus 1 000 francs. Après un fonctionnement de 4 mois vous avez la possibilité de demander le crédit qui vous convient sans en abuser ou tenter de tricher car l'argent qui sera mis à votre disposition n'est venu d'autre part que des membres de la caisse. Ce qui veut dire que le remboursement est obligatoire et sans possibilité d'exemption.

Mesdames et messieurs,

Je ne saurais terminer mon propos sans remercier les responsables de l'Association Manegdbzanga qui n'ont ménagé aucun effort pour la réalisation de cette oeuvre. A mes collègues membres du Bureau Provisoire, je tiens à leur dire que le poste au niveau du bureau est bénévole et que par conséquent ils doivent penser au développement de la région et non à toute autre idée noire.

La Caisse Populaire est aussi une structure apolitique et toute tentative de récupération ou de manipulation ne sera pas tolérée. Car il ne faut pas confondre développer une région et développer quelques individus.

Messieurs les responsables coutumiers
Honorables invités

Les caisses populaires ont, au 20 novembre 1996, une épargne de 6 milliards de francs CFA avec 300 millions de francs de crédits octroyés dont 500 000 aux femmes.

Je vous remercie.

Interpreter's version
(With English glosses provided by the author)
(int.) = interjection

... hey!... bee   Zιyãre, leb n bee   ka.
  (int.) ... *There is one [people's bank] at Ziniare There is also one here.*

Pa naana ye,   waoogame.
It is impressive,   that's a lot.

Bι y wẽ nug-poak n kõ y mense.
So, why don't you clap hands for yourselves.

Masa wã a rat n yeelame, yaa bũmb sẽn ya naana. A malg n wilgame tʋ yaa
Now, he means that the whole thing is just easy. He has explained that whether

rã-kõgda, f yaa talg bio, f yaa ligd soaba, haya! Y vʋʋgame, yaa y vʋʋgr ziig
you sell millet beer, whether you are rich or poor, (int.) You are saved, this place [the bank]

la ka. Marsã f sã zĩnd pĩiri, n paam koabga, f sãnda f yik n ta
has brought you salavation. Now, if you make a mat and sell it for 500 francs, and feel like going

rã roogẽ wã, walla f yik n ta a Gẽnẽba nengẽ, ... hey! yet tʋ õ? Yals tʋ m
to spend it on millet beer, or you want to pay a visit to Geneba, ...(int.) Tell yourself No, let me

yek ka nanda n bas pis-nũ yaa la m yaool n sãage. Fo lebga arzek soaba.
stop by the bank first to deposit 250 francs before carrying on. This will make you rich.

Woto la a gomdã. ẽe! Rẽ wã, f sã n be ka la f tolg n pelga f pʋga,
That was his message. (int.) Therefore, if you live here and sincerely want to become a member

wa yãk ligdi, yaa kobs-yi la f na n pak keesã.
bring some money, you need one thousand francs to open your account

Aya, f sã n yalse n wa yõk f foto ti tõnd pek a n kõ-fo tʋ f wa ne a yiib
OK, if you have your photograph taken and we develop it for you give them two prints

ka tʋ b rʋk n tabl f sebrã zugu, ẽhẽe! Fo sã n paam wakʋr-wakʋr tʋ f wat n
to stick them on your papers, (int.) When you have some spare money and come here

ningdẽ, fo tõeeme, ka la kiis a naas pʋgẽ, n wa lebg arzek soaba. Bala fo tõee
to deposit it, you can, within four months, become rich. Indeed you can

n wa rʋka samde, tusri. Sã n yaa wa gurupma woto n date, tõeeme n dʋk tusri, tʋ
obtain a loan, say 5 000, or in the case of village groups they can get between

5000

ta wa milyõ, tus kẽema piiga, yaa wʊsgo, pa naana, waoogame, tɪ y rɪk n lagem
and one or ten million,   that's a lot, isn't it?   quite huge, you can use it to

taab n tʊm sõma tɪ y fãa sũur yɪ noogo.
to work together and become happy.

Sã n ya nin yenga, woto wã, leb n tõeeme, woto wã, leb n dɪk tusri, maa tus-kẽema a tãabo.
As for individuals [woto wâ] they can [woto wâ], borrow between 5 000 and three million,

Waooga! Pa tõe n dɪ f yembre,   f zak rãmb me pa tõe n dɪ n sa.
That's a lot! You can't spend it all alone,   even your family can't spend it all

Ralla f rɪk n tʊmdẽ. ẽhẽe!   Dẽnd a gomdã yɪla woto.
You will have to put it to work, (int.)   So, that's what he said.

La a sẽn malg n wilg bala yẽ, ad keesã sẽn dɪgã yaa, pa nin yeng rẽnd ye.
What he also explained is that the bank you see here does not belong to a single individual.

Pa tõe n yik bala n wa yet tɪ ẽe! wẽ f yãoogo, yaa mãam... Neb sã n loog n bas-fo,
You can't just get up and claim that (int.) it's only yours... If other people desert you, only

sã n pa sʊy n na n kẽ-fo, ned fãa pa na n wa ye. Ya y fãa n so.
you will only have locusts for company.   It [the bank] belongs to you all.

La y sã n leb n data tɪ y roogã yɪ sõma t'a yʊʊrã yi beoog Burkĩna ka,
And if you want your local bank to prosper and become well-known throughout Burkina,

bãmb sã n na kẽng tẽng a to n tɪ pak keesa, n yet tɪ b na n maana kees a to bɪ b yãk
so that when they go to another village to open a new branch of the bank   they can

Lumbil yʊʊr n togse, n wilg tɪ ya sɪda, Lumbil keesã sẽn pakã, nebã sẽn dɪkd

give Lumbila as an example and say that since the people's bank opened at Lumbila, people have

ligdi n ningd ka wã, b rata vʊʊg-m-menga, b rata maneg-m-menga,
been depositing their money because they want to develop, they want to secure their well-being

b sũur ya noogo.
and this has brought them happiness.

Bι y zoe Wẽnnaam la y maan wa Lumbil rãmbã.
They will then advise them to take example on the inhabitants of Lumbila.

A gomdã tɛk la woto.
That's all he has said.

Oranda Tsûji and the Sidotti Incident
An Interview with an Italian Missionary by a Confucian Scholar in Eighteenth-century Japan

YUKINO SEMIZU

> *From 1641 to 1867, Japan was virtually closed to the outside world except for trading with the Dutch, and Christianity, which had gained a considerable number of followers in the preceding hundred years, was strictly forbidden by the government. In 1708, an Italian missionary was captured when he landed on a small island in southern Japan. He was first questioned by the local magistrate, then sent to the capital following a request from one of the most prominent scholars of the time. The scholar was also an advisor to the* shogun, *the head of the government. The interpreters for both interviews were a group of Dutch-speaking Japanese officials known as Oranda tsûji (Dutch language officers). These translator/interpreters administered the trading with the Dutch and carried out any necessary work involving the Dutch language. The language required for this occasion was, however, not Dutch. The contents of the interviews were such that the incident led to a publication of the first influential study of the West by the Japanese. This article presents an interpreting event in which, in contrast to many assumptions made of them today, interpreters played a pivotal role in cultural transfer and the consequent intellectual development of the country. The historical background of translation in Japan is outlined, and the interpreters' position and their expected roles in the society are examined.*

1. Historical background of translation in Japan

The Japanese had been translating from Chinese over a century before the country's first constitution was written in 604. The translated texts were initially writings on Buddhism. Works of literature and philosophy soon followed. These translated works of Chinese classics formed the foundation of education in Japan right up to the mid-20th century. However, the Japanese do not usually consider reading Chinese classics as reading translation. This is due to the fact that the Japanese, who did not originally have their own script, adopted Chinese characters for their writing system. Whilst the characters used in Japanese are pronounced differently from their Chinese originals, the meanings of individual characters are mostly recognisable. Once the basic rules of Chinese word order were learned, the text could be read as Japanese in its original (Chinese) form. In order to aid less experienced readers, a method was invented to indicate the correct word order by adding Japanese phonetic script and signs in a form of superscript. The origin of the method is not clearly known but it had been well developed by the time the first constitution was written.[1] This traditional method of reading Chinese classics by following the meanings of individual words may have had significant influence when the Japanese began translating Dutch in the 17th century.

In 1543, a Portuguese ship drifted onto a small island in the south of the country. They were the first Europeans to reach Japan. The Portuguese soon established trading with Japan and the Jesuit missionaries who followed the traders met little resistance from either political or Buddhist establishment in the country. For the next hundred years, overseas trading and Christianity grew considerably in Japan but by the 1630s, the Japanese rulers began to see both activities as a threat to their own authorities. In 1639, the government finally outlawed Christianity and persecuted its followers, expelled all Europeans, with the exception of the Dutch, and closed the ports against foreign ships. Thus Japan's two hundred-year isolation began. Translation before the country's closure was mostly of religious texts translated into Japanese by the Portuguese missionaries. These translated texts were often written in the Roman alphabet, which meant that readers were limited to the privileged few who had an opportunity to learn the script from the Portuguese missionaries. On the whole, the Japanese contributed little to translation in this era. However, quite independently of religious activities, a number of Japanese had learned Portuguese in order to act as interpreters to the traders around the ports in southern Japan where the overseas trading took place. Despite the fact that they spoke the language of the 'forbidden religion', they escaped persecution and became the government's official language mediators for the Dutch thereafter.

In 1641, the Dutch were ordered to move their trading station to Deshima, a small artificial island joined to Nagasaki on the main land by a bridge. Despite the seemingly privileged status as the only Europeans in the country, the Dutch had to endure prison-like restrictions. They were not allowed to go across unaccompanied to the mainland. No Japanese except for the officials from Nagasaki and the interpreters were allowed to go into Deshima. The interpreters were no longer employed by the Dutch themselves but were the government's officials, whose loyalty was unquestionably to the government of Japan. The Dutch accepted these hardships, as trade with Japan was vital to the Netherlands' economy at the time. To the Japanese, however, overseas trading was not essential since Japan had always been self-sufficient. It is generally thought that the Japanese government kept the trading link with the Dutch in order to keep open the information channel to the outside world. The government monopolized the information by forbidding the people to learn Dutch, and by placing those few who had become the official interpreters under the direct control of the government. In this context, translation in this era was primarily a part of

---

[1] For more detail of this reading method, see Engels (1998).

the government's foreign policy. In the beginning, the translators' work consisted mostly of day-to-day trade administration. Later, it extended to translation of scientific and technical texts, including medical texts and an encyclopaedia.

2. The Edo period and *Oranda tsûji*

In the Edo[2] period (1603-1867), in which the incident related in this article took place, Japan became free from warfare for the first time in centuries. In this new state of peace, commerce grew rapidly and art and craft thrived. Learning was encouraged by the government and education was made available to people from outside the traditionally educated classes. New Confucianism, which was pragmatic in nature and emphasized the importance of loyalty, was regarded as the ideological foundation of the Edo government. From the cultural perspective, there seemed little need to acquire any knowledge outside traditional studies based on Chinese classics. From a political perspective, however, the government was well aware of the importance of obtaining information about the development of Western nations. They were especially interested in the activities of the Spanish and Portuguese in South-East Asia because of these two countries' strong association with Christianity, which was regarded as a serious threat to Japan's national security. Accordingly, the Dutch were ordered to submit a report on the latest world affairs on their arrival in Japan.[3]

When the Dutch became the only European trading partner, a few Japanese who had been Portuguese interpreters were selected to become the government's official Dutch interpreter/translators, known as *Oranda*[4] *tsûji*, the Dutch language officers. As most professions in feudal Japan, *Oranda tsûji* was hereditary and about twenty families from the educated officials' class held the position throughout the Edo era. By the 1660s, they had established their own professional hierarchy. They were based in Nagasaki where the Dutch traders were stationed. Their language skills in Dutch were probably no more than a few words and phrases when they began working for the government. No learning resources existed except for the Dutch staff at the trading station. It took over a hundred years for generations of *Oranda tsûji* to accumulate enough linguistic knowledge to compile the first Dutch-Japanese dictionary and to write texts on the Dutch language. For some years at the beginning, communication

---

[2] The old name for Tokyo. The government's base was moved to Edo by the first of the Tokugawa *shogun* family, who held the title until the country was opened in 1867.
[3] Once a year and later, once every five years.
[4] The word '*Oranda*' derives from Holland. The term *Oranda tsûji* in this article refers to both the group and individuals. The word *tsûji* is used sometimes to refer to individual interpreters. Both words are treated as collective nouns. For details of the organisation and work of *Oranda tsûji*, see Engels (1998)

between the Dutch and *Oranda tsûji* was mostly in Portuguese and, when possible, in Chinese. With these basic, miscellaneous language skills, *Oranda tsûji* managed to translate trade documents and the report on the outside world that the Dutch submitted to the government. Besides these official duties, they also worked for the Dutch as interpreters and mediators in day-to-day matters. The Dutch, for their part, made considerable efforts to improve the situation by cooperating with *Oranda tsûji*. They assisted with translation of the report and gave language lessons to apprentice *tsûji*. More importantly, they provided *Oranda tsûji* with the knowledge and language of Western science when *Oranda tsûji's* translation tasks extended beyond routine clerical work. In particular, the succession of chiefs of the trading station, known as *Kapitan* (Capitão / Captain), and the station's physicians played a vital role in a number of significant translation events which introduced the Japanese to knowledge from and about the West. The incident described below is one example of these contributions made by the Dutch to *Oranda tsûji's* interpreting activities, which influenced intellectual development during the Edo period.

3. The missionary from Rome and his interviewer

Giovanni Battista Sidotti was a missionary from Rome. He travelled to Japan to preach, knowing that Christianity was forbidden in the country. He reached Japan in 1708 but was caught as he landed. He was questioned in Nagasaki first, then in Edo and subsequently, placed under house arrest. In 1713, the elderly couple who looked after Sidotti confessed to the authorities that the Roman had converted them to Christianity. Following this confession, Sidotti was sent to a dungeon, where he died the following year. Although he did not succeed in his original mission, his meeting with Arai Hakuseki, who interviewed him in Edo, was widely regarded as a landmark in the intellectual history of Japan.

Arai Hakuseki (1657-1725) is indisputably one of the greatest thinkers in Japanese history. His writing includes philosophy, economics, politics, linguistics, geography and history. He was also an accomplished poet in classical Chinese. Hakuseki was one of the most prominent Confucian scholars at the time. He was also an adviser to the *shogun* when Sidotti arrived in Japan. Hakuseki was said to have had an insatiable interest in the West. He was deeply impressed by Sidotti's integrity and scholarship and, after the interviews, made his opinion public that Western science and technology must be distinguished from Christianity. Hakuseki not only distinguished between the two but also praised highly the scientific knowledge of the West. Few to-day would argue with the view that this declaration opened the way for the study of Western science in Japan. Hakuseki wrote a number of works related to the meeting with Sidotti. Amongst these, *Seiyô Kibun* (Report on the Occident)[5] is considered to

---

[5] The translation of the title is by Goodman (1967).

be the most immediate result of the meeting. The work is in three parts; the account of the interviews with Sidotti, geography of the world and history of Europe, and the Christian doctrine with Hakuseki's own criticism of the religion. It was the first influential study of the West by the Japanese.

4. The interview

We now turn to the interview itself. In this section, the event is described following Miyazaki (1968), a study of *Seiyô Kibun*, unless otherwise stated. All translation from Japanese is my own. The interview as an interpreting event will be discussed in the following sections.

In 1708 on a small island in southern Japan, two farmers found a man in Japanese clothes and carrying a Japanese sword. He was unusually tall, did not understand the language and his face was unmistakably that of a European. The foreigner was taken to the nearby town where the officials attempted to question him. No interpreters were available. The officials understood 'Nippon (Japan), Edo, Nagasaki' and managed to catch a few other words including 'Roma, Kirishitan (Christian)'. The foreigner pointed at himself with the word 'Rama'. He drew a map and said a few more words. All these words were written down in Japanese script and, together with drawings of the foreigner's possessions, were sent to the Nagasaki magistrate.

4.1 The interview in Nagasaki

In Nagasaki, the report from the island town was shown to eight *Oranda tsûji*. Also present were the chief, the physician and two other staff from the Dutch trading station. They could only guess that 'Roma' must be a place in Italy and 'Kirishitan' must be the name of a religious sect. The report from the island stated that the foreigner's possessions were 'quite un-nameable'. A few days later, the foreigner was sent to Nagasaki with five hundred guards accompanying him (Katagiri 1995). He was the first foreigner to have entered the country unofficially since Japan closed itself off from the outside world over seventy years previously.

The account of the interview at Nagasaki magistrate's office was recorded in a diary kept by the chief of the trading station. On the first day, a senior *Oranda tsûji*, Imamura Genuemon, carried out a preliminary questioning to assess the feasibility of interview with the foreigner. The questioning lasted several hours. When he was asked in which language the interview was conducted, Genuemon answered 'I cannot say quite which language'. This was probably because the foreigner claimed to know Portuguese but Genuemon did not, and the Japanese that the foreigner insisted on using amounted to no more than incomprehensible fragments. Genuemon would select a word from a Latin dictionary and show it to the foreigner. Genuemon eventually understood that the man was a priest and had been chosen from more than ten ranks of his fellow priests. He also spoke about the death and resurrection of *Yaso* (Jesus) but little else was comprehensible.

On the second day, the chief and four members of the staff of the trading station were asked by the magistrate to attend the interview. One of the staff, Adrian Douw, spoke some Latin. A high official took the trouble to meet the Dutch before the interview began. He warned them that the foreigner might become hostile towards the Dutch and asked them to keep calm if this happened. The Dutch promised they would. Six officials and several *Oranda tsûji* were present at the interview.

Twenty-four questions had been prepared by the Nagasaki magistrate. The same senior *tsûji*, Imamura Genuemon, questioned the foreigner in several languages[6] including Japanese. He would repeat the same question over and over again but little seemed to be understood between the foreigner and Genuemon. The session lasted for an hour and a half. Later on the same day the Dutch received a request from the magistrate that Adrian Douw give Latin lessons to *Oranda tsûji* in preparation for the next session of the interview. It was to be held in eight day's time.

On the eighth day, the second session was held. This time, Adrian Douw questioned the foreigner in Latin in the presence of *Oranda tsûji* and officials. The questions were the same twenty-four questions as those that were asked at the previous session.

The foreigner's answers were made into an official report by *Oranda tsûji* and sent to the head of the government in the capital, Edo. These answers can be seen in a document known as *Roma jin kanjô* (the Roman's appeal), which also contains the drawings of the foreigner's possessions. The report contains fourteen answers with a confirmation at the end;

> A Dutchman by the name of Adrian Douw questioned the foreigner in a language that is called Latin. Douw informed us of the answers, which we have translated here as on the right[7]

This is signed by *Kapitan*, Adrian Douw, *Oranda tsûji* and their supervisor.

These answers have always been known to historians but, as for the questions, they came to light only recently (Katagiri 1995). They were found in the form of a personal copy by one of the *Oranda tsûji* who attended the interview. The contents of the questions are as follows (apart from the first group, the questions have been re-grouped for the purpose of this article).

- The foreigner's nationality, name, age, family, rank and position in the religious order.

---

[6] It is not clear what other languages he used and how he had learned them.
[7] The original document is written vertically and from right to left.

- The journey to Japan: nationality of the vessel that brought him, whether it was the same vessel that had been seen from the island he landed, where it was sailing to after he left.
- Whether he was on his own in carrying out this plan, or whether there were others with the same intention as his, either before or after this incident.
- Where he obtained the sword and the clothes.
- Whether he gave money to those who found him, attempted to preach either to the islanders or the guards while he was being detained.
- The reason for coming to Japan, what he wished to do in Japan, why he wished to go to Edo. (Katagiri 1995)

At this interview, the Japanese learned that the foreigner was from Rome in Italy. His name was Giovanni Battista Sidotti. He was forty-one years old and a Roman Catholic priest. At home, he had a mother, brothers and a sister. His father had died and he had neither wife nor children. Although the questions and answers do not match in their order and number, all twenty-four questions appear to have been answered. Katagiri (1995), however, points out that the answer to the seventeenth question cannot be found in the report. The question is about whether there were more plans to send missionaries to Japan. Katagiri (1995: 115) suggests that, on the whole, the answers concerning Christianity are strangely brief considering the impact this incident must have had on the authorities. It is generally believed that Arai Hakuseki's wish to discover Sidotti's precise intention in coming to Japan prompted him to advise the *shogun* that the Roman should be sent to the capital for more questioning.

4.2 The interview in Edo

Ten months after the interview in Nagasaki, Sidotti arrived in Edo with the senior *tsûji* Imamura Genuemon and two other *tsûji* who had been receiving Latin lessons. Adrian Douw, their tutor, had been ordered to remain in Nagasaki. The chief of the trading station wrote in his diary on the eve of their departure:

> The senior *tsûji* Imamura Genuemon, with two other *tsûji*, came to take leave. They are to accompany the Italian priest to Edo tomorrow. I advised them to take particular care with the questions concerning the difference between the religion to which the priest belonged and that to which we do. They promised they would. (A. Imamura, quoted in Miyazaki 1968: 204).

In Edo, while waiting for Sidotti's arrival, Arai Hakuseki read three books written in 1675 by Giuseppe Chiara,[8] an Italian usually known by his Japanese name

---

[8] Chiara was a Jesuit missionary who renounced his religion and stayed on in Japan.

Okamoto Sanuemon. Hakuseki noted that there were some references to religion that might be of use. The interview was held in four sessions over two weeks. On the day of the first session, Hakuseki met the court officials and the *Oranda tsûji* before the interview began. At this briefing, he told *Oranda tsûji* and the officials:

> From the map of the world, I see Italy and Holland are both in Europe. I imagine, therefore, that seven out of ten words in the language of Italy might be understood in the language of Holland. Even so, for an official purpose, speculations in a language that is not learned correctly must not be spoken. However, today is different. What will be said today is not for an official purpose. Today, you, *Oranda tsûji* are speaking for me, therefore if there are matters that you are not certain of or matters that the Roman does not put into words, you must speak to me as you understand these matters to be. I will not assume that all that you say is exactly what he says. If there are mistakes, you will not be blamed for making them. And I request you, court officials, that since *Oranda tsûji* are not expected to have learned the language fully, if there are mistakes in what they say, they must not be accused of misapprehending. (Miyazaki 1968:7)

The interview began in the presence of the court officials and several guards. In the first interview, Hakuseki asked Sidotti, through *Oranda tsûji*, about his place of origin. Some of Sidotti's answers were in Japanese but it was in the dialect of western Japan and pronounced with the accent of his own language. Sidotti would repeat his words to ensure that what he said would be understood. Towards the end of the first interview, Hakuseki himself took part in the exchange and asked Sidotti a few questions.[9] When the officials left, Sidotti told *Oranda tsûji* at length how he regretted causing troubles for the officials and hardship for the guards, contrary to his wish to save the people of this country. On the following day, Hakuseki summoned *Oranda tsûji* to his own house to review and clarify Sidotti's answers from the first interview. In the second session of the interview, Hakuseki showed Sidotti a map of the world. Sidotti commented that the map was seventy years old and very rare, and should be preserved carefully for the use of the future generations. The third session was spent by Hakuseki asking Sidotti for some additional information to the previous day's answers. The officials were not present on this occasion. During this session, Sidotti attempted to talk about his religion but Hakuseki avoided the subject.

For the fourth session, Hakuseki summoned the officials and informed them that this day's interview would include questions about Sidotti's religion and his intention in coming to Japan. When he was asked about religion and how he had

---

[9] Although there is no record to indicate which language Hakuseki used, it was most likely Japanese. Sidotti's Japanese must have improved since he was first interviewed.

intended to preach in Japan, Sidotti could not suppress his excitement in telling them how he finally reached his destination six years after he had been ordered to travel to Japan. This interview included an extensive range of subjects, including the contents of the Bible and a detailed description of the Christian doctrine. Sidotti tried to teach *Oranda tsûji* Latin pronunciation. He would repeat the word until *tsûji* managed the correct pronunciation and when they did, he praised them generously. He would laugh when *tsûji's* Latin was affected by a Dutch accent, and kindly commented on how difficult it must be for them to discard their old habits. It is generally believed that this interview had a decisive influence on Hakuseki's view of the knowledge of the West.

After the final interview, the magistrate requested *Oranda tsûji* to ask Sidotti another set of questions. They were mostly geographical. They include:

- The distance and locations of various places, including Italy, India and the point at which The Plough and the Southern Cross can be seen.
- Whether ginseng, aloeswood and sugar are grown in Italy.
- What makes (Sidotti) consider Japan to be superior to other islands in the world.
- Whether there are strange and large sea animals in the ocean. (Miyazaki 1968:207)

On the following day, *Oranda tsûji* were ordered to produce an additional report based on the interview. It contains Sidotti's statement that he had no intention of conspiring to invade Japan.

Sidotti's commitment and dignity deeply impressed Hakuseki. One of the consequences was that Hakuseki advised the *shogun* that the Roman should be placed under house arrest for life. Being a Christian missionary, Sidotti would have been executed were it not for this advice. Another consequence was that Sidotti's scholarship inspired Hakuseki to search for further knowledge of the West. He visited the Dutch on their annual visit to Edo[10] and interviewed the *Kapitan* and the physician with the aid of *Oranda tsûji*. He questioned them in detail on the history and geography of Europe, as well as about the principles of Christianity. He also asked about Dutch. These visits confirmed what he had learned from Sidotti, which resulted in the writing of *Seiyo Kibun*.

5. Sidotti's interview as an interpreting event

Sidotti's interview displays a number of features which are unusual by today's standards. At the same time, it has characteristics that are surprisingly similar to many of today's interpreting situations, in spite of its unique context. In this

---

[10] One of their obligations to the Japanese government.

section, interpreting at Sidotti's interview will be examined from the perspective of discourse interaction.

5.1 Role and status of the participants

Role and status in social interaction are not independent entities but determined by the participants' perception of themselves and of each other (Wadensjö 1998). Sidotti's position at the earlier interview was that of an arrested person but there is no record to suggest that he was frightened and disorientated as an arrested person in the police station often is (Gentile *et al.* 1996:91). Instead, he acted according to the status he held as a priest in his own society and made continuous efforts to communicate with his 'audience'. Sidotti gained considerable 'status' in his new circumstance too, due to the fact that his coming was seen by the authorities as a possible threat to national security. The significance of his presence was confirmed by the fact that when he was sent to Nagasaki he was accompanied by five hundred guards.

The Dutch in Nagasaki assumed a different status from that of traders in a foreign country when some members of their staff were asked to attend the interview. The high official's personal request to them to keep calm if the Roman became hostile indicates that the Dutch were being accorded the status of being on the side of the authorities. How the presence of the Dutch affected the interaction of the interview cannot be determined from the record available. It can be speculated, however, that by attending an event of such importance, the Dutch must have considerably increased their status. It has been pointed out that interpreters often gain from the reflected status of those with whom they work (Gentile *et al.* 1996:11). This could well have been the case of the Dutch, not only of the individuals who attended the event but the Dutch in Japan as a group.

The prestigious status of Arai Hakuseki in Edo was unquestionable. This meant that, at the interview, Hakuseki was clearly dominant over Sidotti, who was officially a detainee. The description of the interview in *Seiyô Kibun* does not indicate, however, that Sidotti saw the power relationship between Hakuseki and himself in this way. The way in which he cooperated with Hakuseki suggests that although he regarded Hakuseki highly, he did not see himself as subservient.

5.2 Oranda tsûji as intermediary

The role of *Oranda tsûji* as intermediary at the interviews in Nagasaki and in Edo seems to differ considerably. In Nagasaki, they had more autonomy in the way they took part in the interviewing process. In the preliminary interview in particular they could hardly be said to have adopted an intermediary role, since the senior *tsûji*, Imamura Genuemon, was not carrying messages between the two parties but assessing the situation for his own professional purposes. Although the questions for the main interview had been prepared by the authorities, the actual questioning on the first day was conducted on the initiative of Imamura Genuemon. The fact that Sidotti's answers in the official report were organized quite differently from the order in which the questions were presented suggests that *Oranda tsûji* were responsible for the assessment and presentation of the outcome of the interview. *Oranda tsûji's* role in the first interview can be described as that of 'brokers', who act more independently and have more influence on the process of interaction than do mere 'messengers' (Bailey in Wadensjö 1998:63).

Oranda tsûji's role at the second interview became less autonomous and nearer to that of 'pure messenger', whose performance is more dependent on the prime party's action (ibid.). Their task was to pass messages from Adrian Douw, in Latin, to the officials, in Japanese. There was little room for their own initiative. Nonetheless, the fact that they produced the official report of the interview as a part of their duties, suggests that *Oranda tsûji* were expected to take more responsibility than that which is normally assigned to today's court interpreters.

Interpreting for Arai Hakuseki in Edo, *Oranda tsûji's* role becomes even closer to that of 'pure messenger'. In fact, their role here can be described as 'non-person', that is, present during the encounter but assuming the role neither of performer nor of audience (Goffman in Wadensjö 1998:66). This change in *Oranda tsûji's* role was not caused by the involvement of Arai Hakuseki, since contact with high officials was a part of their normal work. Rather, it was due to the difference in the purpose of the interview. The interview in Nagasaki was basically administrative in nature, a part of *Oranda tsûji's* regular duties. The interview by Hakuseki was, in contrast, academic in nature and few routine formulae in *tsûji's* professional resources could be applied. The interpreters' function on this occasion was more focused on the contents of the interview than on the process of the interaction. *Oranda tstûji's* interactional role may have been 'non-person' but their function as intermediaries for communication was indispensable. The different settings in Sidotti's interview demonstrate how the interpreter's role changes in relation to the varying factors governing each interpreting situation.

5.3 The interpreting process in Sidotti's interview

By today's standard, it would be hard to expect a successful outcome if the interpreter's language competence were as inadequate as that of *Oranda tsûji's* Latin. Yet, considering the significance the event has had in the intellectual history of Japan, the interpreting at Sidotti's interview has to be judged a success. In discussing the cognitive process of communication based on the relevance theory proposed by Sperber and Wilson (1986), Gutt (1990: 157) describes the translator's task as being to arrive at the intended interpretation of the original, and then determine in what respects his translation should interpretively resemble the original ... for his target audience with its particular cognitive environment.

The cognitive environment in communication refers to all the information to which an individual has access whether consciously or unconsciously. This includes the knowledge the individual already has (Sperber and Wilson 1986: 39). The larger the cognitive environment shared between the speaker and the hearer, the more chance there is of successful communication (Gutt 1990). On this basis, if Sidotti's message had been presented to *Oranda tsûji* as a written text, the translation would have had little chance of becoming a successful communication, since the means of arriving at the intended interpretation of the original would hardly have been available to *Oranda tsûji*. As it was, notwithstanding the difficulties they had in communicating in an unfamiliar language, *Oranda tsûji* were able to access the original interpretation intended by the author/speaker, as the speaker was physically present while the translation was taking place. The particular cognitive environment of the target audience, in this case that of Arai Hakuseki, included the knowledge he had gained from the books he read before the interview. In what respects the translation should interpretively resemble the original was also determined by Hakuseki. In his statement before the interview, he directed *Oranda tsûji* to speak in the manner they understood the original messages to be. In terms of relevance theory, one could say that all participants in the interview were aware that successful communication depends on more *explicatures* than *implicatures*. Explicatures are assumptions that could analytically be implied by the utterances, while implicatures are contextual implications and contextual assumptions of the utterances (Gutt 1990:144). This awareness forms an important part of the shared cognitive environment. It could be concluded that the participants in Sidotti's interview, including the interpreter *Oranda tsûji* Imamura Genuemon, utilized the available shared cognitive environment to optimal effect and communicated successfully across the language barrier.

5.4 Sidotti's interview as translation history

From the historical perspective, Sidotti's interview has characteristics that are similar to interpreting events during the conquest of the New World. They are both cultural encounters of the West and the non-West that took place in non-Western cultures. The interpreters in both cases did not, at first, speak the language of the outsiders who came into their society. Looking at some of the issues in more detail, however, Sidotti's interview presents a number of unique aspects that distinguish it from the interpreting that took place in the 'New World'.

Cultural encounters in history are often seen as one culture's dominance over another. Interpreters were often recruited from the vulnerable members of the native society, such as women or slaves. Many of those who became the interpreters to the newcomers from outside found themselves becoming outcasts from their own society. These interpreters were almost always individuals who had little power over those for whom they interpreted. Their loyalties were often divided and they were looked upon with suspicion by both the newcomers and the people in their own society (Delisle and Woodsworth 1995; Karttunen 1994). In contrast, despite the impact Sidotti's arrival had on the Japanese authorities, it had little immediate influence on the society itself. Sidotti was an individual in an alien society and had no power over its people. For their part, *Oranda tsûji* were not vulnerable individuals and their loyalty was never in doubt. In many respects, therefore, the relationship between Sidotti and his interpreters has more in common with that between interpreters in fieldwork[11] and their clients. Traditionally, fieldwork encounters involve a European researcher and interlocutors from non-Western cultures. These encounters, like Sidotti's case, do not usually result in one culture's dominance over the other. Furthermore, unlike the conquest context, interpreters in fieldwork are less vulnerable and have more potential power to influence the event, since the researchers have no means of dominating their interpreters. On the contrary, they are entirely dependent upon them. Sidotti too, had to depend on *Oranda tsûji*.

There are, however, two major differences between the fieldwork situation and Sidotti's interview. One is the 'direction of culture'[12] in interpreting, that is, whether interpreters translate their own culture 'out' or others' 'in'. In the fieldwork situation, interpreters translated their own non-Western culture 'out' for the researchers from outside, who collected information from the culture that was alien to them. In Sidotti's interview, the direction of culture was the reverse. The interpreter translated an alien culture into his own language and culture. The implication of this is that in the fieldwork situation, the context of the interpreting is physically available to the researchers to substantiate what is alien to them. In Sidotti's interview, there were few resources from which *Oranda tsûji* could draw necessary information in order to comprehend the original message. In this respect, there is a similarity to the missionary context. In the missionary context, interpreters translate outsiders' culture 'in' to their own culture and the context of the original message was not easily available. On the other hand, in the missionary context, the outsiders were often dismissive towards the societies they worked in (Delisle and Woodsworth 1995:256; Robinson 1997:85), which created unequal power relationships. Conversely, there is no evidence

---

[11] Wadensjö's (1998) term to refer to researchers in anthropology
[12] The concept has been borrowed from 'direction of translation', which refers to whether translation is into or out of the translator's native language (Shuttleworth and Cowie 1997:42) The term 'direction of culture' refers to the translator's relation to the contents of the translation and not to the language.

that either Sidotti or Arai Hakuseki considered his own culture and language to be dominant over the other's.

Another difference between *Oranda tsûji* and the interpreters in fieldwork is the question of loyalty. Anderson (1976: 220) cites Phillips (1960) who observes that an anthropologist who is 'working through a native interpreter, must encourage his translator to ally with him' or else the interpreter's own society 'may seek to 'save' him from the outsider's corrupting influence'. Anderson points out that the interpreter is often called upon to take sides with an offering of benefits of one sort or another. The question of interpreters' loyalty and the influence of their personal interest on interpreting performance are still prevalent issues in interpreting today (Gentile *et al.* 1996; Wadensjö 1998). *Oranda tsûji's* loyalty was unquestionably to the Japanese government and their personal interest was to stay loyal to it. This does not mean, however, that they interpreted Sidotti's words to suit the government, since there was no personal benefit for them in taking such an action. There is, however, one occasion in the whole event of Sidotti's interview in which *Oranda tsûji* may have taken sides. Before Sidotti was put on trial, *Oranda tsûji* were ordered to produce an additional report, which was sent to the court ahead of Sidotti. This report stated clearly that Sidotti's intention was solely of a religious and not a territorial nature. Katagiri (1995: 123) considers that Arai Hakuseki may have instigated the report as a strategy to save Sidotti's life. If that was the case, Hakuseki was exercising his personal influence on the trial. Had *Oranda tsûji* chosen to be loyal to their employer, the government, and reported Hakuseki's act, it might have brought them a considerable reward. But *Oranda tsûji's* decision was disloyal to their own employer. What benefit they expected from this decision is impossible to say but one would like to imagine that *Oranda tsûji* also wished to save the life of the Roman who risked his life for a religious belief. It may just be possible that, on this occasion, their sense of duty took second place to their humanistic interest.

6. Conclusion

Sidotti's interview as translation history is interesting in that it can be seen as a prototype of dialogue interpreting, the purpose of which was first and foremost to enable communication in an encounter of different cultures. Studying interpreting in the historical context, therefore, can be one way to re-examine the assumptions and expectations made today about interpreters and interpreting. Some useful insights into the perception of translation held in a particular society can also be gained, since the main participants in the translation event, the clients, the interpreter and others present, can be studied together. This allows us to observe a whole process of translation in a relatively compact context. Moreover, interpreting events in history are fascinating human stories, from which we can learn a great deal about the fundamentally humanistic activities of translating and interpreting.

References

Anderson, Bruce (1976) 'Perspectives on Role of Interpreter', in Richard Brislin (ed) *Translation, Application and Research*, New York: Gardner Press, 208-225.

Delisle, Jean and Judith Woodsworth (ed) (1995) *Translators through History*, Amsterdam: John Benjamins.

Engels, Yukino (1998) *A Study of Oranda Tsûji: in preparation for an extended study of translation history in Japan through Oranda tsûji*, Unpublished MSc dissertation, Manchester: UMIST.

Gentile, Adolfo, Uldis Ozolins and Mary Vasilakakos (1996) *Liaison Interpreting. A Handbook,* Victoria Australia: Melbourne University Press.

Goodman, G.K. (1967) *The Dutch Impact on Japan*, Leiden: E.J. Brill.

Gutt, Ernest-August (1990) 'A Theoretical Account of Translation – Without a Translation Theory', *Target* 2(2): 135-164.

Karttunen, Frances (1994) *Between Worlds: Interpreters, Guides, and Survivors*, New Jersey: Rutgers University Press.

Katagiri, Kazuo (1995) *Oranda Tsûji Imamura Genuemon Eisei: Tostukuni no Kotoba o Wagamono to shite [Learning Languages of Land Afar]*, Tokyo: Maruzen.

Miyazaki, Michio (ed) (1968) *Seiyo Kibun [Report on the Occident] by Arai Hakuseki*, Tokyo: Heibonsha.

Phillips, H. (1960) 'Problems of Translation and Meaning in Field Work', *Human Organization* 18: 184-192.

Robinson, Douglas (1997) *Translation and Empire: Post-Colonial Theories Explained*, Manchester: St Jerome Publishing.

Shuttleworth, Mark and Moira Cowie (1997) *Dictionary of Translation Studies,* Manchester: St. Jerome Publishing.

Sperber, D. and D. Wilson (1986/1995) *Relevance : Communication and Cognition,* Oxford: Basil Blackwell.

Wadensjö, Cecilia (1998) *Interpreting as Interaction*, London & New York: Longman.

Part III

Issues in Training

First Steps on Firmer Ground
A Project for the Further Training of Sign Language Interpreters in Austria

NADJA GRBIC

> *This article focuses on a further training project for sign language interpreters[1] implemented from February 1997 to March 1998 at the Institute of Translation Studies at the University of Graz. This one-year project, the subject of detailed analysis in this article, was the first attempt to be undertaken in Austria to teach and observe sign language interpreters who had received no formal training but had mainly worked as natural interpreters, very often in complete isolation and without any opportunity to reflect upon and discuss their work. In order to be able to analyse the different effects of this project in a useful context, it is outlined here against the background of the ever-changing perception of the social practice of sign language interpreting in Austria.*

1. Social Background

That fact that today, sign language interpreting is no longer characterized by complete invisibility in the scientific community is not only confirmed by recent publications (for instance Brennan and Brown 1997; Brennan 1999), which were published and disseminated in the field of translation and interpretation studies, but also by conferences explicitly inviting the involvement of researchers dealing with sign language interpreting (for instance the *Critical Link* Conference series – see Carr *et al.* 1997). In spite of this gradual opening up of interpretation studies to previously more peripheral fields of research, sign language interpreting remains one of the least systematically investigated areas in this field.

As regards the social practice of sign language interpreting, only few data are available which permit a meaningful comparison of the situation in different countries to the extent required. A study on the status and use of sign language in seventeen European countries, which was commissioned by the EUD (European Union of the Deaf) and published in 1997, makes it possible (despite the relatively small sample) to draw upon concrete material and determine at least some general trends with regard to certain crucial questions of interpreting

---

[1] The project was funded by the European Social Fund and the Austrian Ministry of Labour, Social Affairs and Health (Project number EMPLOYMENT HORIZON 0056109008). The author wishes to thank Sonja Pöllabauer for the translation into English of this article.

(Kyle and Allsop 1997). Within this study, three groups of informants were requested to give their perceptions of the use of sign language in their countries: deaf people on the basis of in-depth interviews, and hearing persons and institutions with an involvement in deafness (schools, hospitals, social security offices etc.) via questionnaires.

The interviews with the deaf people on their views on the use of sign language in certain settings (deaf schools, family, work, deaf associations etc.) revealed that Sweden, Ireland, Denmark and the UK were seen as countries in which sign language is used quite often. Least use of sign language can be observed in France, Italy, Spain, Portugal and Austria (Kyle and Allsop 1997: 63). Regarding the use of sign language in public life (TV programmes, public sign language courses, legislature, university etc.), Austria was once again shown to have the lowest ratings from the point of view of the deaf informants, followed by France and Luxembourg. The Scandinavian countries received the highest ratings (ibid.: 65). The survey among the institutions showed that 76% of the surveyed institutions use interpreters very often or on a daily basis; in Great Britain the rate is 73%, whereas in Austria 50% of all institutions indicated that they never or very seldom used interpreters (ibid.: 77). One third of the Austrian institutions also indicated that they did not know where to request interpreters. The European average here was 7% (ibid.: 78). Finally, only 7% of all deaf people surveyed in Austria were of the opinion that full-time professional sign language interpreters were available in Austria, whereas the rate in Sweden and Denmark was 100%. The figure varied between 80 and 90% in Norway, Great Britain, Finland and Germany (ibid.: 66).

These first comparative data show that the use of sign language and sign language interpreters has always been and, in many cases, still is very rare in Austria. Moreover, the lack of consolidation in the profession, which among other things includes training, further training, professional associations, accreditation and licensing, resulted in the parties involved in the different interpreting situations having entirely diverging opinions of what interpreting actually involves. According to Tseng (1992), this first phase of professional practice, which precedes the process of professionalization, is characterized by market disorder:

> Practitioners in the market cannot keep outsiders from entering practice. They themselves may have started practice as outsiders or quacks. Recipients of the service either have very little understanding of what practitioners do or very little confidence in the service they receive. It is very likely that the public simply does not care about the quality of the services. Hence, distrust and misunderstanding permeate the market. What matters more to clients, in the absence of quality control, is usually price. Whoever demands the lowest fees gets the job. (Tseng 1992: 44-45, as cited in Mikkelson 1997: 78).

2. Before professionalization

When we started thinking about training courses, Austrian sign language interpreters were mainly 'natural interpreters' (Harris 1977), recruited from highly motivated family members, friends, social workers, teachers, clerics, etc. No training programmes, no clearly defined professional profile and no group identity existed, and there was little contact between the different groups. Owing to this lack of monitoring mechanisms, many of those who occasionally work as sign language interpreters had highly diverging views on the basic competencies which we tend to regard as essential for any professional interpreting practice. These divergences originated from their individual experiences as well as from the historical mythologizing of deafness and sign language.

In an anonymous survey of 33 Austrian sign language interpreters (Grbic 1994), involving information gleaned from questionnaires[2] conducted in 1993, various data were obtained which could be used for the purpose of informing curriculum design. In the course of the data evaluation process the participants were divided into two groups. One group had been brought up in a deaf environment and had thus had contact with the Deaf Community from an early age (18 persons). The second group had not learned sign language before becoming adults (15 persons). The decision to split the participants into two groups was based on two assumptions. In the first place, children of deaf adults (CODA) were assumed to be bilingual and therefore have fewer problems with both languages. Secondly they were assumed to have a different approach to their role as interpreters because of their close emotional ties with the Deaf Community. While the second assumption was clearly confirmed, the first had to be completely re-evaluated.

The difference between the two groups was already obvious in the evaluation of the data on the participants' school education. In the CODA group (Group 1), the highest educational level of the majority of the participants was that of an apprenticeship (67%); in Group 2, the majority had completed a university education (67%). Of the 33 interviewees, only 6 were full-time sign language interpreters, of whom 5 were CODAs. As had been assumed, the Group 2 participants were mainly involved in the Deaf community (7 in the school system, 2 in religious education, 3 social workers, 1 missionary, 1 student). The representatives of the CODA group had in general 8-10 years professional practice, the second group on the whole 2-3 years.

As regards fields of activity, the interpreters were found to be working in the

---

[2] In total, 50 questionnaires were sent out, 34 were returned, which means an overall response rate of 68%. Altogether, 33 questionnaires were evaluated.

settings listed in Table 1 in descending order of frequency (minimum = 0, maximum = 99).³

Setting	extent
Official settings/authorities	66
Court, police	54
Everyday situations	52
Business	46
Lectures	42
Medicine	41
Church	41
Further training, courses	38
Professional training	37
Culture	36
Professional activity	33
School	28
Driving school	21
TV	16
Conferences	13

Table 1: Frequency of fields of activity

3. The language problem

As mentioned above, in the evaluation process we had to revise the hypothesis that the CODA group were persons who were bilingual, at least to the extent that they had basic language skills to draw upon (as for instance is very often the case with children of migrants).
It became clear, however, that only one-third of the CODA group (27.8%) communicated with their parents in sign language. The majority used a form of *total communication,* a mixture of simultaneous speaking and signing using the structures of both language systems. Nevertheless, the self-appraisal of their language competence was relatively high compared to the second group: 44% stated that they understood communication between deaf people in most cases, 56% indicated that they had no problem in understanding. Their active sign language competence was estimated even higher: 28% believed that they were able to communicate with deaf persons in most situations, 72% even indicated that they were able to do so effortlessly, in any situation and on any given topic. Group 2

---

³ The informants had to mark the frequency of 15 given settings on a scale (never = 0, seldom = 1, sometimes = 2, often = 3). The top rate of 99 would have been reached if all interpreters (n=33) had worked often (3) in one of the settings.

had lower self-appraisal scores. With regard to passive competence, 47% said they usually needed some time to understand deaf people they had not met before, 53% had no problems in most situations. Active skills were rated lower, i.e. 40% indicated being able to understand sign language to a limited degree, 40% in most situations and 20% effortlessly, in any situation and on any topic. As regards their personal estimation of their interpreting competence, the direction of interpreting from sign language into German received lower scores in both groups. Of the CODA group, 83% were convinced that they were able to translate in most cases or with no problems at all from German into sign language, as compared with 53% in Group 2. With regard to the direction sign language into German, the result was 67% as opposed to 20%.

Observations of real interpreting situations indicate that the interpreters' problems with both languages were more serious than they had assumed. As mentioned above, many of the active interpreters, especially those of the CODA group, had a relatively low level of education. This resulted in problems with the German language: those areas especially affected were formal register, lexis, morphology, syntax and discourse. Some had great difficulties in avoiding dialect and/or socio-cultural variants when interpreting and the majority had no experience in producing coherent texts in German in front of a large audience. One last difficulty was that the interpreters' lack of awareness of the contrastive differences between both languages very often engendered interference and a strictly word-for-word rendition of the manual surface structures of the sign language (very often without additional non-manual grammatical markers).

A brief example can serve as an illustration of some of these problems.[4]

Austrian SL[5]   SELBST FRÜHER SCHULE BEREICH FRÜHER WIR JUNG NAIV
When I went to school, when we were still young

Int.   Er hat früher schon in der Schule, früher
He has already earlier in school, earlier

Austrian SL   OFT-SCHAUEN BALL FUSSBALL WILL ALLE AUCH
we very often watched football. Of course we also wanted

---

[4] The text is a transcription of a video recording of an Austrian TV charity show called *Help TV*, in which people are given the opportunity to discuss their problems and money is collected. This particular contribution was about a football club for the Deaf which was in financial difficulty. Interpreting was provided by an official court interpreter.

[5] In the column Austrian SL, a gloss transcription in capitals of the signed output of the Deaf person is presented; beneath it, an acceptable English version is given in italics. **Int.** shows the interpreter's German output with a rough translation into English in italics.

Int.	Immer Fußball gespielt, *always played football*
Austrian SL	MITSPIELEN DABEI FREILICH SPIELEN GLEICH SPIELEN FUSSBALL *to play, to join in simply.*
Int.	das ist für ihn einfach das, die Erfüllung. *that simply is for him that, the fulfilment.*

The text produced by the interpreter (Int.) is unusual in many respects. It is very obvious that it is extremely difficult for the interpreter, who is introduced to the audience by the presenter as an 'expert in his field' at the beginning of the TV show, to produce a coherent German text which is adequate to a formal situation (e.g. the utterance 'that simply is for him that').

If an interpreter uses a great part of his capacity for the production of the translation, perception and analysis of the source text may assume a more marginal role. As a translation strategy, this interpreter opts for a simplifying summary of what he perceives as the core meaning (= playing football in school) without referring precisely to the source text. This strategy of simplifying summariszing can also be observed at other passages of the interview when the interpreter repeatedly marks his utterances with introductory sentences: 'Well, he thinks that...' or 'for him it is like that:..'. This indirect third-person orientation not only has an effect on the language and content but also greatly influences the relation between the interlocutors. Thus the hearing TV presenter hardly ever addresses the Deaf person directly but always turns to the interpreter: 'Can you ask him...' or 'You say he thinks that...'.

Another interesting aspect, apparent in this example, is a frequently observed tendency not to interpret what the Deaf person actually said but to translate the intention one perceives in the Deaf person's utterance. When the latter says that he watched football matches when he was in school and really would have liked to join in, this is translated as 'fulfilment', a special vocation for this sport he had already felt at a very early stage. Although this may seem fitting in the context of the TV show, which aims at moving the audience to tears, it was not actually said by the Deaf person.

As noted above, a further problem is interference from the source language system on the interpreter's output. This is especially obvious in the first part of the example when the interpreter renders the reduplication of the time period marker, a common feature in Austrian Sign Language, in a word-for-word fashion into German: 'He has already earlier in school, earlier'. This translation holds strictly to the word level and does not reflect sign language elements to a sufficient degree. In Austrian Sign Language, German word forms exist but most of them have developed independent meanings which differ greatly from the respective German lexemes. In the case of the signed utterance FRÜHER SCHULE BEREICH FRÜHER ('He has already earlier in school, earlier') what is important is the marking of the period of time in question as an adverbial modification. In German, this can be expressed more adequately by 'Während meiner Schulzeit' ('When I was still at school'). Thus, important grammatical markers are obscured or lost in any one-to-one transfer of sign language text.

As regards sign language competence, most interpreters did not acquire their skills through formal training but rather as a result of their natural communication with Deaf people. These, however, generally had a less developed linguistic awareness, as evidenced by the fact that they did not regard their own language as language but as an inferior derivative of German. This can be explained by two factors. On the one hand, there is the influence of traditional language theory with its phonocentric attitude towards sign language, which for its representatives was at best a phylogenetic precursor of language (see Jäger 1996). On the other hand, there is the official banishment of sign language from Austrian deaf education since 1866 (see Grbic 1994: 126) and the resulting taboo and stigma attaching to this language code. The deliberate denigration of sign language in the entire German-speaking world still has many supporters even today, as can be seen from the quote given below from a book written by a teacher of the Deaf with the misleading title *Sign Language of the Deaf and Psycholinguistics*.

> No sign languages are genuine and autonomous systems but they are always direct or indirect derivations of spoken languages, i.e. derivations of language which do not meet the standards of the original and cannot substitute it. Sign languages can only transfer a small part of the semantic features, which constitute the content of the utterance, into visual forms of expression. In theory, it may be possible to express all the semantically relevant elements in a visual manner but this would lead to a completely uncontrollable torrent of signs, the use of which would take up so much time that this would no longer be feasible. (Gipper 1987:15 – my translation)

As the majority of the Deaf attended special Deaf schools – the European average is approximately 78% (Kyle and Allsop 1997: 49) – this view was very often internalized and transmitted to hearing children. At that time, even deaf people giving sign language courses regarded it as natural to offer *signed German*, a mixture of Austrian Sign Language and German with a large share of German syntax but also morphology (see Boyes Braem 1990), instead of Austrian Sign Language.

4. The restrictive force of received role models

Apart from the communication problems and misunderstandings experienced by both groups of recipients (hearing and deaf), inadequate interpretations also contributed to reinforcing the general stereotype of Deaf people as mentally retarded, needy groups on the fringes of society. Owing to the fact that the representation of Deaf people in our societies is also influenced by the interpretations people are confronted with, it is not surprising that the deficiency model of deafness has remained the hitherto dominant view. Unlike differentiation or cultural models, founded on descriptive, sociological, cultural or linguistically-oriented approaches, the deficiency model suggests that Deaf people require assimilation and remedial teaching in order to become inconspicuous, functioning members of society (see Lane 1992; Grbic 1997a).

Sign language interpreters in Austria were largely unaware of the far-reaching consequences of their work. They saw themselves as benefactors, helpers and advocates of the Deaf, and were convinced that their duties included giving advice and support – either because they considered their protégés to be unable to cope with life on their own (i.e. they had internalized the deficiency model), or because they were of the opinion that society had oppressed Deaf people long enough and believed they had the moral obligation to act as advisors and take decisions for the Deaf. In each of these situations, they acted rather partially and thus, very often undermined the normative system of the 'strong' (hearing) culture.

In the above-mentioned study (Grbic 1994), the interpreters were also asked to give a personal appraisal of their role. They were given a choice of six statements and were asked to mark the statement they regarded as being most appropriate. The results of the analysis are presented in Tables 2.1 and 2.2.

Tasks of the interpreter	A=18	%
A sign language interpreter should always be a social worker as well	10	55.56
A sign language interpreter should always be an advisor as well	9	50.00
A sign language interpreter must remain neutral regardless of circumstances	8	44.44
A spoken language interpreter must remain neutral regardless of circumstances	5	27.78
A sign language interpreter should also always be advocate for the Deaf as well	3	16.67
A spoken language interpreter should also always be the client's advocate as well	0	0

Table 2.1: Interpreter role, Group 1

Tasks of the interpreter	B=15	%
A sign language interpreter must remain neutral regardless of circumstances	8	53.33
A spoken language interpreter must remain neutral regardless of circumstances	6	40.00
A sign language interpreter should always be an advisor as well	4	26.67
A sign language interpreter should always be advocate of the Deaf as well	4	26.67
A sign language interpreter should always be social worker as well	3	20.00
A spoken language interpreter should always be the client's advocate as well	0	0

Table 2.2: Interpreter role, Group 2

Once again differences between the two groups' personal estimation of their roles could be seen. Whereas the CODA group had the highest scores with regard to the statements 'interpreter = social worker' and 'interpreter = advisor', in Group 2 the norm of neutrality was predominant. Interestingly, nearly one third of this group also viewed the role of an interpreter as an advocate for the Deaf, as opposed to almost 17% of the CODA group. This can perhaps be attributed to the fact that members of this group did not so much consider themselves to be helpers (as do the children of deaf parents, who have to learn this role at a very early stage of their socialization into the Deaf Community), but rather as protectors of the Deaf from an unfair majority which doesn't understand and discriminates against them.

What is striking is the fact that many of the study participants chose two or more statements which exclude or contradict one another, such as remaining neutral and acting as an advocate at the same time.

In the four years that elapsed between this survey and the start of the further training project, a new generation of untrained sign language interpreters had grown up. These interpreters were critical of the paternalism inherent in the role of interpreter as helper, benefactor, advocate or protector and committed themselves to a strictly regulated interpreter role model and to promoting the professionalization of sign language interpreting. The first meetings concerning the possibility of founding a professional association took place. These interpreters took their conceptual models and role ideals from the field of simultaneous conference interpreting which they regarded as the standard form and a case of 'pure interpreting'. Thus, they adopted a very mechanistic view of interpreting. A sign language interpreter and researcher who had observed a similar phenomenon in Great Britain described the consequences of this role model as the 'cult of professional expertise' (Scott-Gibson 1994).

Thus, when we started designing the training course we had two groups of potential participants. On the one hand, the group of the CODA tended to act on paternalistic and charitable grounds. Although they apparently supported the interests of the weak party, in reality they adopted the view that Deaf people were in no position to assume responsibility for their personal, social and professional affairs without their help. This attitude, which they regarded as extremely loyal, was in reality *pseudo-loyal* (Grbic 1997b: 301).

On the other hand, there was the second group of interpreters who believed in an 'ideal form' of language communication as neutral and transparent transmission of content. They saw themselves in the role of non-participants and thus attempted to relieve themselves of the obligation of becoming actively involved in the interaction process with all its attendant problems. I shall refer to this attempt at total personal detachment as *double pseudo-loyalty* (see Grbic 1997b: 302).

Obviously, the boundaries between these two groups were not as rigidly defined as my remarks suggest. In many cases it is obvious that the diverging interests of the parties involved in the interpreting process lead to a series of conflicts for the interpreter, which as far back as the mid-1970s had rightly been referred to as role overload (Anderson 1976).

As mentioned above, similar developments can also be observed in other countries. The fact that other European countries have taken the lead in the fields of Deaf Studies and sign language research makes it possible for latecomers such as Austria to recognize trends and changes more distinctly and to react faster.

As comparative data, let us briefly review the results of a similar study conducted in Germany (Ebbinghaus and Heßmann 1989). I have chosen this study due to its linguistic and socio-political similarity to the situation in Austria. Concerning general attitudes towards deafness, the similarity can be seen in the fact that from the middle of the 19th century onwards, Austrian deaf education oriented itself closely towards Germany and teaching models used there, which focused purely on spoken languages. The ideological consequences of this tradition are still apparent and have clearly shaped the representation of deafness in our society. The results of von Ebbinghaus and Heßmann's study conducted from 1986-1988, based on in-depth interviews with natural interpreters (most of them belonging to the CODA group) and Deaf people, as well as on exemplary analyses of short interpreting sequences, confirm our own experiences – not only with regard to linguistic problems but also concerning the interpreters' self-perception. In both languages, the analysed target texts are grammatically defective, simplified, incoherent and fragmentary and the wide range of grammatical possibilities of both languages is used only to a very limited degree (ibid.: 149-193). Meanwhile the interpreters' role model oscillates between the 'helper's syndrome', resulting from the exacting experience of having to assume responsibility for Deaf parents from early childhood onwards, and a paralysing helplessness due to the role overload which interpreters experience (ibid.: 125-148). Empirical data are scarce, yet on the basis of quite numerous descriptions in the literature we can assume that similar situations preceded attempts at professionalization in other countries (see e.g. Roy 1993 for the development of role models in the US).

5. The course

5.1 Curriculum design

The unsatisfactory social practice of sign language interpreting in Austria described above, the increasing dissatisfaction of parts of the Deaf community and the express wish of a group of committed interpreters, who were aware of their lack of qualifications, confronted us with the task of developing (in addition to the design of a five-year university curriculum for sign language interpretation)[6] further training courses for interested and dedicated interpret-

---

[6] The Institute of Translation Studies at the University of Graz has offered sign language

ers who until now had not had the opportunity of receiving formal training. This chance presented itself within the framework of a transnational project of the European Community Initiative EMPLOYMENT HORIZON. Being able to cooperate with 13 institutions from 9 European countries[7] has had major advantages. In areas in which Austria had little experience, we were able to draw on the expertise of other countries and so avoid some of the problems that otherwise would have been inevitable.

The literature on sign language interpreter training was less helpful than we expected. There were few recent publications and these were usually of a rather general nature. Moreover, they pertained mainly to the United States and, due to the great historical, linguistic and socio-political differences in the adoption of models and contents, had to be treated with great caution. Yet it was possible to draw upon a series of insights and incorporate these into the programme, especially in certain fields of sign language interpreting, which at that time seemed to be of minor importance in Austria, such as for instance interpreting in the field of education, or interpreting for persons with minimal language skills (e.g. Frishberg 1994). Even more interesting were a few distinctly problem-oriented publications about the causes and consequences of study reforms and the idea of re-structured course profiles (Brennan and Brien 1995).

Completely lacking in this literature was the discussion of the chances and difficulties involved in the integration of sign language courses into existing interpreting study courses. In this respect we were something of an exception, as interpreting courses for sign language are usually organised at institutes or in disciplines which adopt a different focus, e.g. sociology, educational theory or linguistics. Thus, the special challenge in the design of the curriculum was to combine the experience of existing training institutes for sign language interpreters with the experience of a traditional interpreter training institute for interpreters, resulting in a completely innovative approach.

After talks with the individual interpreters of the different Austrian provinces, the model adopted was a two-term part-time training course. We were aware of the fact that we could only touch on problems in this short time. On the other hand the advantage was a relatively compact programme which, due to the short time scale, would also attract interpreters from more remote regions.

As suggested above, the target group had a series of features in common but still needed to be regarded as a heterogeneous group of individual competitors. By means of a common training course they were supposed to develop a group awareness which would enable them gradually to change their social practices.

---

courses since 1990 and has dealt with the gradual integration of courses on sign language and Deaf culture into the curriculum since then.

[7] Within an ERASMUS project, study exchanges had already been organised with Denmark, Germany and Great Britain.

The overriding aim of this training course was, then, apart from the provision of knowledge, to increase the interpreters' awareness of the tasks they are faced with and to offer them help in reflecting upon and discussing their work. Another central aim was to choose the most motivated participants of the group to recruit them as teachers for the planned five-year university course.

The general framework and recurrent theme of the course was interpreting as problem solving. In real interpreting situations, sign language interpreters are confronted with a complex dynamic system, requiring problem solving at sites of discoursal conflict. In this case problem solving means that interpreters constantly have to overcome barriers between actual and required conditions in order to reach their aims. These barriers and problems can arise at different levels of the interpreting interaction: on a personal level, the interpreter him/herself as an individual with all his/her cognitive, emotional and motivational characteristics, on the level of the socio-cultural framework (including the roles and role expectancies under which the interpreter operates), and finally due to the system involved, which includes the respective interpreting assignment with all its variables (see Risku 1997). These aspects were to be dealt with throughout the course.

The course was organised in the form of twelve modules (part-time weekend seminars) each composed of 22.5 contact hours at the Institute of Translation Studies at the University of Graz. The seminars listed in Table 3 were designed following discussions with hearing and deaf experts from Austria and our partner institutes:

	Module	Trainers from	Deaf	Language
M 1	History and Sociology of the Profession	Graz & Vienna	-	German
M 2	Communication and Rhetoric	Graz	-	German
M 3	German Discourse Analyses	Graz	-	German
M 4	Introduction to (Sign) Linguistics	Linz	-	German
M 5	Sign Language Grammar	Hamburg & Graz	+	ÖGS[8]
M 6	Deaf Sociology and Deaf Culture	Hamburg & Graz	+	ÖGS
M 7	Community Interpreting	Hamburg	-	German
M 8	Introduction to International Signing	Bristol	+	IS, English
M 9	Interpreting into Sign Language	Copenhagen	-	IS, English
M 10	Interpreting into German	Graz	-	German
M 11	Court Interpreting	Vienna	-	German
M 12	Introduction to Interpretation Studies	Graz	-	German

Table 3 : Training modules

The order of the modules was based on the following considerations: as a first introduction to the topic, we planned a general theoretical seminar on profes-

---

[8] Austrian Sign Language.

sional issues which dealt with the history and development of interpreting and sociological considerations concerning spoken and sign language interpreting (role models, stereotypes, translation norms, work in asymmetric interactions, etc.). In addition, factor models (Vermeer 1990, Salevsky 1998) as tools for the analysis of individual interpreting actions were to be presented and applied on the basis of video recordings. The seminar was also intended to help the participants orient themselves by offering them a first impression of the training course. The final registration did not take place until after this first unit. In order to be able to offer a very broad initial introduction, the seminar was conducted by two persons teaching in tandem: an interpreting researcher with a focus on conference interpreting and community interpreting and another researcher specialized in sign language interpreting. At the end of the seminar, the participants drew up a list of the fields they were interested in. These were then ordered according to topic area and given to the teachers.

The next module group focused on German language (M2 and M3), since (as the 1994 study and initial talks with interpreters had shown) the target group's greatest fears and self-doubts were linked to their mother tongue skills. After a short theoretical introduction, the first of the two seminars focused on exercises on communication and rhetoric. In the second seminar we attempted to provide a theoretical basis for discourse analysis and to apply these basics to concrete texts.

The third module group (M 4-6 and M8)[9] focused on sign language and Deaf culture. As the sign language-related problems were much bigger than the target group had estimated (see section 3), and owing to the fact that it could be assumed that nobody had dealt with sign language grammar before, this module group required a relatively long period of time. In seminar 4, the basics were provided via an introduction to simple linguistic concepts and contrastive comparisons of spoken and signed languages with the help of video material. Seminar 5 focused mainly on the grammar of Austrian Sign Language and included many exercises, and seminar 6 dealt with the history of deafness and aspects of Deaf culture from the point of view of Deaf people. Seminar 8, *Introduction to International Signing*,[10] was not originally conceived as a course for

---

[9] The block had to be split due to the working commitments of one trainer.

[10] IS is a not very standardized supra-regional variant of sign language. From a language policy point of view it can be compared to Esperanto or another artificial (planned) language. It is used e.g. at international conferences as a language for those Deaf people who cannot be accompanied by interpreters speaking their regional sign languages due to financial or other reasons. From a linguistic point of view IS is based on a strong sign language, for instance the ASL (American Sign Language). Compared to traditional sign languages, however, it has more iconic elements and spatially motivated structures. As regards its informative content, even Deaf researchers doubt its communicative value (see Allsop *et al.* 1995).

IS. The main aim was to increase the participants' awareness of the specific grammatical features of visual-gestural languages in general. As the varieties of IS rely to a far greater extent on space as source of grammatical reference, while lexis is of minor importance, we hoped that IS would also help to increase the participants' competence in Austrian Sign Language grammar. Apart from the first seminar in this block, all modules were taught by Deaf trainers.

The fourth group (M7 and M9-11) included several different interpreting settings. Due to lack of time we had to focus on certain topics. All four seminars included a theoretical introduction, practical exercises and the joint analysis of the resultant interpretations. The first seminar of the block concentrated on a special domain of interpreting considered to be prevalent in this field, namely community interpreting. The next two seminars concentrated on special problems of interpreting into sign language or into German, and the last seminar of the group focused on court interpreting. The reason for choosing court interpreting was twofold. Firstly, according to the Austrian Deaf Association, only few interpreters are prepared to work in court. On the other hand, we aimed to offer those who had been working in court without prior training the opportunity to reflect upon the complexity and problems of this setting with the help of experts. The seminar consisted of a theoretical introduction and a mock trial which was filmed and subsequently analysed.

The course was completed with a seminar on interpreting studies. Theoretical aspects were treated in all modules but in the last seminar these individual aspects were to be taken up in a more systematic way. The following contents were chosen together with the trainer: history of interpreting studies, specific research areas for sign language interpreting, studies on interpreting quality, process models, including Gile's effort model (Gile 1995).

The training course led to the award of a certificate for successful completion of each seminar. The participants' performance was assessed by the teachers of each seminar by means of an examination, a written paper or a video.

5.2 The participants

Information about the project and registration forms were sent to institutions (Deaf associations, schools for the Deaf, etc.) and sign language interpreters. Successful candidates needed to have worked as sign language interpreters for at least two years, have excellent sign language proficiency (applicants were asked to send in a video), be integrated into the Deaf community, have relevant proof of their experience and be highly motivated to engage in further training.

The group comprised 20 women and 4 men from 8 of 9 Austrian provinces. Approximately half of them had taken part in the study in 1994 (see section 2). Table 4 provides details on the participants' professional experience.

The division of the participants into two groups, mentioned above (section 2), is apparent. Group 1 (7 years professional experience and more) mainly

Years of professional experience	Number
Since childhood	9
for 15 years	1
for 8 years	1
for 7 years	1
for 4 years	2
for 2 years	8
for 1 year	2

Table 4: Professional experience

had family ties with the Deaf community, whereas Group 2 showed a greater distance. Most participants did not work as full-time interpreters, but in educational and social professions (see Table 5).

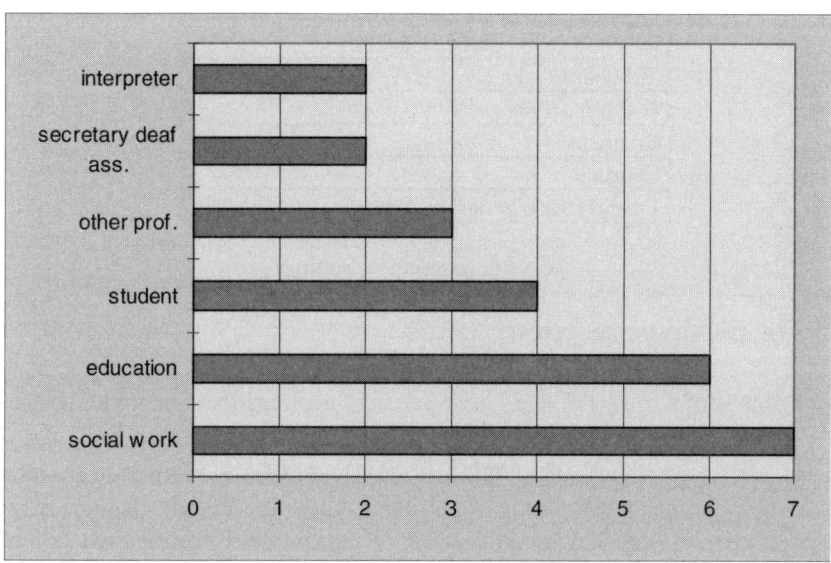

Table 5: Main professions of the participants

When they entered the training programme, the participants worked as interpreters in the areas listed in Table 6.

As regards the frequency of the various different settings, there had been a shift since the study conducted four years earlier. While in the earlier study, traditional settings dominated (such as official settings/authorities and court/police – i.e. areas in which interpreters are mainly recruited by institutions), there is now a distinct shift towards interpreting in educational settings. Although great care must be taken in drawing conclusions from a comparison of the two study populations, certain assumptions could be made, due to the overlapping of informants of both studies by more than 50%. Results are also largely confirmed by interpreting agency statistics.

Setting	%
Further training, workshops	17.29
Everyday situations	12.00
Social work	11.45
Vocational training	9.70
Workplace	9.50
Deaf association	7.45
Health	6.45
Police, court	4.58
Religious settings	3.75
Politics	3.45
Art and culture	3.25
Lectures and conferences	2.20
Psychotherapy and counselling	2.25
Television	1.29
Driving schools, driving tests	1.20
Business	1.08
Sports	0.70
Primary and secondary schools	0.50

Table 6: Interpreting settings

5.3 The participants' view

After each seminar, participants were asked to evaluate the content and organization. The evaluation was, on the one hand, considered as feedback for the trainers and a source of information for the team of organisers. On the other hand, it offered us an interesting opportunity to monitor certain changes in participants' perception of various aspects of training and professional practice covered during the training programme.

The participants had to evaluate 8 aspects for each seminar on a scale from 5 (excellent) to 1 (poor). I should like to concentrate on just the four curriculum-related questions, which focus on issues of more general interest, leaving aside comments on purely local, organizational matters. The questions are 1. Practical relevance of the seminar, 2. Extent of new things learnt, 3. Satisfaction with course content and 4. Overall assessment. Table 7 shows the results of this survey (standard deviation is shown between brackets).

The evaluation of the seminar received higher ratings than expected. Our assumption that certain seminars might possibly receive a low assessment was based on a series of initial talks with the future participants, in which they often expressed a very negative attitude towards theoretical aspects, interpreters who usually worked in other fields, experiences of colleagues abroad, etc.

	Module	Practical relevance	Informativity	Content	Overall assessment
1	Introduction and Sociology of the Profession	4.53 (0.61)	4.21 (0.79)	4.47 (0.62)	4.53 (0.51)
2	Communication and Rhetoric	2.95 (1.28)	2.25 (0.85)	2.15 (0.81)	2.40 (0.82)
3	German Discourse Analyses	4.55 (0.61)	4.72 (0.46)	5.00 (0.37)	5.00 (0.00)
4	Introduction to (Sign) Linguistics	4.33 (0.59)	4.44 (0.70)	4.55 (0.59)	4.44 (0.73)
5	Sign Language Grammar	5.00 (0.00)	4.85 (0.49)	5.00 (0.00)	5.00 (0.00)
6	Deaf Sociology and Deaf Culture	4.80 (0.56)	3.40 (0.98)	4.73 (1.14)	4.87 (0.52)
7	Community Interpreting	4.45 (1.10)	3.85 (1.14)	3.95 (0.70)	3.95 (1.32)
8	Introduction to International Signing	4.65 (0.70)	4.58 (0.62)	4.76 (0.37)	4.76 (0.44)
9	Interpreting into Sign Language	4.89 (0.31)	4.53 (0.70)	4.84 (0.44)	4.95 (0.23)
10	Interpreting into German	4.89 (0.31)	4.84 (0.37)	4.84 (0.00)	4.84 (0.37)
11	Court Interpreting	4.40 (0.84)	4.20 (0.79)	4.40 (0.70)	4.60 (0.52)
12	Introduction to Interpretation Studies	4.33 (0.87)	4.44 (0.73)	4.50 (0.53)	4.50 (0.51)

Table 7 : Assessment of the module

Only the seminar *Communication and Rhetoric* received below-average ratings. This would suggest that either the content of the workshop did not seem relevant to the participants, or that something was missing in the design and running of the course. The comments and suggestions for improvement made by the participants are not very helpful, because the points of criticism ranged from complaints about uncomfortable chairs to doubts about the trainer's competence. After the evaluation we assumed that the negative assessment of the seminar could be put down to various reasons. First, un-cued production of texts belonging to a variety of text types, genres, registers and intended for different purposes in one's mother tongue presents a major psychological hurdle for people who have received no academic training and have never had the opportunity to formulate their thoughts about complex issues in a coherent fashion. Secondly, communication and rhetoric in one's mother tongue without a connection to interpreting might at first seem irrelevant for professional practice. Thirdly, the timing of the seminar was perhaps not ideal. This kind of seminar possibly ought to be offered at a later stage, when the participants have had time to get to know each other and feel less inhibited when asked to perform in front of the group, and when, as a result of discussions in other workshops, they are already beginning to comprehend the great complexity of interpreted interactions and the wide range of skills these require. And fourthly, there was the possibility of dissatisfaction with the trainer. Another seminar on this topic offered approximately one year after this training course by a different trainer received nearly the highest ratings.

I should now like briefly to discuss the participants' responses to the four questions (practical relevance, informativity, content, overall assessment) in relation to the changes in attitude mentioned above and our assumptions before training commenced.

5.3.1 Practical relevance

As far as the results regarding the practical implementation of the contents are concerned, we were surprised that all seminars except for the unit *Communication and Rhetoric* (2.95) received a score of at least 4.33, including the two intellectually most difficult seminars and the almost completely theoretical seminars: *Introduction to (Sign) Linguistics* (4.33) and *Introduction to Interpreting Studies* (4.33). This clearly contradicts the above-mentioned negative attitude of the participants towards theory. The highest possible score, and thus of greatest practical relevance, was assigned by the participants to the theoretical seminar on sign language grammar which was taught by two Deaf people in sign language (5.00). This clearly shows the need for a systematization of a naturally acquired sign language competence. With regard to professional practice, it would be desirable to offer seminars on the contrastive grammar of German and Austrian Sign Language and translation exercises from sign language into German in order to facilitate a systematic comparison of the structures and to avoid word-for-word renditions.

5.3.2 New information

The participants attributed the lowest degree of informativity to two of the key modules, namely *Community Interpreting* and *Deaf Sociology and Deaf Culture*. The reason for this, we believe, is that the content of these two courses is closely related to their daily work.

Most participants felt that they had learnt most in those workshops aimed at enhancing sign language grammar (4.85) and mother tongue proficiency (interpreting into German – 4.84, German discourse analysis – 4.72). This is in accordance with assumptions made before the start of the training programme, namely that the interpreters do not have a sufficiently high potential for reflection in either of the two languages involved.

5.3.3 Content

Course content generally received high ratings. Again, mother tongue proficiency and sign language competence were regarded as the two most important aspects. *Introduction to International Sign* (4.59) ranks fourth even though none of the informants had ever worked in this field. This confirmed our assumption that IS might help to increase the participants' knowledge about the grammatical structure of their own sign languages.

5.3.4 Overall assessment

Highest rates for the overall assessment of the modules were assigned to *German Discourse Analyses* and *Sign Language Grammar* (both 5.00), followed by *Interpreting into Sign Language* (4.95) and *Deaf Sociology and Deaf Culture* (4.87). In a special category 'additional remarks', participants expressed the view that it was especially important that three seminars had been taught by

Deaf trainers in sign language (see Table 3). Most interpreters had never experienced a similar situation. Thus, they suggested that more Deaf people be recruited as trainers for future training courses. This enhances the participants' passive and active language competence on the one hand, and on the other hand also contributes to dismantling the traditionally hierarchical relationship between 'strong' interpreters and 'weak' Deaf people.

Another possible improvement would be to use teams of hearing and Deaf experts for seminars dealing with different aspects of interpreting (community interpreting, court interpreting etc.). Our approach had been limited to inviting Deaf people as guests to these seminars to teach certain exercises in tandem with hearing trainers. There is a consequent need for more trainers with a knowledge of translation and interpreting studies.

5.3.5 Final Evaluation

One month after completion of the course we sent a final evaluation sheet to all participants. We asked them to answer some basic questions about their perception of their profession, current interpreting practice and changes in their professional practice after having attended the course. Twenty participants returned the forms.

All indicated that they felt more confident in their work since they had attended the training programme. 50 percent said that the number of interpreting assignments they were asked to do had increased, and all except one agreed that it was highly desirable to offer a sign language interpreter training programme at university level. The main reasons given were that a university-level degree programme would provide the necessary theoretical foundations. Secondly, it would guarantee the methodical and systematic acquisition of knowledge and skills, and thirdly it would be easier to convince the general public that sign language interpreting is a fully-fledged profession.

Finally it was important for us to find out which qualities the course participants associated with the sign language interpreter profession now. We asked them to indicate between one and five qualities which, from their point of view, are crucial for a fully qualified and professional sign language interpreter. We deliberately did not offer any possible answers as is usual in a multiple-choice system, for example. The qualities listed in Table 8 were indicated in descending order of frequency.

6. Conclusion

Finally, it must be said that this training course was an incentive for a range of changes to be made in the social practice of sign language interpreting in Austria, as described in section 4. Many activities resulting from this training programme suggest that the consolidation of the profession has already begun. One of the most important indicators of this is the founding of the Association

Quality	number	percent
Willingness for further training	14	70
German language proficiency	11	65
Sign language proficiency	12	60
General knowledge	9	45
Self-confidence	9	45
Conscientiousness & self-assessment	8	40
Advanced social skills	8	40
Knowledge of deaf culture	7	35
Adhering to code of professional practice	7	35
Flexibility	7	35
Interpreting techniques	5	25
Interpreter's own culture	5	25
Intellectual curiosity	5	25
Techniques for crisis/stress management	5	25
Ability to work in a team	5	25
Clear idea of professional profile	4	20
Respect for others	4	20
Discourse analytical skills	3	15
Basic knowledge in translation/interpretation theory	3	15
Willingness to accept criticism	3	15
Willingness to face conflict situations	3	15

Table 8: Interpreting qualities

of Sign Language Interpreters in March 1998, after the end of the training course. This association was founded jointly by all the course participants with the aim of establishing a common forum for the professionalization and institutionalization of sign language interpreting. In this respect, the association aims at the consolidation of the profession from the inside as well as the outward representation of the profession. To date, the association has initiated the following measures: establishment of a comprehensive code of professional practice, organization of further training seminars (especially in fields where the interpreters had realised during the training course that they had great shortcomings), development of an Austria-wide, officially recognized system of accreditation and examination for future members, publication of a newsletter, development of legal regulations concerning the remuneration of accredited interpreters together with the respective ministry and the establishment of a commission for complaints. The effects of the course on the quality of interpreting cannot yet be ascertained due to a lack of empirical studies.

As far as the training course itself is concerned, it can only be regarded as an impetus for a series of changes. We touched upon various topics which, of course, could not be dealt with in detail. The course content offered a wide range of topics and was thus able to meet the needs of a relatively heterogeneous group of participants. Nevertheless, the organisers need to recognize that such a training course can only be a temporary solution on the path towards the implementation of a fully-fledged academic training programme for sign language interpreters. A definite advantage was that the course could be offered at an Institute of Translation and Interpretation Studies. For the domain of sign language interpreting it was very positive that the course offered on the one hand, an opportunity to exchange ideas with representatives of other interpreting professions and on the other hand, that it provided an integration of theoretical concepts and models from other domains which previously had wrongly been thought to be incompatible. For a traditional institution which had previously trained only spoken language interpreters, the training course proved to be an important impetus for the revision and change of conventional and, to a certain extent, old-fashioned curricula and didactic concepts.

The scientific community is now faced with the task of eradicating another white spot from the map. In the future, it will be important to focus increasingly on the Deaf community as a consumer of interpreting services in order to avoid too narrow a focus on the professionalization of the profession, which would obscure our view of the real objective, namely to offer Deaf people access to information, knowledge and education. In this respect, Mairian Corker, one of the few Deaf people who also deals with theoretical aspects of sign language interpreting, claims that it is important "to re-emphasize the role of sign language interpreting as a service (...) which should therefore be led by and responsive to a range of user concerns and user preferences" (Corker 1997: 13), rather than adhere to strict concepts of interpreting which only serve to reinforce old hierarchical structures or create new positions of power.

References

Allsop, Lorna, Bencie Woll and Jon Martin Brauti (1995) 'International Sign: The Creation of an International Deaf Community and SL', in Heleen Bos and Trude Schermer (eds) *SL Research 1994*, Hamburg: Signum, 171-188.

Anderson, R. Bruce W. (1976) 'Perspectives on the Role of Interpreter', in Richard W. Brislin (ed) *Translation. Application and Research*, New York, London, Sydney & Toronto: Gardner Press, 208-228.

Boyes Braem, Penny (1990) *Einführung in die Gebärdensprache und ihre Erforschung*, Hamburg: Signum.

Brennan, Mary and David Brien (1995) 'MA/Advanced Diploma in BSL/English Interpreting', *The Translator* 1(1): 111-128.

------ and Richard Brown (1997) *Equality before the Law: Deaf People's Access to Justice*, Durham: Deaf Studies Research Unit.

------ (1999) 'Signs of Injustice', *The Translator* 5(2): 221-246.

Carr, Sylvana E., Roda Roberts, Aideen Dufour & Dini Steyn (eds) (1997) *The Critical Link: Interpreters in the Community. Papers from the First International Conference on Interpreting in Legal, Health, and Social Service Settings*, Amsterdam & Philadelphia: Benjamins.

Corker, Mairian (1997) 'Deaf people and interpreting. The struggle in language', *Deaf Worlds* 13(3): 13-20.
Ebbinghaus, Horst and Jens Heßmann (1989) *Gehörlose Gebärdensprache Dolmetschen. Chancen der Integration einer sprachlichen Minderheit*, Hamburg: Signum.
Frishberg, Nancy (1994) *Interpreting: An Introduction*, Silver Spring, Maryland: RID Publications.
Gerver, David and H. Wallace Sinaiko (eds) (1978) *Language Interpretation and Communication*, New York & London: Plenum Press.
Gile, D. (1995) *Basic Concepts and Models for Interpreter and Translator Training*, Amsterdam & Philadelphia: John Benjamins.
Gipper, Helmut (1987) 'Vorwort', in Antonius van Uden, *Gebärdensprachen von Gehörlosen und Psycholinguistik. Eine kritische Bestandsaufnahme*, Heidelberg: Edition Schindele, 11-18.
Grbic, Nadja (1994) *Gebärdensprachdolmetschen als Gegenstand einer angewandten Sprach- und Translationswissenschaft unter besonderer Berücksichtigung der Situation in Österreich*, University of Graz: PhD Thesis.
------ (1997a) 'Academic Acceptance of Sign Language in Austria', in Zavod za gluhe i naglusne (ed) *The Right to Knowledge for the Deaf. Proceedings of the International Conference, 3-5 October 1996, Brdo pri Kranju, Slovenia*, Ljubljana: Zavod za gluhe i naglusne, 65-73.
------ (1997b) 'Von Handlangern und Experten. Die soziale Praxis des Gebärdensprachdolmetschens im Wandel', in Nadja Grbic and Michaela Wolf (eds) *Text – Kultur – Kommunikation. Translation als Forschungsaufgabe*, Tübingen: Stauffenburg, 293-305.
Harris, Brian (1977) 'The Importance of Natural Translation', *Working Papers on Bilingualism* 12: 96-114.
Jäger, Ludwig (1996) 'Linguistik als transdisziplinäres Projekt: das Beispiel Gebärdensprache', in Hartmut Böhme and Klaus R. Scherpe (eds), *Literatur und Kulturwissenschaften. Positionen, Theorien, Modelle*, Reinbek bei Hamburg: Rowohlt, 300-319.
Kyle, Jim and Lorna Allsop (1997) *Sign On Europe. A Study of Deaf People and Sign Language in the European Union*, Bristol: Centre for Deaf Studies.
------ and Bencie Woll (1989) *Sign language: The study of deaf people and their language*, Cambridge: Cambridge University Press.
Lane, Harlan (1992) *The Mask of Benevolence: Disabling the Deaf Community*, New York: Alfred A. Knopf.
Mikkelson, Holly (1997) 'The Professionalization of Community Interpreting', in Muriel M. Jérome-O'Keefe (ed) *Global Vision. Proceedings of the 37th Annual Conference of the American Translators Association. October 30 - November 3, 1996*, Colorado Springs, Colorado, 77-89.
Risku, Hanna (1997) 'Übersetzen als komplexes Problemlösen: Kognitive Anforderungen', *TextConText* 11 = NF 1: 59-71.
Roy, Cynthia (1993) 'The Problem with Definitions, Descriptions, and the Role Metaphors of Interpreters', *Journal of Interpretation* 6(1): 127-154.

Salevsky, Heidemarie (1998) 'Translationsmodelle – Basis für die Bewertung von Übersetzungs- und Dolmetschleistungen?', in Peter Holzer and Cornelia Feyrer (eds), *Text, Sprache, Kultur*, Frankfurt am Main: Peter Lang, 55-68.

Scott-Gibson, Liz (1994) 'Open to Interpretation: The Cult of Professionalism', Keynote paper presented at *Issues in Interpreting* conference, University of Durham, 17-20 April, 1994.

Tseng, Joseph (1992) *Interpreting as an Emerging Profession in Taiwan. A Sociological Model*, Fu Jen Catholic University, Taiwan: Master's Thesis.

Vermeer, Hans J. (1990) *Skopos und Translationsauftrag*, Heidelberg: Universität Heidelberg.

Teaching Liaison Interpreting
Combining Tradition and Innovation

ANNALISA SANDRELLI

> *In the light of ever-increasing interest in liaison interpreting both as a professional activity and as a process, the issue of training has acquired paramount importance. The Department of Italian of the University of Hull offers its final year students a first exposure to interpreting techniques in a module combining traditional approaches and dedicated computer technology. The paper discusses issues of curriculum design and illustrates them with samples of actual teaching materials and students' work.*

1. Introduction

In recent years researchers have taken a particular interest in dialogue interpreting as a specific form of communication, gaining insight into its distinguishing features with respect to other types of interpreting (Gentile *et al.* 1996; Del Rosso 1997; Linell 1997; Wadensjö 1998a; Hatim and Mason 1997; Mason 1999a; and many others).[1] This improved understanding of the dialogue interpreting process has led to growing interest in the issue of training as a key element to ensure better quality of interpreting services. But what do we mean by 'training'? And how do we make sure that curriculum design reflects real training needs?

This paper discusses one approach to training, namely the use of this type of interpreting as a language learning technique for advanced foreign language students. In this sense, the term **liaison interpreting** will be used, since it defines the basic function of the interpreter (i.e. liaising between the two parties), without tying it down to any specific professional setting. In this paper the interpreting situation is referred to as an **interview** and the interpreter's interlocutors are called the **clients**. The article describes the liaison interpreting module offered by the Department of Italian of the University of Hull, defining its objectives and its limitations and discussing the role played by each component within the curriculum.

2. Liaison interpreting as a language learning technique

First of all, a distinction must be made between **professional training** and **basic training**. Traditionally, **professional training** courses are organised in

---

[1] See the bibliography in the special issue of *The Translator* on dialogue interpreting (Mason 1999a) for more references.

non-academic settings, often with the involvement of local authorities. They are most common "... in countries where the need for reliable interpreting is recognized by the society at large rather than just by members of the linguistic minorities" (Wadensjö 1998b: 34). Teachers include professional interpreters and staff from local bodies who are likely to employ interpreters (courts, police, hospitals, schools, etc.). Participants are usually members of the community with some interpreting experience, but no formal qualifications. Courses of this type often offer some form of accreditation, in an attempt to regulate the market and increase professionalism.

On the other hand, **basic training** in liaison interpreting techniques is offered by higher education institutions in many countries. Translation and interpreting departments tend to introduce liaison interpreting early on in the degree programme as a preparatory exercise for consecutive and simultaneous interpreting.[2] By contrast, within a modern languages degree liaison interpreting is usually introduced in the final year as a language learning technique for advanced students (Thomas and Towell 1985). It is, of course, beyond the scope of such modules to produce professional interpreters: their aim is to present the basic features of liaison interpreting and developing practical skills.

In some UK universities liaison interpreting has been used as a language learning technique for at least twenty years (Griffiths 1985). Its key strength lies in the fact that it provides an opportunity to use communicative skills in an activity which has connections with the real world (Parnell 1989). Moreover, teaching does not require specialised equipment and can easily be integrated with other language learning activities. Because this technique requires students to use several skills at the same time, a liaison interpreting exercise lends itself to several learning goals:

- it improves students' ability to analyse and understand speech, both in the foreign language and in the native language;
- it forces students to concentrate on their production in both languages, thus developing their oral fluency and ability to express themselves. In particular, the exercise provides an opportunity for students to improve their understanding and active use of the more formal varieties of language, with which they are not always familiar (Keith 1985; Hanstock 1985);
- it can be used to increase students' knowledge and understanding of specific cultural differences.

The easiest way of employing liaison interpreting as a language learning

---

[2] For example, in Italy both the Trieste and the Forlì Schools for Interpreters and Translators offer liaison interpreting in year 2, before students start training in conference interpreting in years 3 and 4. At Heriot-Watt University in the UK, liaison interpreting is introduced in year 2 and a more advanced training programme is offered in final year.

technique is to use it as a form of advanced role play (Thomas and Towell 1985; Parnell 1989). The two teachers (one for each language) take the roles of the clients, and students take turns to act as liaison interpreters. A common format for the role play is the journalistic interview, but others are possible, such as an interview for a job, a meeting with a bank manager, and so on (Hanstock 1985: 54). The teachers should have a spontaneous (although partly planned) conversation rather than reading a fully-scripted dialogue (Keith 1985; Hanstock 1985; Layton 1985; Parnell 1989). If the teachers have scripts in front of them, students tend to forget that liaison interpreting is meant to be an exercise in communication. Moreover, from a language learning perspective, scripted dialogues can be too difficult to interpret, since written texts lack the redundancy typical of spoken discourse and have a higher information density.

Since effective communication is the goal of the exercise, the teachers act as if they really need the services of the student interpreter: this has the effect of placing responsibility for each verbal exchange on the student. It is essential that the teachers respond to what is being said by the student interpreter and not to what he/she should have said. Therefore, if the student's interpretation is unclear, incoherent or incomplete, the teacher/client to whom it is addressed will ask for clarifications or refuse to understand. Likewise, students are encouraged to request information (a repetition or an explanation) from the clients in the appropriate way, since such occurrences are quite common in professional interpreting (Wadensjö 1998a: 106).

Teachers should not interrupt students to correct mistakes, since this would destroy the illusion created by the role play (Keith 1985; Layton 1985; Parnell 1989). Corrections can take place in a de-briefing session at the end of the class, or can be inserted into the interview itself. If the mistake is of a grammatical nature, the teacher/ client can use the correct form in his/ her reply. If the student interpreter distorts the meaning of the original utterance, it may be possible for the teacher/ client to make him/ her aware of the misinterpretation in the ensuing exchange.

This exercise encourages students to use the two languages creatively and flexibly, since the emphasis is on communication and meaning, rather than form. However, there is always a risk of turning liaison interpreting into an artificial linguistic exercise – a sort of 'oral translation' – if the non-linguistic elements of liaison interpreting are overlooked in the curriculum. The following section identifies the different sets of skills at work in liaison interpreting.

3. Liaison interpreting: process and skills

An interpreted interview is essentially a dialogue that involves two clients and an interpreter. Communication flows from one client to the other and back, with the interpreter facilitating the process. This means that the level of interactivity in liaison interpreting is high compared with other types of interpreting (Del

Rosso 1997; Wadensjö 1998a). The contents of the interview may be partially pre-determined, because both clients have usually prepared 'something to say' in line with their goals and expectations (Gentile *et al.* 1996). However, the development of discourse is influenced by every participant's reaction to each verbal exchange, which in turn may be influenced by the interpreter's translation choices. Furthermore, the very presence of the interpreter can influence the speakers' discourse strategies (Linell 1997). Thus, dialogue is characterized by many of the features of spontaneous speech, such as interruptions, comments, sudden changes of topic, etc. In this sense, when discussing the interpreter's text-processing strategies, Hatim and Mason (1997) talk about the prominence of context over structure and texture in liaison interpreting.[3] The interpreter has to process every segment of the interview, treating it as a completed statement, but making sure it is consistent with the segment that preceded it: "(...) on the basis of separate instalments of input, linked with each other only at the highest level of text organisation (i.e. that of the entire interaction) each chunk of output is expected to be coherent in its own right contextually" (Hatim and Mason 1997: 50-51).

Owing to the highly interactive nature of the interview, the role of the liaison interpreter is not always clear to the clients or, indeed, to the interpreter him/herself. Wadensjö (1998a) has identified two main roles, **relaying** others' talk and **co-ordinating** others' talk. The two roles are not mutually exclusive, but complementary, since in any given exchange the liaison interpreter usually performs both. However, many definitions of the interpreter's role take into account only the relaying aspect: this can be seen in several professional codes (Mason 1999b, Wadensjö 1998a) which insist that the interpreter's task is to provide a literal translation of what is said. In short, the interpreter is seen as a sort of "translating machine" (Mason 1999b: 149) and not as an active participant in the dialogue. His/ her aim must be to remain 'invisible', thus making the interpreted interview similar to a normal interview between two speakers of the same language.

By introducing the concept of talk co-ordination, Wadensjö acknowledges the presence of the interpreter in the interview and redresses the balance in the direction of a three-party interaction. The development of the interview is influenced by the interpreter, a fact that becomes evident "… when the DI [dialogue interpreter] provides utterances with no counterpart in the preceding discourse,

---

[3] The authors define texture, structure and context as follows: "The term 'texture' covers the various devices used in establishing continuity of sense and thus making a sequence of sentences operational (i.e. both cohesive and coherent)." (Hatim and Mason 1997: 36); "[structure] assists us in our attempt to perceive specific compositional plans in what otherwise would only be a disconnected sequence of sentences." (Hatim and Mason 1997: 37); "contextual factors (...) determine the way in which a given sequence of sentences serves a specific rhetorical purpose " (Hatim and Mason 1997: 39).

explicitly co-ordinating moves ..." (Wadensjö 1998a: 102). The products of relaying are called **renditions** and those of co-ordinating **non-renditions**. The latter are usually provided in one language, as they are aimed at one client only: for example, the interpreter may address one of the clients and ask for clarification; or the interpreter may add an explanation, if he/she perceives the client does not understand what is happening, and so forth (Wadensjö 1998a: 111-113).

In order to perform his/her task, the interpreter needs a number of skills. It is useful to refer to Gile's Effort Model for consecutive interpreting (Gile 1995) to identify some of the skills needed in liaison interpreting. Clearly, there are differences between consecutive interpreting as used in a conference setting and liaison interpreting. The most obvious one is that in consecutive conference interpreting the interpreter usually works only in one language direction and hears the whole speech (or at least a large part of it) before beginning to interpret. In liaison interpreting on the other hand, the interpreter works in two language directions with a text that is developing 'in real time'. However, the technique used by the liaison interpreter to interpret each part of the exchange is consecutive interpreting. In this sense, an interpreted interview is made up of a series of short consecutive interpretations. When the liaison interpreter listens to Client 1, he/she uses the following skills:

- Listening and Analysis;
- Note-taking;
- Short-term Memory;
- Co-ordination.

When the interpreter produces his/her interpretation for the benefit of Client 2, he/she uses the following skills:

- Remembering;
- Note-reading;
- Production (in L2).

The process is then repeated in the opposite language direction (L2 to L1) and so on. Owing to the nature of discourse in liaison interpreting (partly planned, sharing some of the features of spontaneous speech, such as simpler sentence structure, fewer subordinates, redundancy, etc.), there is no need for a very elaborate **note-taking** system. Indeed, it has been claimed that note-taking diverts the interpreter's attention away from the message and therefore should not be taught at all (Keith 1985; Parnell 1989). However, it can be argued that whether one's memory resources are sufficient to perform the interpreting task depends on the type of information contained in the message, since even a good interpreter cannot be expected to store lists of figures, proper names and other types of non-contextualized information (Schweda Nicholson 1990: 137) in his/ her short-term memory without the help of notes.

From this brief overview it will be clear that there are several sets of skills at work in liaison interpreting. Firstly, the interpreter needs very high linguistic competence in the two languages. This covers knowledge of technical language (e.g. legal, medical, financial, economic, etc.), but also familiarity with colloquial language and language varieties related to the socio-cultural background of the clients (Gentile et al. 1996)

Secondly, he/she needs very good domain knowledge, that is deep knowledge of the field(s) in which he/she works and of the topics discussed in the interviews.[4] Thirdly, he/she needs excellent interpreting (or relaying) skills, viz. the ability "(...) to receive a message which is not formulated for the interpreter and to deliver that message in a form and a character indistinguishable from the original" (Gentile et al. 1996: 38). Listening skills, a good note-taking technique and good memory are among the essential ingredients. Furthermore, the interpreter must be able to analyse the clients' statements to establish what is relevant information and what is redundant: therefore, the ability to summarize is also important.

In addition to the above relaying skills, the interpreter needs dialogue management skills to facilitate communication between the two parties without betraying the intentions of either of the clients. The interpreter will need to be familiar with all aspects of cultural differences, both at an institutional level (differences between the legal systems, educational systems, social services, etc. of the two countries) and at a personal level (different values, expectations, social roles, etc.). In order to co-ordinate talk successfully, the interpreter must be able to recognize possible sources of misunderstandings in the different conceptual systems of the two clients or in the ambiguity posed by certain lexical choices, and produce his/ her interpretation accordingly. This ability must be accompanied by a clear perception of the specific requirements of every interview.

To summarize, liaison interpreting does not involve only a language transfer. Other skills are required which have to be developed through specific training. The liaison interpreting module described in this paper was designed on the basis of this principle.

4. The module

In our department the teaching of basic liaison interpreting techniques is incor-

---

[4] However, while for conference interpreters the knowledge acquisition process takes place almost entirely before the interpreting assignment, the face-to-face interaction with clients enables liaison interpreters to continue building up their knowledge during the interview, through feedback or direct questions (Del Rosso 1997).

porated into the Year Four language core module (Advanced Language Skills).[5] At this stage, students have just returned from an academic year spent abroad and can be expected to have achieved a high degree of fluency in Italian. Students study the characteristics of languages for special purposes (e.g. economics, advertising, medicine, etc.) in the reading and writing class first; then, in the liaison interpreting class students are faced with the challenge of working on oral texts on similar topics. As contact time is limited, they are expected to practise assiduously on their own to achieve the standards required.

At the beginning of the course, students are given a list of class topics, so that they can prepare for the oral class in advance by reading relevant newspaper articles, watching television programmes or listening to the radio. This background work has the aim of simulating the liaison interpreter's preparation process before a professional assignment and therefore includes both domain knowledge and terminological information. Students are encouraged to come to class with their own word lists and to try and anticipate the contents of the interview on the basis of their knowledge of the topic (Keith 1985).

The choice of texts is influenced by their relevance to Italian culture and society and by their high topicality, as most of them are selected from the press. In both parts of the module (written and oral), texts become more specialised in Semester II, as can be seen in Table 1, which lists the topics studied in the academic year 1997-1998.

In the first few weeks of training, students work on a number of preparatory exercises, both in class and in their own time, to strengthen their relaying skills separately (see 5.1). The texts used in the preparatory exercises are usually articles from newspapers and magazines, selected and graded in order of ascending difficulty. The first few texts are very short, with simple syntax and a low information density; gradually texts become longer, with more complex syntactic structures, more information and some lexical difficulties.

After a few weeks of practice on the preparatory exercises, students start working on the **interview**. The role-play requires students to employ all of their relaying skills at the same time as their dialogue management skills and awareness of body language. For the exercise to be successful, the dynamics of the interview must be clearly explained at the outset of the course, dwelling upon the relationship between the liaison interpreter and the two clients. The triangular model suggested by Gentile (Gentile et al. 1996: 51-53) is clear and provides

---

[5] The are usually 35 students attending this module, divided into two groups, to make class size more manageable. Contact time is two lectures per week: one is devoted to the analysis and the production of written texts and the other one introduces students to basic liaison interpreting techniques. The liaison interpreting class is taught by two teachers, an Italian native speaker and an English native speaker. The module is taught over two consecutive semesters, with exams at the end of each one.

	Semester I	Semester II
w 1	[Introduction. Explanation of module aims]	Business and finance (general)
w 2	The EURO	The EURO and Italian businesses
w 3	Italian political parties	Business: Alitalia
w 4	An Italian Nobel Prize for Literature: Dario Fo	The wine-making industry. Organic agriculture
w 5	Reform of Italian universities	Technological research and development
w 6	Introduction to *InterprIt*: trade fairs in Italy	Technological research and development: video
w 8	Federalism and secessionist movements in Italy and Spain	Medicine: organ transplants
w 9	Italian cinema: its stars and governmental policies	Medicine: allergies
w 10	The Internet: use and abuse	The environment and the tourist industry
w 11	The Italian fashion industry: Giorgio Armani	The Catholic Church and contemporary social issues
w12	Revision	Mock exam

Table 1: Course schedule

a simple graphic representation of the interview, with the interpreter placed in a pivotal position, the clients in the other two corners, with arrows indicating the directions in which communication flows. From a practical point of view, a flexible seating arrangement in the classroom can help reduce tension and add credibility to the role-play setting (Parnell 1989).

The source materials for interviews are also taken from the press. The chosen format for the role-play is that of the journalistic interview, with one of the teachers playing the role of an English-speaking reporter and the other one playing the role of an Italian interviewee (a government minister, a writer, a film actor, a scientist, an entrepreneur, and so on). Teaching notes are then prepared, including suggested English questions and the outline of oral-style responses. In class, both teachers have a copy of these notes and use them as guidelines for the unscripted, spontaneous development of the interview. A key factor in the success of the exercise is the choice of a suitable topic. A comparison between some aspect of Italian and British lifestyles or institutions (e.g. reform in Italian universities, in Table 1, above) not only presents the student interpreter with a number of translation difficulties, but may also induce him/her to take on a co-ordinating role. For example, the student may need to explain some institutional differences to one of the clients, or may have to ask for additional information before he/she can translate the client's statement. Therefore, careful selection of topics may contribute to developing students' sensitivity to cultural differences as well. Lastly, as far as body language and other aspects of delivery and presentation are concerned, the video-camera has already proved useful in filling this gap in the related field of consecutive interpretation training (Kellett 1995). In Semester II a liaison interpreting class was filmed: this experience is described in section 5.2 below.

From this brief overview, it is easy to see that the preparatory exercises can be performed outside of class hours without any great difficulty, particularly if students work in pairs or in small groups. On the other hand, it is difficult for students to replicate the interview situation outside of the classroom. As a response to students' requests for suitable practice materials to be used in their own time, the Department looked into the possibility of supplementing interpreting classes with a dedicated software package. The result was the integration of *InterprIt* into the module (see section 6.1 below).

The following two sections (5 and 6) outline classroom activities and individual practice, discussing samples of teaching materials and students' work from the academic year 1997-1998.

5. Class practice

5.1 Preparatory exercises

Traditional exercises for developing students' listening and analysis skills are **oral summaries,** which are also useful to train their short-term memory skills and language production. The teacher reads out the first paragraph of an article and asks students to summarize it in the same language, without the aid of notes. The aim of the exercise is to train students to listen for meaning and to identify key ideas in a passage. When students can confidently identify units of meaning, elements of **note-taking** can be gradually introduced. In line with what was said in section 3, only the basic features of the note-taking technique devised by Rozan (Rozan 1979) are presented to the students as a general framework. Students learn to identify the macrostructure of the text and write down only the skeleton of discourse. They are encouraged to keep their notes to a minimum and to make full use of arrows, symbols, acronyms, and abbreviations.

As a general rule, students are instructed to write down key words directly in the target language, as this facilitates the re-reading of the notes. However, as Gran notes (Gran 1985), for some language combinations (including English into Italian), the target language word may often be longer than the source language word. In such cases, it is advisable to note it down in the shortest possible form, irrespective of the language. Indeed, most professional interpreters take notes using a mixture of words from all the languages they know, together with a number of symbols (Gran 1985; Allioni 1998; Darò 1999). The main criterion underlying every note-taking system is intelligibility of the notes for the interpreter:[6] therefore, no specific system is imposed on students, who are encouraged to experiment and develop their own technique.

When teaching note-taking, it is important to ensure that it does not become the sole focus of the students' attention in the interview. This can be done by presenting an oral summary drill and then asking students to write down only the key words in every paragraph, as illustrated in example 1.

Example 1
Il ministro dei Beni Culturali e vicepresidente del Consiglio Veltroni è un grande appassionato di cinema: è stato critico cinematografico per il quotidiano *La Repubblica* e ha scritto vari libri dedicati al cinema.
The Minister for Cultural Heritage and Deputy Prime Minister Veltroni is a big fan of cinema: he was film critic for the daily La Repubblica and has written several books on film[7]

Min/ Cul & vice Prime Min   ♥   cinema (critic / Repubblica, books)

Even if the interpreter does not catch Veltroni's name, his governmental posts are sufficient to identify him. His passion for the cinema only needs to be recorded once in the notes; after that, the words 'critic' and 'books' should be enough to suggest 'film critic' and 'books about film'. Similarly, advanced students of Italian can be expected to know that *La Repubblica* is one of the main Italian dailies. Example 1 also shows that when faced with culture-bound items (such as *vicepresidente del Consiglio*), it is advisable to try and identify a solution during the note-taking phase, to avoid translation problems or an uneasy calque, like 'vice-president of the Council'.

Most interpreters do not write their notes from left to right on the same line. Instead, a very common convention is to arrange the elements vertically and in a diagonal line across the page (vertical *décalage*, see Gran 1985; Darò 1999). Thus, the subject of the sentence is placed in the top left corner of the page, the verb is placed in the centre, a little lower down, and the object on the right-hand side of the page. This means that just by looking at the page, the interpreter can

---

[6] A sign is acceptable if it is easy to use and if it activates a spontaneous association between form and meaning in the interpreter's mind (Allioni 1998: 86).
[7] The translations given in italics are the author's translations. They are intended as a help for readers with no knowledge of Italian.

reconstruct the structure of the sentence, since the position of each segment on the page indicates its function. The other advantage of a visually based note-taking system is that it helps students to distance themselves from the structure of the original and to produce a clear target language text. Therefore, it is essential for students to be able to identify the function of each segment during the listening phase and to arrange the notes accordingly. Example 2 illustrates the need for a clear hierarchy of the elements in the notes, particularly when the source language structure is complex.

Example 2
È crisi 'nera' qui a Tokyo, ma non per tutti. Per il vino italiano, purché rosso (i giapponesi sono convinti che sia un toccasana per le malattie cardio-vascolari ...) si respira aria di boom: nei primi sei mesi del '98 le vendite sono cresciute quasi del 200%.
These are hard times in Tokyo, but not for everybody. Italian wine, but exclusively red wine (Japanese people are convinced that it works miracles with cardio-vascular diseases), is enjoying a boom: during the first six months of 1998, sales have increased by nearly 200%.

While it is common in Italian to start a sentence and then interrupt it with a series of subordinates and parenthetical remarks, the same structure reproduced in English would be clumsy and not very clear. If, on the other hand, priority is given in the notes to the fact that the sales of Italian red wine in Japan have recently doubled, it becomes easier to produce a well-structured TL version:

bad ⊥ in Jap,
but no all.
_____

6 m / 1998,

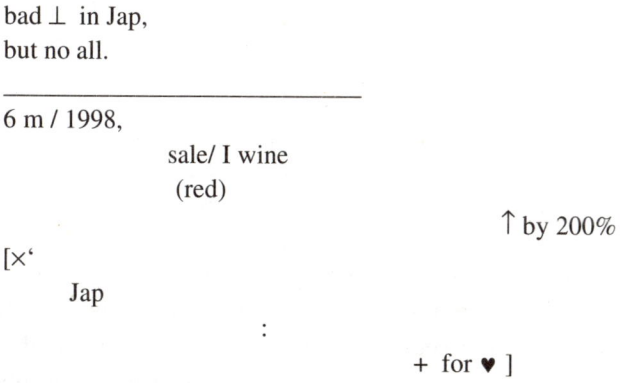

The above are the author's own notes, shown to students as an example: the symbol ⊥ indicates 'situation, circumstance'; ↑ means 'increase, growth'; ×' means 'because, since, as, on account of' (causal relation); + indicates 'positive, beneficial, favourable'; and ♥, fairly obviously, 'heart'. A possible TL version, based on these notes is:

These are hard times in Japan, but not for everyone. In the first six months of 1998, sales of Italian red wine have increased by almost 200 %, as Japanese people are convinced that it greatly helps to prevent heart disease.

Note-taking skills can be developed by **report writing** exercises. Students take notes while a text is being read live, or while a tape is playing a recorded passage and then they write a summary of the text. This is a useful preparatory exercise for consecutive interpreting, with which it shares the listening and note-taking phase and the reformulation phase, but not the time pressure. Students must be encouraged to read their reports carefully before submitting them to the teacher, to make sure they are consistent and logical. This need is apparent in example 3, from a report writing exercise on spa tourism.

Example 3
In Campania il giro d'affari è di oltre 150 miliardi l'anno con una presenza di turisti-pazienti che supera le 20 mila unità.
In the Campania region the annual turnover is over 150 billion lire, with health tourists exceeding 20 000.
Student's version:
150 billion of these are tourists

The figure indicating the turnover from spa tourism was mistakenly assumed to refer to the number of tourists. This student was clearly not shocked at the idea of 150 billion tourists flocking to Campania spa villages every year.

The acquisition of good note-taking skills must go hand-in-hand with progress in students' language skills. Gile (1995) theorizes in his Gravitational Model of Linguistic Availability that one's command of a language is made up of an Active Zone and a Passive Zone. The former includes linguistic material which is often used and can easily be retrieved; the latter includes vocabulary and structures which can be recognized and understood, but are not always mentally available. It is easy to see why it should be particularly important for a liaison interpreter to try and increase the mental availability of vocabulary and structures of both of his/ her working languages. **Paraphrasing** is one of the most effective exercises to enrich and activate students' language skills. Another useful activity to expand students' language skills is **reading**, particularly when attention is paid not just to vocabulary, but also to structures and the contexts in which they are used. The newly-acquired linguistic material must be actively used, for example in short **presentations** on a topic agreed in advance. Presentations help develop the ability to identify key concepts and present them to others with clarity and concision, essential tools of the interpreter's stock-in-trade. Students' stress management skills are also improved by this exercise, as are their posture, voice modulation and other extra-linguistic features of interpreting.

5.2 The interview

After a few weeks devoted to the exercises focusing on individual skills, students are asked to combine them in a **liaison interpreting exercise**.

In Semester I, this takes the form of a role-play, in which the two teachers act as an English interviewer and an Italian interviewee. Students take turns to interpret a whole verbal exchange each (at least one question and one answer). Listening to other students' interpretations and to the teachers' suggestions is the first step to developing the evaluation tools that interpreters need to monitor their performance. Students learn to assess whether their interpretation is accurate (from the point of view of the informational and pragmatic content), whether it is appropriate to the context (both in linguistic and socio-cultural terms), and whether it is accessible to the client to whom it is addressed (from the point of view of overall coherence and cohesion of the text, clarity of presentation and quality of delivery).

In the examination at the end of Semester I, students have to demonstrate sufficient familiarity with the liaison interpreting technique, including ability to deal with difficulties in a professional manner. Example 4 illustrates what can happen when a student is not aware, or is not thinking, of the conventions at work in interpreting. In an intervention which could be classified as an **explicitly co-ordinating** move (Wadensjö 1998a: 73), a student interpreter (SI) asked the Italian client (C) to repeat a name, without realising that it was the name of the Italian client herself.

Example 4
SI *[to the Italian client]* Ehm, può ripe.., scusi può ripetere il nome della signora Marcega...
     Um, can you ..., sorry, can you repeat the name of Mrs Marcega...?
C   Sono la signora Emma Marcegaglia.
     I am Ms Emma Marcegaglia.

Clearly, the student was finding it difficult to accept the basic rules of the role play and see the Italian teacher as a client.

By contrast, Example 5 is taken from an interview in which the student seemed to be at ease with her interpreting role and the roles of the teachers as clients. The English client (EC) was a journalist, while the Italian client was an expert in market research: they were discussing smoking trends in Italy. The student took the needs of her clients into account, and consistently made additions (underlined below) to the original message for the sake of cohesion and clarity (**expanded renditions**; Wadensjö 1998a: 71).

Example 5
EC I find this statistic very interesting. Could it mean that a fraction of the population is resistant to change and can't be convinced to

	give up smoking?
SI	Questi statistici* sono molto interessanti*. Voleva dire che una frazione della popolazione è resistente di* cambiamenti e non si lasciano convincere a smettere
→	di fumare, oppure c'è un'altra ... spiegazione?[8]
	These statistics are very interesting. Did you mean that a fraction of the population is resistant to changes and do not let themselves be convinced to stop
→	*smoking, or is there another explanation?*

The interpreter decided to make the English client's question more explicit, by adding 'or is there another explanation?'. Then, in the following extract the Italian client (IC) began his answer by partially agreeing with the English client and then went on to introduce another possible explanation for the increased cigarette consumption.

IC	Può darsi, non è l'unica spiegazione possibile. Un'altra ipotesi ricorda che fra il 1992 e il 1993 gli italiani hanno vissuto una svolta stressante, con gli scandali di Tangentopoli, la crisi politica ed economica. Proprio fra il 1992 e il 1993 si è verificata una leggera ripresa nel consumo di fumo, insieme ad un aumento nel consumo di dolci, forse per contrastare l'amarezza della realtà.
	Maybe, it's not the only possible explanation. Another hypothesis reminds us that between 1992 and 1993 Italians went through a stressful period, with the so-called Bribesville scandals and the political and economic crises. Precisely between 1992 and 1993 we found a slight increase in cigarette consumption, together with an increase in the consumption of sweets, maybe to fight off the bitterness of reality]
SI→	Yes, this... these figures may seem ... may mean that there is a number of people that don't manage to give up smoking. But there is not ... there is another hypothesis for this period and that is
→	that Italians lived through a stressful period with scandals in Milan and the political and economic crisis. That was ... resulted in a higher consumption of cigarettes and also sweets. Maybe this can be seen as a contrast to .. the ...bitterness of reality.

In order to make this statement easier to follow for the English client, and being

---

[8] The asterisk (*) indicates a grammatical mistake in the student's interpretation. In this case, wrong gender for the word 'statistics' (masculine rather than feminine) and wrong preposition (*resistente di* rather than *resistente a*).

aware of the considerable time elapsed between question and answer, the interpreter inserted an explicit reference to the question ('these figures may seem ... may mean that there is a number of people that don't manage to give up smoking'). The interpreter also competently handled a culture-bound item in the Italian client's reply, namely the reference to *Tangentopoli*, which is the name invented by the Italian press for the corruption scandals (involving leading politicians and entrepreneurs) which began in Milan and then took the entire country by storm in the years referred to above.

Examples 4 and 5 show that, with the choice of a suitable topic, the role play can highlight most of the aspects of the liaison interpreter's two roles (see section 3), thus making the interpreter a real participant in a triadic exchange. However, this method has the disadvantage that students have to take turns to act as interpreters, and consequently never tackle the full interview.

The language laboratory makes it possible for the whole class to work simultaneously on the same interview (Hanstock 1985: 55). The two teachers play their roles as usual, but this time speaking into a microphone. All the students are equipped with headsets and a microphone and can record their interpretations in the gaps left by the teachers. The two teachers can tune into any student's channel and listen to his/her interpretation of that segment of the interview. At the end of the exercise, students are asked to comment on the interview they have just interpreted from several points of view, including content, style, difficult lexical items, comprehension problems, etc. Then, students play back their recordings, which enable them to monitor some of the extra-linguistic aspects of their interpretations, such as voice pitch, intonation, speed, etc. This method is also less threatening for shy students than an interactive interpreting class.

However, this use of the language laboratory also presents problems, the most important of which is that it eliminates all interaction between the clients and the interpreter. In effect, the student is no longer a real participant in the exchange. Therefore, this method must be used sparingly to consolidate students' relaying skills and as an occasional alternative to traditional class practice. It is not advisable to introduce it in Semester I, when students are still learning the basics of the liaison interpreting technique.

Another tool that can be fruitfully employed in class is the video camera. Video recordings of students' performances can be useful in helping them identify problems with their delivery and posture, such as mannerisms, hesitations, nervous movements, etc., which are otherwise difficult to rectify in an interpreting class. In Semester II a class was filmed. The exercise was aimed at training students' evaluation skills in two stages. In the first stage students were asked to evaluate the performance of their peers. In the second stage students had to carry out a self-evaluation evaluation when watching the video footage of their own performance.

In both cases, students used a **quality assessment form,** which was divided into two sections. The first section included questions on aspects of delivery (fluency, speed, voice features), posture, turn-taking technique and situation awareness. The second part of the questionnaire required students to evaluate the interpreter's use of the two languages from several points of view, including grammar, vocabulary choices and style. Students were also asked to indicate whether the information content of the interview had been reproduced accurately, focusing in particular on figures, proper names, and culture-specific references. A class discussion followed, in which the assessment criteria were thoroughly discussed with the teachers.

Thus, the form provided students with a yardstick against which to evaluate the quality of their work not only in liaison interpreting classes, but also during their individual study hours. The following section illustrates the specific tools developed in the department to assist students in their individual practice hours.

6. Individual practice

The limited contact time available for this module means that students are expected to practise intensively on their own. In order to provide students with some guidance and useful practice material, two training tools were developed in the Department, namely *InterprIt* and the glossary project, described below.

6.1 InterprIt

InterprIt is a self-access course aimed at beginners in interpreting, designed by two teachers of the Italian department (Cervato and De Ferra 1995) and developed in co-operation with the CTI Centre for Modern Languages, which is the lead site for the TELL Consortium, a major centre for the development of language learning software.

As mentioned in section 4, the original impetus behind the development of the program was the need to provide students attending the module with suitable training material in liaison interpreting to be used on a self-access basis. Thus, *InterprIt* was devised as a solution to a specific problem. However, this does not mean that the program cannot be fruitfully employed by a different type of user. Indeed, its authors note: "It may also prove especially suitable for the many untrained yet practising community interpreters wishing to brush up their skills" (Cervato and De Ferra 1995: 201).

If the program is to be used as part of a module, as originally intended, *InterprIt* needs to be well-integrated with class activities. The course schedule distributed at the beginning of each semester (see section 4) includes references to sections of the program that students are asked to review each week. Whenever possible, teachers select interviews for class practice on topics related to those contained in *InterprIt*. Thus, students study each topic and the related terminology in the reading and writing class, in the liaison interpreting class and by using *InterprIt* during their self-access hours.

The program offers a choice of eight interviews on a variety of different situations: an Italian woman trying to buy a house in England; an English businessman at an Italian trade fair; an English journalist meeting an Italian wine-maker; etc. After selecting one interview from the Main Menu, students do some background reading on the topic chosen, to acquire information and terminology they are likely to need in the following screens.

In Screen One, students hear a brief description of the situation, including who the clients are, where the interview is taking place and the general aims of the interview. Then, students can listen to a simplified version of the answers that the Italian interviewee will give in the next screen and try to guess the questions asked by the English client, thus re-constructing the structure of the interview. By presenting the answers first and having students work out the questions, the exercises raise awareness of the need for coherence and cohesion throughout the interview and provides students with an overview of the main topics which will be discussed.

Screen Two presents the full interview, which is broken into questions and answers. Students listen to a question, take notes in an on-screen box and record their interpreted version. They can also hear a simplified version of the same segment before they record their interpretation: the simplified version has a simpler syntax, has a lower information density and only includes the main ideas in the passage. They then go on to interpret the answer, and continue until they reach the end of the interview. Their recorded interpretation is stored in temporary sound files, which are made available to students in Screen Four for self-assessment. Although the program does not include a specific facility for saving students' work to disk, it is possible to do so by accessing the temporary file directory of the program and copying the relevant files (the procedure is described in detail in a handout distributed to students). Despite the objective technical difficulties, in the academic year in question several students decided to save their work in this way in order to receive feedback on their performance from their teachers.

Throughout the whole exercise, students have access to on-screen linguistic help, including a glossary (in Italian), a vocabulary section (Italian into English and English into Italian) and language notes. All of this material is presented in the same order as it appears in the interview, so that students can look at the terminology used in Question 1 while interpreting the latter.

When students reach the end of the interview, they move on to Screen Three, where they are presented with two tasks, which have the aim of training them to identify the main ideas in a text and strengthening their skills in report writing from oral sources. The first task is listening to the whole interview and writing down the key words in an on-screen box. Students can compare their work with the program's key words, which are not meant as an answer key, but only as suggestions. Indeed, students are encouraged to write down the words they feel they will need to reconstruct the text: therefore, one student's work is never exactly the same as another one's (see section 5.1 on note-taking). On the basis of the identified key words, students type up a written translation in a larger on-screen box. The translation work can be saved to disk or printed and handed in for assessment or suggestions.

Screen Four is the self-assessment screen. Students can compare their own written translation (from Screen 3) and their recorded interpretation (from Screen 2) with a transcript of the original interview and/ or with the teacher's suggested translation and interpretation. Once again, the versions offered by the program are only suggestions for a possible translation and a possible interpretation.

After describing the overall structure of *InterprIt*, let us give an example of materials from the program. In this extract taken from *Alla fiera campionaria* ('at a trade fair'), an English buyer for a chain of department stores is visiting the Milan trade fair in the hope of placing some orders. He has stopped at a leather goods stand and, through an interpreter, he has asked for a price list. What follows is the Italian client's answer and the student's interpretation, transcribed from a sound file saved to disk by the student herself (IC: Italian client; SI: student interpreter):

Example 6

IC   Sì certo. Ecco, questo è il nostro catalogo con l'ultimo listino prezzi. In esso troverà prezzi di assoluta convenienza e di gran lunga inferiori a quelli che oggi la concorrenza pratica sul mercato. Vorrei aggiungere che per il pagamento in contanti lo sconto che pratichiamo è del 5% sui prezzi del nostro listino, purchè l'ordinazione sia di importo superiore a Lit. 1.000.000.
Certainly. Here is our catalogue with the latest price list. You will find that the prices are very reasonable and much cheaper than those of our competitors. I should like to add that there is a 5% discount on these prices if you pay cash, and as long as your order is for more than one million Italian lira[9]

SI   Yes, sure. Here is our new catalogue and the price list. Our prices are extremely reasonable compared to those of our competitors. You will have a 5% discount for cash payment for goods totalling about 300 pounds.

If the student's version is analysed as a product of her relaying activity, it could be described as a **close rendition** (Wadensjö 1998: 70-71): the essential pieces of information have all been preserved. The student chose to omit certain phrases

---

[9] The English translations in italics in examples 6 and 7 are the ones suggested by the program.

(*In esso troverà* / 'You will find that'; *Vorrei aggiungere che* / 'I should like to add that'), which do not contribute any new information. The resulting English interpretation is more direct than the original Italian, but nevertheless accurate. Moreover, it is interesting to note that the student tried to take the needs of the English client into account, by providing a currency conversion (one million lira / three hundred pounds), which, although not entirely correct, gives an idea of the sum involved.

Let us now look at another example, taken from an interview about holidays and the habits of Italian holidaymakers. The two clients are a Scottish student who is writing a dissertation on holiday patterns in different European countries and an Italian travel agent who has accepted to provide information to help with the project. This time both the interpretation and the translation were saved to floppy disk, so the two versions can be compared. In the following extract the Italian client describes what her job involves (IC: Italian client; SI: student interpreter; ST: student interpreter's written translation):

Example 7
IC I lavori che vengono svolti da un'agenzia turistica sono svariatissimi. Comprendono prenotazioni semplici di passaggi aerei, passaggi ferroviari, passaggi marittimi, prenotazioni alberghiere, viaggi in gruppo, viaggi in comitiva, viaggi individuali costruiti ad-hoc per ogni cliente che ha delle esigenze particolari.
The tasks undertaken by a travel agency are varied. They include simple bookings of air fares, rail tickets, ferry crossings, hotel bookings, group travel, package holidays and individual holidays tailor made for customers with specific needs
SI There are various tasks involved including booking ... plane, train, boats, and hotels. We cater for groups, individuals and those people with special needs.
ST The work of a Travel agent varies enormously. The tasks include booking flights, railway tickets, sea crossings, bookings for groups, individuals, package tours and specifically prepared packages for those customers with special needs.

The interpretation includes most of the information of the original, albeit in a slightly compressed fashion. The interpreter merged the first sentence and the opening clause of the second sentence into a new, streamlined utterance. By contrast, in the written translation the student decided to keep the original paragraph structure.

What is also noticeable is that terminology is more precise in the translation than in the interpretation (e.g. booking trains vs. booking railway tickets): the student tackled the translation exercise after the interpreting exercise and therefore had been able to study the topic and the relevant on-screen terminological information. However, the student's translation of the Italian phrase *che ha delle esigenze particolari* by the expression 'with special needs', both in the translation and in the interpretation, is potentially misleading. The Italian phrase does not refer specifically to customers with disabilities and in need of special care, but rather to any special arrangements requested by a customer, such as a business travel package.

The above examples give an idea of the teaching and learning potential of *InterprIt*, and of its limitations as well. Starting from the latter, the first, obvious shortcoming of the program is that it primarily targets the skills that the interpreter needs to perform his/her relaying role. All the interviews are pre-recorded, so there can be no real dialogue between student interpreter and clients. Since the clients are not physically present, they cannot react to the student's interpretation as they would do in a real life situation. Students have no opportunity to address the clients to ask for additional information or explanations. Moreover, the absence of the two interlocutors can be a psychological hurdle for some students, resulting in lack of motivation. Lastly, in a software package of this type some features of communication, such as body language and facial expressions, are lost (Cervato and De Ferra 1995: 193).

Being aware of the program's limitations, its authors included a number of features to partially simulate a real liaison interpreting situation. One of them is a pause button in the interpreting screen: students are allowed to interrupt a passage at any stage. This was because "… in [professional] liaison interpreting the interpreter is allowed to intervene, to seek help, to ask for clarification and repetition; giving our students some sort of control seems to reflect as closely as possible (within the limitations we have already discussed) a real life situation" (Cervato and De Ferra 1995: 197). Similarly, the on-screen linguistic help partially reflects the possibility of seeking help from the clients themselves. As far as the loss of non-verbal information is concerned, the inclusion of video clips of the two speakers could be explored for future development of the program.

With all its limitations, *InterprIt* offers possibilities that are not granted by a traditional class situation. The most important of these is that the program allows self-pacing: although each interview is structured around the four screens, users can skip parts of the program or go over each section more than once if they so wish, at their own speed. Therefore, the program caters for different learning styles and enables students to concentrate on improving their interpreting technique, without the pressures that can be induced by a class situation. Indeed, it was noticed during the testing of *InterprIt* that the absence of the teacher contributes to reducing stress and anxiety: "That they feel confident with the machine is suggested in the early stages by the improvement in their voices which become immediately more relaxed than in a traditional class situation" (Cervato and de Ferra 1995: 193).

The program presents students with situations in which there is a real-life communication problem. This is a good incentive from the point of view of students' motivation, as it gives the exercise a sense of purpose and enhances their sense of responsibility. The last Screen of the program is also helpful in developing the students' self-assessment skills: by comparing their work with the versions provided by the program and with the original, students can better identify their weaknesses and concentrate their efforts on the latter.

All of the above benefits were confirmed by the students themselves in questionnaires distributed at the end of the course. As *InterprIt* was thoroughly tested before its commercial distribution, the questionnaire did not focus on technical aspects of the software, but on its training content and its integration into the liaison interpreting module. There was an almost unanimous agreement on the overall usefulness of *InterprIt*. All the respondents appreciated the program for providing extra practice material outside class hours, thus showing that the primary goal that its authors pursued had been achieved. The freedom granted to learners was recognized as one of the key strengths of *InterprIt*. One user stated that "you can take your time for notes and translations, the pressure is much less", thus confirming that the program contributes to make interpreting less of an intimidating experience for beginners. Other users stressed the individual focus allowed by the program, as opposed to traditional classes. When using *InterprIt*, students found that the training is "possibly more beneficial in that practice is more private". The majority of students expressed the view that the program is particularly useful for developing note-taking skills and improving their vocabulary. Out of all the students who completed the questionnaire, only one declared a preference for traditional class practice, on the grounds that "it is off-putting speaking to a computer".

Other comments included suggestions for improvement of the program. Among them was the request to include an in-built facility for saving students' work to disk, to replace the rather cumbersome procedure currently used (see above). Another request was to try and devise a way to increase the amount of feedback received through the program: one solution would be to save one's work and then send it to the teachers by e-mail attachment. Lastly, one student remarked that when using *InterprIt* students do not get the benefit of comparing their performance with that of their peers. Indeed, the authors of the program have suggested that one of the possible uses of the program would be in a normal class situation: students could work in pairs, tackling one verbal exchange each and commenting on each other's performance (Cervato and de Ferra 1995: 201).

This brief overview has highlighted the program's key benefits and limitations. *InterprIt* provides an opportunity for individual intensive practice in relaying skills, including listening and analysis, memorising, note-taking and production. On the other hand, the program does not directly target the co-ordinating skills that a liaison interpreter also needs to develop. However, since the program was developed for use alongside interactive liaison interpreting classes, students have a chance of honing such skills in class, under the guidance of their teachers.

6.2 The glossary

Another way in which technology is being used to help our students in their individual study hours is the electronic glossary. The glossary project was first introduced in the module in the academic year 1997-1998, to train students in the terminological search methods used by interpreters.

Students are divided into small groups at the beginning of every semester to produce short glossaries on the various class topics. The teams are asked to look for relevant vocabulary in newspapers, on-line resources, dictionaries, etc., and to draw up a glossary including the original Italian word, its English translation(s), a usage example and sub-language. Every week, one or two days before the class, two groups hand in their work, both in printed form and on floppy disk. After being checked and (if necessary) corrected, the material is transferred into a main database, which is made available to the whole class on the campus computer network. Students can access the glossary to brush up their vocabulary in preparation for a class topic, thus complementing the extra-linguistic preparation done through background reading. The glossary can also be printed out and used for revision before exams.

The key advantage of a glossary created on an electronic support over traditional pen-and-paper ones is the higher flexibility. An electronic glossary can be constantly updated with new entries, it is easily accessible by the whole class and it offers several search options. Students can search for an Italian word in column 1; or they can start the search from the English term (column 2); they can focus on the usage of a given term (column 3); finally, they can obtain separate print-outs of glossaries of terms belonging to the same sub-language by searching in column 4.

The glossary compiled in the first year of its introduction in the module included over 600 terms. Students' feedback on the project was extremely favourable: compiling a glossary was considered a useful vocabulary-expanding exercise, which also had positive repercussions on the acquisition of interpreting skills. Feeling more knowledgeable about the vocabulary likely to come up in the interviews increased students' confidence when tackling interpreting on that topic, and contributed to reducing anxiety.

7. Conclusions

The module described in this article offers basic training in liaison interpreting through a combination of traditional interpreter training techniques and new methods relying on computer technology.

This mixture, developed primarily to overcome the problem of time constraints, has received favourable reactions from students since its introduction. In particular, *InterprIt* seems to contribute to making the interpreting class less of an intimidating experience for beginners. As discussed in this paper, the program does have some shortcomings and is only a first tentative step towards the integration of computer technology into the interpreting curriculum. No grand claims can be made about the effectiveness of the program or about the overall training content of the module. We do not produce interpreters, but we try to give our students an idea of what interpreting is about. Moreover, students who attend this module develop a number **transferable skills**, such as oral fluency in the foreign language, sensitivity to cultural differences, mediating ability, a good note-taking technique, summarising skills, report-writing skills, and a degree of familiarity with computer technology. As language graduates are increasingly expected to have acquired practical skills by the end of their degree courses, a module in basic interpreting techniques can enhance their 'marketability' in the eyes of potential employers.

References

Allioni, S. (1998) *Elementi di grammatica per l'interpretazione consecutiva* [Elements of a grammar for consecutive interpreting], SERT 10, Scuola superiore di lingue moderne per interpreti e traduttori, Trieste: Università degli studi di Trieste.

Cervato, E. and D. de Ferra (1995) "InterprIt': A Computerised Self-access Course for Beginners in Interpreting', *Perspectives: Studies in Translatology* 3(2): 191-204.

Darò, V. (1999) 'Aspetti procedurali dell'annotazione grafica' [Procedural aspects of note-taking], in C. Falbo, M. Russo e F. Straniero Sergio (a cura di), *Interpretazione simultanea e consecutiva. Problemi teorici e metodologie didattiche*, Milano: Editore Ulrico Hoepli, 289-298.

Del Rosso, G. (1997) 'L'interprete di trattativa' [The liaison interpreter], in Laura Gran e A. Riccardi (a cura di), *Nuovi orientamenti negli studi sull'interpretazione* [New Perspectives in Interpreting Studies], Università degli Studi di Trieste, Scuola Superiore di Lingue Moderne per Interpreti e Traduttori: Padova, 237-249.

Gentile, A., U. Ozolins and M. Vasilakakos (1996) *Liaison Interpreting – a Handbook*, Melbourne: Melbourne University Press.

Gile, D. (1995) *Basic Concepts and Models for Interpreter and Translator Training*, Amsterdam & Philadelphia: John Benjamins.

Gran, L. (1985) *L'annotazione grafica nell'interpretazione consecutiva* [Note-taking in consecutive interpreting], Strumenti Didattici e Scientifici (2), Trieste: Università degli Studi di Trieste.

Griffiths, B. (1985) 'The Ear has its Reasons – Interpreting and the Modern Languages Curriculum', in G. Doble and B. Griffiths (eds) *Oral skills in the modern languages degree*, London: CILT, 89-111.

Hanstock, J. (1985) 'Liaison interpreting problems specific to French', in N. Thomas and R. Towell (eds), 52-56.

Hatim, B. and I. Mason (1997) *The Translator as Communicator*, London: Routledge.

Keith, H.A. (1985) 'Liaison interpreting as a communicative language-learning exercise', in N. Thomas and R. Towell (eds), 1-12.

Kellett, C. J. M. (1995) 'Video-Aided Testing of Student Delivery and Presentation in Consecutive Interpretation', *The Interpreters' Newsletter* 6, Università degli Studi di Trieste, Scuola Superiore di Lingue Moderne per Interpreti e Traduttori, 43-66.

Layton, A. R. (1985) 'Interpreting and the communicative approach', in N. Thomas and R. Towell (eds), 69-78.

Linell, P. (1997) 'Interpreting as communication', in Y. Gambier, D. Gile and C. Taylor (eds) *Conference Interpreting: Current Trends in Research*, Amsterdam & Philadelphia: John Benjamins, 49-67.

Mason, I. (ed) (1999a) *The Translator. Special issue on Dialogue Interpreting*, 5(2).

------ (1999b) 'Introduction', in I. Mason (ed), 147-160.

Parnell, A. (1989) 'Liaison Interpreting as a Language Teaching Technique', in L. Gran and J. Dodds (eds) *The Theoretical and Practical Aspects of Teaching Conference Interpretation*, Udine: Campanotto Editore, 253-255.

Rozan, J. (1979) *La prise de notes en interprétation consecutive*, Genève: Université de Genève, 4th ed.

Schweda Nicholson, N. (1990) 'Consecutive Note-Taking for Community Interpretation', in D. Bowen and M. Bowen (eds) *Interpreting – Yesterday, Today and Tomorrow*, American Translators Association Scholarly Monograph Series, Binghamton: State University of New York (SUNY), 136-145.

Thomas, N. and R. Towell (eds) (1985) *Interpreting as a language teaching technique*, London: CILT.

Wadensjö, C. (1998a) *Interpreting as Interaction*, London & New York: Longman.

------ (1998b) 'Community Interpreting', in M. Baker (ed) *Routledge Encyclopaedia of Translation Studies*, London & New York: Routledge, 33-37.

Notes on Contributors

Nadja Grbic has studied linguistics and Slavic languages and is currently Assistant Professor in the Department for Translation Studies at the University of Graz, Austria. She is responsible for further training of sign language interpreters in Austria and has developed a five-year full-time interpreter training course at University level, due to start in the next two years. She also teaches translation and interpreting studies. Research interests include sign language interpreting, translation history, issues of translation/interpretation and power.
Address: Institut für Translationswissenschaft, Karl-Franzens-Universität Graz, Merangasse 70, A-8010 Graz. E-mail: nadja.grbic@kfunigraz.ac.at

Sandra Hale is senior lecturer in Interpreting and Translating at the University of Western Sydney and co-ordinates the Graduate Diploma (I&T), MA (Interpreting and Linguistics) and MA (Translation and Linguistics). She worked as a community/legal interpreter for many years before becoming an academic. She also works as a conference interpreter. Her research interests lie mainly in discourse analysis of court interpreting and translation. She holds a BA (I&T), Grad.Dip.in Trans., Dip.Ed. (Italian & Spa), M.Applied.Ling. and has recently completed her PhD in court interpreting. She is a NAATI accredited Interpreter and Translator.
Address: University of Western Sydney, School of Languages and Linguistics, P.O. Box 555 Campbelltown, Sydney, New South Wales, Australia 2560. E-mail: S.Hale@uws.edu.au

Pierre Kouraogo has completed a Ph.D. in ESOL at the University of London Institute of Education and is senior lecturer in applied linguistics in the Modern Languages Department of the University of Ouagadougou. He is also co-ordinating a professionalization project that includes a translation programme. He has published on education and ESOL and is currently interested in the issues and practices of translating into a foreign language and more generally the interface between language teaching and the training of professional translators.
Address: Déptartment de Langues Vivantes, Université de Ouagadougou, 03 BP 7021, Ouagadougou 03, Burkina Faso. E-mail: pierre.kouraogo@univ-ouaga.bf

Ian Mason is Professor of Interpreting and Translating at Heriot-Watt University, Edinburgh. He has taught translating and liaison interpreting for many years and has been involved with the validation and accreditation of degree programmes in interpreting and translating in Hong Kong, Ireland and the United Kingdom. In addition to collaborations with Basil Hatim, also of Heriot-Watt University, (*Discourse and the Translator*, Longman 1990; *The Translator as*

Communicator, Routledge 1997), he has published on various aspects of the linguistics and pragmatics of translating and interpreting. He was guest editor of a special issue of *The Translator*, vol. 5(2), entitled *Dialogue Interpreting*.
Address: School of Languages, Heriot Watt University, Edinburgh EH14 4AS, United Kingdom. E-mail: I.Mason@hw.ac.uk

Bernd Meyer has a M.A. in Portuguese Language and Linguistics and is writing a dissertation on the use of medical terms in interpreted doctor-patient communication. He is currently working as a research assistant on the project 'Interpreting in hospitals', which is being pursued in the Research Centre on Multilingualism at the University of Hamburg (www.rrz.uni-hamburg.de/SFB538).
Address: Universität Hamburg, Research Center on Multilingualism, Project A2, 'Interpreting in Hospitals', Max-Brauer-Allee 60, 22765 Hamburg, Germany. E-mail: Bernd_Meyer@public.uni-hamburg.de

Cynthia Miguélez has been a member of staff at the University of Alicante (Spain) for 12 years, where she currently teaches interpreting at both undergraduate and postgraduate levels. She also collaborates regularly with the U.S. *National Center for Interpretation Research, Testing and Policy* and has been an invited member of staff at the *Summer Institute for Court Interpreting* sponsored by this Centre for the past four years. She has published and lectured in Europe, Asia and America on topics related to professional interpreting standards and interpreter training.
Address: Dpto. de Filología Inglesa, Sección Traducción e Interpretación, Universidad de Alicante, Apdo. Correo 99, 03080 San Vicente del Raspeig, Alicante, Spain. E-mail: giambruno@ua.es

Annalisa Sandrelli is a graduate of the *Scuola Superiore di Lingue Moderne per Interpreti e Traduttori* of the University of Trieste (English and Spanish). Between 1996 and 1998 she was Lector in Italian at the University of Hull. In 1999 she was awarded a Training Grant to undertake doctoral research on simultaneous interpreting, under the Marie Curie Training and Mobility of Researchers programme of the European Commission. She teaches liaison interpreting and consecutive interpreting in the Department of Italian of the University of Hull. Her main research interests are conference interpreting and film translation (both subtitling and dubbing). She is a free-lance conference interpreter and media translator.
Address: Department of Italian, The University of Hull, Hull HU6 7RX, East Yorkshire, United Kingdom. E-mail: A.Sandrelli@selc.hull.ac.uk

Yukino Semizu is preparing a MPhil/PhD at University College London in the field of translation history. Born and educated in Japan, she has lived in the UK

since 1975. She completed a MSc in Translation Studies at UMIST in 1998.
Address: Church House, Church Hougham, Dover, Kent CT 15 7AH, United Kingdom. E-mail: yukino@gtwiz.co.uk

Miranda Stewart is Senior Lecturer in the division of Spanish and Latin American Studies at the University of Strathclyde. She trained as an interpreter and translator and teaches translation studies and liaison interpreting as well as the sociolinguistics of Spanish. She has published on interactional pragmatics in Spanish and French and on applied linguistics. She is author of *The Spanish Language Today* (Routledge 2000).
Address: Department of Modern Languages, University of Strathclyde, Glasgow G1 1XQ, United Kingdom. E-mail: M.M.Stewart@strath.ac.uk

Cecilia Wadensjö is a researcher in the Department of Communication Studies at Linköping University, Sweden. She is also a Certified Interpreter between Swedish and Russian. Her previous publications on the subject of interpreting include *Interpreting as Interaction* (Longman 1998).
Address: Department of Communication Studies, University of Linköping, S-581 83 Linköping, Sweden. E-mail: CecWa@Tema.LiU.SE

Index

accommodation 9, 102
accreditation v, 150, 168, 174
acquisition 167
action systems 90, 95, 103
Active Zone 184
adjacency pair 48
adversarial courtroom 21
Afoloyan, Adebisi 111
Africa 109
AIIC i
Alarcos Llorach, E. 62
Alexandre, Pierre 109, 110
Algonquins iv
Allioni, S. 182
Allsop, Lorna 150, 155, 161n
ambiguity 4
American Sign Language 161n
anaphora 4, 11-12
Anderson, Bruce 144, 158
animator 52n, 64
anticipation 83
Anyaehie, Evaristus 112
Apfelbaum, B. 83
apology 54
artificial language 161n
Ashanti 115
assimilation 156
assumption 88
Australia v, 24
Austria v, 150-171
Austrian Deaf Association 162
Austrian deaf education 158
Austrian Sign Language 154
author 52n
autonomous learning v

bademda 116
Baker, Mona iii
Bamgbose, Ayo 111
Bandia, Paul 109, 112, 115
Bartels, O. 93
basic training 174

'being-with' 82
Bennett, M.S. 21
Bentivoglio, P. 63
Berk-Seligson, Susan ii, 5, 24, 34, 53, 55-56, 66
bilingual interactions 95
bilingualism 111
body language 179, 181
Bogoch, B. 23, 33
Boretti de Macchia, S. 29
Boyes Braem, Penny 155
Brennan, M. 53, 149, 159
brief 83
Brien, David 159
Britain 55, 64, 150
broker 141
Brown, Penelope 53, 56, 67
Brown, Richard 149
Brûlé, Etienne iv
Bühler, Karl 89
Bührig, Kristin 89, 101
Burkina Faso v, 110-130
burn-out iv, 73
business negotiation iii, 51-52

Canada 52
Candlin, N.Ch. 49n, 73
Cantonese 87
Capps, L. 73
Carr, Sylvana i, 149
Cervato, E. 188-193
Chafe, Wallace 94
Chamot, Anna 120
Charrow, R. 4n
Charrow, Veda 4n
Chiara, Giuseppe 137
Chinese 131
Christianity 132
Cicourel, A. 87
clarification 15-18
close rendition 76, 190
code-switching 113

cognitive environment 142
coherence iii, 12-13, 17-18
commitment 61-62
communicative effectiveness 116
communicative needs 91
communicative radius iv, 82-84
communicative pas de trois 73
community interpreting iii, 88, 103, 161, 162
compensation 114
competence 152, 167, 178
competing discourses ii, iv
comprehensibility 12
computer-based learning v
conference interpreting v, 161
   simultaneous 157
Conley, J.M. 4
consciousness-raising v
consecutive interpreting 8n, 110, 112, 174, 177
context 116, 176
contrastive grammar 166
co-ordination 83, 88, 102, 176, 185
Corker, Mairian 169
Cortés, Hernán iv
counterfactuality 62n
courtroom interaction iii
courtroom interpreting ii-iii, 3-19, 21-50, 51-70, 162
Cowie, Moira 143n
Crandal, J. 4n
credibility 63
cross-cultural encounters iv
cross-cultural misunderstanding 61
cross-examination iii, 21-50, 48, 54
cross-lingual communication 116
cultural differences 178, 181
cultural encounters 142
culture-bound item 182, 187
Crystal, David 4
Cummins, Jim 111
curriculum design 151, 158-162, 173

Danet, B. 4n, 23, 33
Danquah, J.B. 115

Darò, V. 182
Das Gupta, J. 110
Davy, Derek 4
Deaf community 151
décalage 182
declaratives 25-26
de Ferra, D. 188-193
deficiency model of deafness 156
Delisle, Jean iv, 114, 116, 143
Del Rosso, G. 173, 175-176
Denmark 150
detachment i, 157
dialect 79, 153
dialogic interaction iii
dialogue interpreting iii, vi, 51-55, 88, 110, 120, 144, 173
   consecutive 110
diction 13-18
diplomatic interpreting iii
direction of culture 143
direction of language 177
direction of translation 143n
discourse analysis 73, 161
discourse organization 97
discourse strategies 176
disempowerment 66
dissociate processing 6
distance ii, iv, 51
distancing 80
doctor-patient communication 87-106
Douw, Adrian 136, 141
Dunstan, R. 22
Dutch iv, 132

Ebbinghaus, Horst 158
Edo period 133
Edwards, D. 74
effort model 162, 177
Ehlich, Konrad 89-90, 92n
electronic glossary 194
embedding 14
Engels, Yukino 132n
English iii, 24, 53
English/Cantonese 87
English/Spanish see *Spanish/English*

equivalence iv, 24, 48, 78
   cross-cultural 68
   pragmatic iii, 30, 26, 48-49
Erickson, F. 82
Esperanto 161n
European Union of the Deaf 149
examination-in-chief 21-50
exhortation 118
expert witness 3-19
explicature 142
explicitation 114
eye-contact 83, 118

face iii, 51-70
face-threatening 52, 88, 118
face-to-face interaction v
factor models 161
Fahey, R. 23, 26, 37
false start 15-16
Feldman, W.L. 21
fieldwork encounter 143
Finland 150
fluency 174
footing ii, iv, 51, 54
foreign language students 173
formalese 66
formality 66
frame 91
framework 82
France 150
Fredericks, Cecilia 87-88
free translation 117
French 110
Frishberg, Nancy 159
Fulfide 111
functional pragmatics 89
functional quality 88

gate-keeping 54
gaze 81-83
gender differences 79
Gentile, Adolfo 72, 140, 144, 173, 176, 178-179
German 87, 153
German/Portuguese 92-103

Germany 52, 150
gesture 7, 76, 118
Gibbons, J. 33
Gile, D. 162, 177, 184
Gipper, Helmut 155
'given-new'-format 94
Goffman, Erving 52n, 54
González, Roseann 4, 7n
Goodman, G.K. 134n
Gran, L. 181-182
Gravitational Model of Linguistic Availability 184
Grbic, Nadja v, 149-171, 197
Gricean maxims 57
Griesshaber, Wilhelm 89
Griffiths, B. 174
griot 115-116
Gutt, E.A. 141-142

Hakuseki, Arai 134, 137-144
Hale, Sandra ii-iii, 21-50, 56-57, 66, 197
Halliday, M.A.K. 46
Handlungsqualität 89
Hanstock, J. 174-175, 187
Harris, B. 51
Harris, S. 22, 151
Hasan, R. 46
Hatim, Basil ii, 90, 173, 176
hedges 16-17, 53, 56, 58, 61-63
Herman, J.L. 72
Hessmann, Jens 158
Hoffman 4n
honorifics 53, 68

illiteracy 111
illocutionary force 28-29, 36, 41, 48, 52, 56, 58-59, 64, 89
Imamura, A. 137
Imamura, Genuemon 135, 140, 142
immigration interview 54-55, 64
impartiality i
imperative 25, 46, 60, 65
implicature 58, 60, 63, 67, 142
implicitation 114
indigenous languages v

indirectness 58, 65, 68
institutionalization 168
intention 154
intentionality 62
interactivity 175
interference 113, 153-154
interjection 118
International Signing 161
interpersonal 51, 116
interpreter style iv, 68
interpreting studies 162
InterprIt 181, 188-193
interrogative 25-26, 45
interview 173, 179
interview protocol 120
intonation 58, 60
IRAP 111
Ireland 150
irony 67
Italian 52, 131-145, 179-191
Italian/English 181-191
Italy 150

Jäger, Ludwig 155
Japan iv, 131-145
Japanese 131
jargon iii, 6, 8-9
Jula 111

Kang, M.A. 54
Karttunen, Frances iv, 143
Katagiri, Kazuo 135-136, 144
Keith, H.A. 88, 174-175, 177, 179
Kellett, C. 181
kinesics 58
king's linguist(s) v, 109-130
Knapp, Karlfried 52-53, 88, 102
Knapp-Pothoff, Annelie 52-53, 88, 102
knowledge structures 87, 89
Korean 52
Kouraogo, Pierre v, 109-130, 197
Kundera, Milan 73
Kyle, Jim 150, 155

Lalouschek, Johanna 87

La Malinche iv
Lane, Harlan 156
Lang, R. 51
language laboratory 187
language learning software 188-193
language learning technique 173
language policy 111, 161n
Latin 135, 141
Layton, A.R. 175
Leech, G. 62
legal language 4-5
Levinson, Stephen 53, 56, 67
liaison interpreting v, 88, 173
licensing 150
Lind, E.A. 4
Linell, P. 173, 176
linguistic awareness 155
Lindquist, Peter 6n
literal translation 9, 13, 176
Loftus, E. 23
Löning, Petra 87, 90
loyalty 144, 157
Luxembourg 150

McCann, L. 73
Mackintosh, Jennifer 117
macrostructure 181
Maley, Y. 23, 26, 37
markedness 29-30
Martinet, A.V. 43
Mason, Ian i-vi, 51-70, 90, 118, 173, 176, 197-198
mass communication 120
maxim
    of quantity 57
    of quality 57
medical communication 87-106
medical encounters iv
medical terms 89-92
medizinische Fachsprache 89
memory 177
metaphor 9
Meyer, Bernd iv, 87-106, 198
Middleton, D. 74
Miguel, M.A. 55, 61

Miguélez, Cynthia iii, 3-19, 198
Mikkelson, Holly 150
Miyazaki, Michio 135, 137, 139
modality 42, 61, 63, 65
monitoring i, 11, 151
Moore 110
Moore/French 109-130
Morris, R. 55
Mossi 115
mother tongue proficiency 166
Müller, Frank 95

Naiman, N. 120
Nama, Charles 112
narrative 73
nation-building 110
national languages 110
natural interpreters 151
negotiation
   of face iii, 53
   of role i
nennende Prozeduren 89
neutrality 157
New Confucianism 133
New World 142
Nikiema, N. 111
no-rẽẽsa 115
non-involvement 81
non-person 141
non-rendition 177
Nord, Christiane 119
Norway 150
note-taking 177, 181

O'Barr, William 4,
Ochs, E. 73
official languages 110
off-record 67
Okpewho, I. 112
O'Malley, Michael 120
opacity 95
oral summaries 181
oranda tsûji iv, 131-145
Ouagadougou 112
Oxford, Rebecca 120

pace 80
Palmer, F.R. 63
Papua New Guinea 51
paralinguistic 5
paraphrasing 184
Parnell, A. 174, 175, 177, 180
participant role 88-104
participation 103-104
participation framework iv, 51, 54-55
particle 53, 56, 58-59
Passive Zone 184
paternalism 157
Pearlman, L.A. 73
perception space 93, 94-95
perlocutionary effect 60
Pförringer, W. 97
Phillips, H. 144
phonocentric attitude 155
pitch 76, 80
planning 97
Plimer, D. 73
Pöchhacker, Franz 88
Polish iii, 64-68
Polish/English 55, 64-68
politeness iii, 46, 51ff
polysemy 10
Pórtoles, L. 29
Portugal 150
Portuguese 92, 132
Portuguese/German 92-106
position 72
power ii, iv, 21, 51, 59, 66, 143
powerplay 61
pragmatic effects iii, 62
pragmatic force 24, 40
pragmatic function 22, 30, 46, 89-92
pragmatic mismatch 67
preposition 11
presentation 184
presente de anticipación 62
principal 52n, 64, 118
private verbs 63, 65
problem solving 160
pro-drop 62
professional code 176

professional interpreting 112
professional practice 150
professional stance iv
professionalism 174
professionalization 150, 157
proficiency 166
pronoun 62
proxemics iv
pseudo-loyalty 157
psychotherapy iv, 71
Pym, Anthony ii, 53n, 56

question 20-50
   confirmation seeking question 26, 48, 57
   declarative question 27
   information seeking question 26, 48
   tag question 27, 33
   wh-question 23, 27, 59, 65, 67
   yes-no question 23, 27, 57, 59
question form iii
question type 22-23
Quirk, R. 27-28, 34-35, 37, 41

raag-naaba 115
Real Academia Española 28, 36
redressive action 54
redundancy 14
reformulation 184
refugee 73
register 5
Rehbein, Jochen 87, 88, 89-90, 96, 101
relaying 88, 102, 176-177, 192
relevance theory 141
remedial teaching 156
remembering 73-74, 78, 80
rendition 153, 177
   close 76, 190
   expanded 185
   taxonomy of 102
renumeration 168
repair 15-16, 61, 97
repetition 4, 14, 42, 67
responsibility 52, 61, 83-84, 103, 141, 157-158, 175

report writing 184
re-telling 72
Rigney, A.C. 24, 26, 33, 54n, 56
Risku, Hanna 160
Robinson, Douglas 143
role 54, 64, 88, 92, 101-102, 140, 176
   supportive 101
role conflict v
role model 155
role overload 158
role play 175, 179
Roma jin kanjô 136
Romance languages 62
Rönsch, W. 93
Roy, Cynthia 54, 158
Rozan, J. 181
Rubin, Joan 120

Salevsky, H. 161
Sandrelli, A. v, 173-196, 198
Sanou, B. 111
Sanou, F. 111
Schegloff, E. 22
Schultz, J. 82
Schweda Nicholson, N. 178
Scott-Gibson, Liz 157
Searle, John 89
Seleskovitch, Danica 117
semantic ambiguity 17-18
semi-professional expressions 90
Semizu, Yukino iv, 131-145, 198-199
Seiyô Kibun 134-135, 139, 140
Sherwood, B. 51
shift ii, 9, 12, 52-54, 103
Shuttleworth, Mark 143n
Sidotti, Giovanni 134-144
sign language 53
sign language competence 155
sign language grammar 161, 166
sign language interpreters 149-171
signed language 53
sign language interpreting v
simplifying 88, 154
Simpson, O.J. iii, 24, 55
simultaneous interpreting 8, 13, 55, 157, 174

skills v, 18, 91, 113, 152, 174, 177
social identity 79
social practice 90, 149, 158-159, 167
sociolect 79
socio-textual practices ii
Spain 150
Spanish iii, 8, 24, 53
Spanish/English 8-19, 21-50, 53, 55-70
speech act
  indirect 47
  theory 89
speech actions 89, 98
speech event 21, 63, 68
speech genre 66
speech situation 88
speech style 5
Sperber, D. 141-142
status 140
Stenhouse, Lawrence 120
stereotype 156
Stewart, Miranda iii, 51-70, 199
stigma 155
stress iv
style 13-18, 118
sub-dialogue ii
subject-verb agreement 11
subject-verb order 29
summarize 178
Svartvik, J. 62
Sweden 72, 150
Swedish 72-85
synchronization 84

taboo 155
Tebble, H. 53
tenor 46, 65-66, 118
tense 11, 62
terminology iii-iv, 4, 8-10, 87-106
therapeutic encounters 71-85
Thomas, N. 174-175
Thomson, A.J. 43
three-party interaction 176
three-way exchange/interaction 88
total communication 152
Towell, R. 174-175

training v, 120, 149-171, 173-196
training materials 6
training programme iii, v, 151
transferable skills 195
transference 72
transcribing 120
transcription 7, 56
translation (in Japan) 131-133
translation studies 90, 149
translational filter ii
transparency 95, 101
trauma 72
triad iv
triadic exchanges 54-55, 187
triangular model 179-180
Tseng, Joseph 150
Turkish 102
turn allocations 83
turn management i
turn-taking 83
TV show 154

United Kingdom 150
United States 3, 24, 52, 55, 159
units of meaning 117
untrained interpreters iv-v, 51-52, 87-106, 114, 157

van der Veer, G. 73
verbalization of knowledge 89, 91
verbs of cognition 63
Vermeer, Hans 161
vocabulary 4, 87, 194
volition 62

Wadensjö, Cecilia ii, iv, 52n, 54, 71-85, 102, 140, 143n, 144, 173, 174, 176, 199
Walker, A.G. 21-22
Walraven, J. 55
Watzlawick, P. 80
Weber, E. 63
Wiese, Ingrid 90
Wilson, D. 141-142
witness testimony 3

Woodbury, H. 23, 39, 41
Woodsworth, Judith iv, 143

Yugoslavia 72